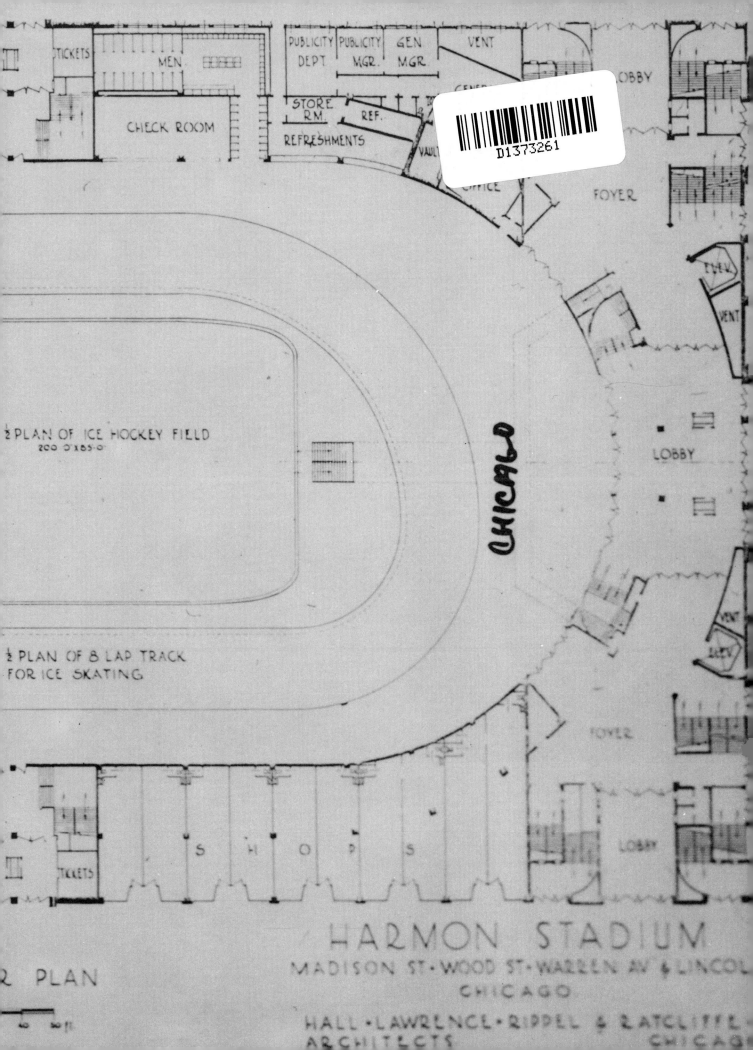

AND NOW, YOUR
CHICAGO BULLS!
A THIRTY-YEAR CELEBRATION!

By Roland Lazenby

1966 CHICAGO BULLS 1996
XXX
30 YEARS AND RUNNING

Jack Smith
Publisher & Director, Fine Books

Bob Snodgrass
Publishing Consultant

Bill Smith
Photo Editor

Jeanne Warren
Editor

Randy Breeden
Design and Typography

Dust Jacket Design by Bonnie Henson

Contributing Photographers: Al Hall, Bill Smith, Nathaniel Butler, Steve Lipufsky, Andrew Bernstein and John Frank

Fiber optic photo Wolf Photo and Chris Dennis

Select photos courtesy of the The Chicago Tribune and NBA photos

Remaining photos courtesy the Chicago Bulls

Published by Taylor Publishing Company, Dallas, Texas

ISBN: 0-87833-113-1(General)
ISBN: 0-87833-114-X(Limited)
ISBN: 0-87833-115-8(Collectors)

fb
TAYLOR

And now...
your Chicago Bulls!
A 30-Year Celebration

By Roland Lazenby

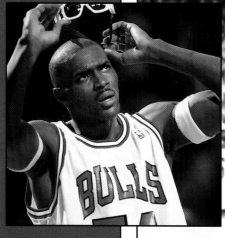

Author's Note to the Reader

TODAY, THE CHICAGO BULLS ARE MORE than the best-loved team in the NBA—they are a phenomenon. But it hasn't always been that way. The Bulls followed nearly a half century of failed basketball teams in the Windy City. From Johnny "Red" Kerr to Phil Jackson, from Dick Klein to Jerry Reinsdorf, from Jerry Sloan to Michael Jordan, the Bulls' story is a strange, winding tale, beginning with disheartening struggles and miraculously cresting with the glory of the Jordan years.

The first part of this text is a quick look back at the Bulls' formation. Parts two and three are an oral history, which allows the players, coaches, owners, staff members and media representatives who witnessed the events to tell the stories in their own words.

My special thanks to Steve Schanwald, the Bulls' vice president of marketing and broadcasting, and to the team's media relations staff, Tim Hallam, Lori Flores and Tom Smithburg. All of you were a tremendous help under trying circumstances. Also Bulls staff members Keith Brown, Dave Kurland, Wendy Knoll and Brooks Boyer were tremendous help.

Also special thanks to Ken Widelka and the *Chicago Tribune* for generous use of photographs.

I also want to thank George Biggers, formerly of the *Chicago Tribune's* book division, who first conceived of this project and hired me to do it.

In addition to thanking the more than 60 people who agreed to be interviewed for this project, I want to acknowledge the work of the dozens of writers who have covered the team for the city's newspapers, including Terry Armour, Lacy J. Banks, Terry Boers, Bill Gleason, Mike Imrem, Melissa Isaacson, John Jackson, Paul Ladewski, Bernie Lincicome, Bob Logan, Jay Mariotti, Kent McDill, Mike Mulligan, Skip Myslenski, Steve Rosenbloom, Gene Seymour, Sam Smith, Ray Sons, Paul Sullivan, Mark Vancil, Bob Verdi, and many, many others. Without their work over the years, the compilation of this history would have been impossible.

Extensive use was made of a variety of publications, including the *Baltimore Sun, Basketball Times, Boston Globe, Chicago Defender, Chicago Tribune, Chicago Sun-Times, Daily Southtown, The Detroit News, The Detroit Free Press, The Daily Herald, Hoop Magazine, Houston Post, Los Angeles Times, The National, New York Daily News, The New York Times, New York Post,*

The Charlotte Observer, USA Today, The Oregonian, Philadelphia Inquirer, Sport, Sports Illustrated, The Sporting News, Street & Smith's Pro Basketball Yearbook, and The Washington Post.

Also of tremendous value were the media guides produced by the Bulls' publicty staffs over the years.

Also vital were several books, including:

24 Seconds to Shoot by Leonard Koppett
Bull Session by Johnny Kerr and Terry Pluto
Cages to Jump Shots by Robert Peterson
Championship NBA by Leonard Koppett
Coach by Ray Meyer and Ray Sons
From Muscular Christianity to the Market Place by Albert Gammon Applin II
From Set Shot to Slam Dunk by Charles Salzberg
Giant Steps by Kareem Abdul-Jabbar and Peter Knobler
Holzman on Hoops by Red Holzman and Harvey Frommer
Honey by John Russell
Long Time Coming by Chet Walker and Chris Messenger
Loose Balls by Terry Pluto
March to the Top by Art Chansky and Eddie Fogler
Maverick by Phil Jackson and Charlie Rosen
Michael Jordan by Mitchell Krugel
Official Spalding Basketball Guide, various editions, 1898-1930
Pro Basketball Encyclopedia by David S. Neft and Richard M. Cohen
Rare Air by Michael Jordan with Mark Vancil
Sportswit by Lee Green
Tall Tales by Terry Pluto
The Bob Verdi Collection by Bob Verdi
The Bulls and Chicago by Bob Logan
The Franchise by Cameron Stauth
The Glory and the Dream by William Manchester
The History of Professional Basketball by Glenn Dickey
The Jordan Rules by Sam Smith
The Official NBA Basketball Encyclopedia, edited by Zander Hollander and
    Alex Sachare
Transition Game by Melissa Isaacson

10

Foreword

by John Paxson

WHAT FOLLOWS IS PERHAPS THE MOST unique story in all of sports, the rise of the Chicago Bulls from the status of a third-rate NBA team to become one of the most successful franchises in the history of American professional sports.

I consider it my great fortune to have been there for the exciting part of the ride.

It was fun playing with Michael Jordan and the Bulls back in 1985-86 when I joined the team. We weren't very good, and that was hard. We didn't have a lot of talent or confidence, and other teams would disrespect us. Especially Boston. The Celtics did that a lot. Michael was so good and Charles Oakley was pretty decent, but outside of that we really didn't have a good team until Scottie Pippen and Horace Grant came into the picture. Then you could see the talent level rise, and we had the feeling that we were going to get better.

Before that could happen we had to defeat the Pistons. Once we did, we claimed three straight championships. What a dream come true. It changed how each and every player on the roster looked at himself. It changed the city of Chicago, too. Winning can do that. I'm not sure what winning did for us outwardly, but inwardly it justified all the effort and hard work that we put into it. It confirmed our belief that we could win, and with that comes a confidence that carries over into your personal life as well as your professional life.

The greatest part about winning is how you feel as a group. You're happy for one another. You look at small plays that happen in a game, the people who come off the bench and provide something that the group needs. In our first championship run, Cliff Levingston provided some key minutes in the games out in Los Angeles. Craig Hodges did the same thing. You understand how important each individual is to your success. It's not just the best player. It's from one to twelve, the coaches included, and your appreciation for each player is very high.

The story of the team begins well before our championship years, but if anything, the story shows just how important the Bulls who came before us were to our success. Without their perseverance, there would have been no Chicago Bulls. In that regard, the championship is all of ours to share. Mostly, though, it belongs to the city of Chicago and the greatest fans in the world.

Introduction

by Jerry Reinsdorf

WELCOME TO THIS CELEBRATION OF the Chicago Bulls' 30 seasons of existence. As I look back over these pages, I'm amazed at the growth and accomplishments of the organization.

I'm very proud of these accomplishments, of the three world championships and the completion of the United Center, a joint venture of the Bulls and Blackhawks, which gives the city of Chicago a state-of-the-art sports arena, among the finest, if not the finest, in the world.

I'm also humbled, because these things wouldn't have been possible without the support of our fans, particularly that small, loyal group who followed the Bulls through their lean decades. Some of my favorite passages here come in reading about the old Bulls, when the roster was filled with tough guys like Jerry Sloan, Bob Love, Chet Walker, Tom Boerwinkle and Norm Van Lier. They didn't win a world championship, but they established a fighting spirit here in Chicago that gave Jerry Krause, our vice president of basketball operations, his staff and the many great players something to build on in the 1980s.

On our 30th anniversary, I salute them and our fans.

Now let's see if we can't get to work on winning that fourth title.

The laser lights dance in the United Center.

The Cast of Characters

Tiny Archibald, a Hall of Fame guard in the 1970s and '80s, lives in New York where he is pursuing a coaching career.

B. J. Armstrong, the former Bulls' guard, was selected by the Toronto Raptors in the 1995 expansion draft, then traded to Golden State.

Johnny Bach, a former Bulls assistant coach from 1986 to 1993, is a Charlotte Hornets assistant coach.

Ed Badger, the Bulls' head coach from 1976-78, lives in Florida.

Ben Bentley, the former Bulls PR man, is retired and lives in suburban Chicago.

Bill Blair, a former Bulls assistant coach from 1983-85, is coach of the Minnesota Timberwolves.

Tom Boerwinkle, a former Bulls center and broadcaster, operates an oil distributorship in Chicago.

Bob Boozer, who played forward for the first Bulls' team, is a lobbyist for the telecommunications industry.

Bill Cartwright, the former Bulls player, is a consultant to the Seattle Supersonics.

Don Casey, the former Bulls assistant coach, is a Boston Celtics assistant coach.

Jim Cleamons is a Bulls assistant coach.

Jerry Colangelo, the Bulls' first scout and marketing director, owns the Phoenix Suns.

Doug Collins, the Bulls' coach from 1986 to '89, is coach of the Detroit Pistons.

Tom Dore is a Bulls radio broadcaster.

Don Dyer coached Scottie Pippen at Central Arkansas.

Bill Gleason is a longtime Chicago sportswriter.

Sidney Green, the former Bull, lives in Orlando.

Matt Guokas, the former Bulls guard, is a color analyst for NBC Sports.

Tim Hallam is the Bulls' director of media relations.

Garfield Heard, a former Bulls forward, is an Indiana Pacers assistant coach.

Phil Jackson is the coach of the Chicago Bulls.

Michael Jordan is Michael Jordan.

Johnny Kerr, the first coach of the Bulls, is a Bulls broadcast color analyst.

Dick Klein, the Bulls' founder, is a scout for the Phoenix Suns. He lives in South Carolina.

Jonathan Kovler, the former Bulls managing partner, lives and works in Chicago.

Jerry Krause, a former Bulls scout, is the Bulls vice president for basketball operations.

Ronnie Lester, a Bulls guard in the early 1980s, is a scout for the Los Angeles Lakers.

John Ligmanowski is the Bulls' longtime equipment manager.

Bob Logan is a veteran Chicago sportswriter and author of the 1975 book, The Bulls and Chicago.

Kevin Loughery was Michael Jordan's first NBA coach.

Bob Love, the former Bulls forward, is the team's community relations director. His jersey number 10 is one of three retired by the team.

Irwin Mandel is the Bulls' vice president for financial and legal affairs.

Brian McIntyre, the former Bulls PR director, is the NBA's vice president for public relations.

Kip Motta, son of Dick Motta and a former Bulls ball boy, is an assistant coach with the Dallas Mavericks.

Dick Motta, Bulls coach from 1968-76, is coach of the Dallas Mavericks.

Jeff Mullins, the former Bulls guard, is the coach at the University of North Carolina-Charlotte.

John Paxson, the former Bulls guard, is a Bulls assistant coach.

Will Perdue a former center for the Bulls was traded to the San Antonio Spurs in 1995.

Mark Pfeil, the former Bulls trainer, is the Milwaukee Bucks' trainer.

Scottie Pippen is a forward for the Bulls.

Jack Ramsay, the former Portland coach, is a broadcaster with the Miami Heat.

Cheryl Raye is a reporter for WMVP in Chicago.

Clifford Ray, the former Bulls center, is a Continental Basketball Association coach.

Jerry Reinsdorf is the chairman of the Chicago Bulls.

Oscar Robertson, the NBA Hall of Famer, is a Cincinnati businessman.

Scotty Robertson, a former Bulls coach, is an assistant with the Miami Heat.

Bob Rosenberg is the longtime official scorekeeper for the Bulls.

Chip Schaeffer is the Bulls' trainer.

Steve Schanwald is the Bulls' vice president for marketing and broadcasting.

Jerry Sloan, the former Bulls guard, is the coach of the Utah Jazz. His jersey number 4 was retired by the team.

Reggie Theus, a Bulls guard in the 1970s and early '80s, is a broadcaster living in Los Angeles.

Rod Thorn, the former Bulls general manager in the 1970s and '80s, is an NBA vice president for operations.

Norm Van Lier, the former Bulls guard, is a broadcaster in Chicago.

Bob Weiss, the former Bulls guard, is Seattle Supersonics assistant coach.

Pat Williams, the former Bulls general manager, is chief operating officer and general manager of the Orlando Magic.

Tex Winter is a Chicago Bulls assistant coach.

James Worthy, the former Laker, lives in Los Angeles.

15

Prologue
Chicago Hope,
March 1995

*T*HE RITUAL BEGINS EACH GAME NIGHT *with the house lights going black and the tape deck kicking in, hammering out those familiar Alan Parsons Project chords, the heavy, synthesized, eerie ones that sound like the score for some science fiction horror flick. You know, like Alien III is on the premises or something.*

Simultaneously, lines of green laser lights begin gyrating wildly and raking across the audience, mesmerizing yet another sellout of 21,711. All the while the spotlight focuses on the giant Bulls face, the team logo, at center court, and soon the laser lights stop their dancing and fall to the arena floor to reshape themselves into giant green Bulls heads.

The problem is, if you watch these lights too closely you risk missing the main show on the scoreboard's massive videoscreens overhead. They, too, fill with the angry visage of a Bull, a computer-designed, nineties kind of animal, who turns and snorts his way through the city's canyons, pausing along the way to scare the bejiggers out of a bronze lion in front of the Art Institute.

From there, the Bull elevates his game on some sort of vacuum-cushioned hooves and whisks his way up and down the streets, like a tourist lost in traffic, looking for that renowned Madison Street. You might even say that he passes some familiar landmarks, except this urban environment is sterile and clean and crisp as a laser print and hauntingly unfamiliar.

Heck, when the Bull finally does locate Madison and storms his way out to the United Center, he finds the building set in a vast, green meadow. To make sure you get the picture, the artist rotates the view of the building as the Bull searches for the press gate. Sure enough, it's green meadows all around, as if hundreds of urban blocks have been plowed under and reseeded.

Just as you're beginning to contemplate the implications of all this, public address announcer Ray Clay brings you back to the business at hand with his patented, deeply etched introduction, "AND NOW...

The grand old building – from renowned Gate No. 3 1/2 to its peculiar acoustics – served Chicago for the best part of eight decades.

YOUR CHICAGO BULLS!!!"

On cue, the crowd pushes the decibel level another notch toward infinity, and just in case there's a need for any extra noise, the United Center's architects have placed sound reflectors

17

The crowds in the Stadium could be lusty.

in the ceiling, which knock the waves back to the arena floor. To say the least, it is oppressive, which makes the players on opposing teams thankful that the lights are down. Otherwise, the home fans might be able to see just how distracted and unsettled they are by this display.

The introduction of each of the Bulls' starting five gooses the crowd a bit higher, and by the time Ray Clay works around to calling out Scottie Pippen's name, the sound in the building has built to a heavy metal quality, one in which the particles are being shoved around so forcefully that the air seems momentarily transformed from gas to solid.

Solid noise. And it hurts.

Then the fireworks in the rafters go off, raining sparks and light and smoke down on 21,711 heads until finally it's over, except for the emergency recovery work going on in your ears.

It didn't used to be this way, of course. Back in the old days, you got your beer and popcorn and your basic four quarters of hoop. Promotions were something employees got if they did a good job.

In 1966, when the Bulls were a new team and attempting to celebrate their first season with a parade, they could muster just two flatbed trucks for the procession—one for the staff and one for a frightened bull they had arranged to borrow for the afternoon from the nearby stockyards, a sight that left local reporters shak-

ing their heads in amusement.

Yes, it seems the Bulls have come a long way in 30 years.

On the other hand, they've merely moved across the street, from one side of the 1900 block of West Madison to the other.

Here, inside the United Center, is the future of pro hoops, but outside, just north across Madison, is the game's past, the remains of Chicago Stadium. In the dusk of this Wednesday night in March, the Stadium stands as silent and eerie as a graveyard. Over the coming months, demolition crews will persistently digest the grand old "sandstone sarcophagus," eating away first at the insides, then attacking the shell, until only the steel framework and neat piles of rubble remain.

Tonight, the old building stands with a gigantic hole knocked in its west wall, revealing that the interior is still largely intact. For the ticket holders arriving for tonight's game, it is unsettling to see the giant wound in this landmark. Even stranger, the lights are on inside, as if the spirits of games past are anxiously awaiting the crowd's arrival for another tipoff.

Just months ago, the buildings' circumstances were reversed. Then, the United Center was a framework under construction, standing silently, while the Stadium, the "Madhouse on Madison," thundered with the exhortations of some 18,676 fans. Tonight, though, the only sound in the Stadium is the relentless Chicago *wind pushing through the vast hole and rattling the lights. Soon the Stadium will fade altogether, into a parking lot.*

Sometimes during his workday, Tim Hallam, the Bulls director of media services, retreats from his spacious new office in the United Center to the sidewalk outside, for a smoke. These retreats are a bit uncomfortable these days because Hallam, who has worked games at the Stadium for 17 years, doesn't like looking at the grand old building in its hour of demise. He couldn't quite bring himself to gather with the crowd that witnessed the wrecking ball first striking the west wall just days ago. "It was a little bit of a funeral," he explained.

Even Bulls' principal owner Jerry Reinsdorf, the man who built the United Center with Blackhawks chairman Bill Wirtz, admits to being unsettled by the sight of the Stadium going down. "But it's just a building," he says. "It needed to be replaced. What's important are the memories of what happened there, and the memories will live for a long, long time."

Research suggests that the senses drive the memory, so the Stadium is destined like her sister building, Boston Garden—which also is scheduled for razing in the coming months—to be remembered for the peculiar smells of old arenas, decades of stale popcorn and spilled beer and sweat.

Pungent as these were, the overriding sensory impact of the Stadium was the noise itself, which helps explain why the team has gone out of its way to make sure the United Center is just as deafening. "There was no place like Chicago Stadium," says former Bulls general manager Rod Thorn. "The acoustics in that old building just drove the noise down right over the floor, and it just hovered there. It made it impossible to hear anything."

Everyone, it seems, has a favorite recollection of this impossibility. When was it the loudest? For many, that date is May 1989, Game 6 of the Eastern Conference Finals, the Bulls vs. the Detroit Pistons. Toward the end of the third quarter, Pistons center Bill Laimbeer, that dastardly villain, stepped to the free throw line, and somehow the same thought was instantly and magically transmitted into the minds of the 18,676 people in attendance.

"Laim-beer sucks! Laim-beer sucks! Laim-beer sucks!" they intoned over and over until, sadly, he canned both shots.

Kip Motta, son of former Bulls coach Dick Motta, likes to think of the 1974 playoffs when he was a young ball boy and the Bulls were facing the Pistons at home for Game 7 of their playoff battle. Jerry Sloan, the team's gutty leader, had been injured in Game 6 in Detroit and was unable to play. "We were warming up," Motta recalled, "and you could tell there was no excitement. It was like a cloud of doom over us because Jerry wasn't gonna play. But when he came up out of the locker room on his crutches, the crowd gave him a standing ova-

The United Center going up and the Stadium coming down.

19

Michael kissed the Stadium goodbye in 1994.

The United Center is a state-of-the-art home for once and future Bulls.

"These days people talk about noisy buildings, but a lot of that is electronic, manufactured noise. There wasn't much going on back in the Stadium except people yelling and raising hell every time they came out to the game. If they came, they came to yell. They didn't come to see who was gonna look at them and see what they looked like. There wasn't very many people sitting there in mink coats, either. It was hard core fans.

"And they'd boo your ass, too, if you didn't play well," Sloan remembers with a grin. "We were getting beat one night against New York. The Knicks had us down 28 points at half time, and our fans booed us off the floor. We responded to it. We came right back out in the second half and beat the Knicks, and that's when New York was good, when they had Willis Reed and Walt Frazier and that bunch."

"The loudest I ever heard it," says Hallam, "was when Jerry Sloan was coaching and we were playing the Knicks in the best-of-three miniseries in the first round of the 1981 play-offs and we went to overtime.

"That was back when people were smoking in the upper balconies and you had the haze hanging over the floor. That's why it was such a great—I don't want to say it—but a great 'sixth man.' It was so loud it was crazy. You weren't exactly fearful, but you could tell that anything could happen. It was very intimidating for officials, for visiting teams, because it looked like all hell could break loose at any time."

Standing here at dusk, you can almost hear the echoes of these and a thousand other events, Blackhawks Stanley Cup victories, prizefights, ice shows, Globetrotter comedy hours, even an NFL game or two. Michael Jordan made his final playing appearance in the Stadium last year, at a charity game hosted by Scottie Pippen. On departing at the end of the game, Jordan got down and kissed the floor, the very platform of his rise to greatness. It was the only sendoff the Madhouse really needed.

Now, these two buildings are passing in the night. How strange. How appropriate. Reinsdorf is right. History isn't special until something changes or someone dies. Tonight the Stadium is dying. But its history lives.

tion. It was the loudest, most intense ovation I've ever heard. It was unbelievable. They went crazy. For four or five minutes, they didn't stop. And it got louder and louder all the time."

Buoyed by the fan support, the Bulls pulled together and beat Detroit to win the series.

"I was reluctant to even go up there," Sloan remembers. "But I wanted to watch the game."

Now the coach of the Utah Jazz, Sloan's fondest Chicago memories are of the Stadium. "I spent a great deal of my life in basketball in that building," he says, "and it was one of the greatest places if you were a player. Having the fan support in that building to me was the height of excitement. The play-off games that we had, even though you remember the losses, the games that we played in there and the games that we won, the feeling was incredible."

The two arenas shared
Madison Street for a few
months.

1966 CHICAGO BULLS 1996
XXX
30 YEARS AND RUNNING

21

The biggest piece in Jordan's jewelry collection.

ACROSS THE STREET, AS THE BULLS prepare to tipoff against the Atlanta Hawks, the fans find themselves quite comfortable in Reinsdorf's grand vision of the future. While the United Center may not cater to their every whim, it comes close, offering a basketball carnival of live bands, interactive games and an array of food and drink.

On this Wednesday night in March, this party atmosphere courses with a new electricity, and the fans have their thoughts turned to the past, not to the Stadium, but to the rumored return of Michael Jordan to basketball.

To them, the Jordan story is as familiar as their own. You, too, may have heard of him. He's the shooting guard who led the Bulls to their days of glory, or more specifically to three straight NBA championships. Remember his flash dance to the basket during the 1991 victory over the Los Angeles Lakers and Magic Johnson? And how about his matter-of-fact shrug after hitting all those threes to dash Clyde Drexler and the Portland Trail Blazers for the 1992 title? Or the way he toyed with the New York Knicks and the Phoenix Suns in '93?

The fans had been a part of all of it, a big part. Jordan had said as much many times over, and for that he had thanked them just a few months ago, on November 1, 1994, the night his jersey number 23 was retired and his statue was unveiled outside the United Center

Perhaps the most special moment came in 1992 after their second championship. The Bulls had vanquished Portland in Game 6, and after the game the players retreated to the locker room to engage in the usual ritual, spewing their champagne, wearing their new hats backwards, doing their media interviews and hugging lots of hugs.

And the fans, as usual, were supposed to go away, to file out the aisles of the Stadium and retreat to their cars to face the post-game traffic. Only this time they didn't want to turn the moment loose. So they stayed, thundering on in celebration. A curtain call for a basketball team? Unheard of.

Still they thundered. So the players and coaches trudged back up the steep, narrow stairs from the bowels of the Stadium and cast themselves into the center of an unprecedented lovefest.

The 1992 championship celebration was a 10,000-goosebump experience.

Bulls fans were ready to revive the Air Show in 1995.

But this season, the team has struggled to stay above .500, leaving frustration and some despair, a sense that the Bulls'—and to some degree the city's—hour of greatness is slipping away, much like the Stadium across the street is slipping into darkness.

Only now, the rumor of Michael's return has evaporated those anxieties and replaced them with golden thoughts. There's no better evidence of this than the recent boom in retail business in Bulls memorabilia, in jerseys and hats and T-shirts and coffee mugs, anything sporting the team's logo or Jordan's No. 23.

"This is all about hope," observes Brad Riggert, manager of Fandemonium, the United Center's fan store, after watching thousands of shoppers plucking items from the shelves in recent days. "Michael's return is bringing back hope to the fans, hope to the whole city."

Hope, indeed. For decades, that has been the fuel driving Chicago basketball. At times it ran high. More often it ebbed low. In the early 1970s, when Jerry Sloan and Norm Van Lier and Chet Walker and Bob Love and Tom Boerwinkle shoved their way to NBA respect, the hope was based on their work ethic, that good old hogbutcher, stacker-of-wheat, city-of-big-shoulders mentality. They were desperate Bulls, willing to sacrifice their health to be winners.

"We went down to the locker room for the presentation of the trophy," Jerry Reinsdorf recalled. "We must have been down there close to half an hour when somebody mentioned the crowd hadn't left. The team went back up on the floor, and the players got up on the scorer's table and started dancing and holding the trophy up for the fans. The crowd just yelled and yelled and yelled. It was a wonderful, exhilirating feeling.

"I've never seen so much love pouring out from a crowd."

It was a transcendent moment, and now Bulls fans understandably want more of them, want Michael to end his 18-month "retirement" from basketball so they can all share in more glory, more special feelings.

Even though it won't come on this night against the Atlanta Hawks, Jordan's impending return has created a noticeable lift in spirts here. During the 1993-94 season, the first without Jordan, the Bulls accomplished incredible things. They stacked up 55 wins and battled their way to the Eastern Conference Finals yet again, only to lose Game 7 to New York on a controversial, last-second call.

Jordan, of course, was none of that. Instead, he brought the hope of flight, of a special magic, of new possibilities, of glass box buildings and laser lights. His talent has built this phantasmagoria of success, the United Center, and it seems only right that he should play here, in this new age of pro basketball that he has helped to create.

That, above all, is on the fans' minds this Wednesday night in March of 1995. The special feelings are abundant. The fans know that hope is back. Bigger than ever. And, once again, it has wings.

Part One

Hoop Schemes

Birthing the Bulls, 1962-66

THE STORY OF THE CHICAGO BULLS IS really the story of a city attempting to come to terms with an incongrous, unruly game that it was destined to love. That it has taken decades for that love affair to flower only confirms the charm, dedication and foolhardiness of the parties involved.

Perhaps no one was more foolhardy than a promotional salesman whom the newspapers referred to as "Dick O. Klein," the man who brought the Bulls to life with the opening of the National Basketball Association's 1966-67 season.

No less of an authority than The Sporting News had declared that same year that Chicago was "long regarded as the burial grounds of professional basketball."

Interred in the city's memory was a long list of failed teams with strange names. The Bruins, the Duffy Florals, the Studebakers, the American Gears, the Stags, the Packers, the Majors, the Zephyrs. All had lived briefly—and some even won championships—only to starve in Chicago's seeming indifference.

Unfortunately, the failed teams served to obscure the city's many major contributions to basketball. After all, it was Amos Alonzo Stagg, that famous football coach, who is credited with first bringing the game to Chicago. Stagg, in fact, served with Dr. James Naismith, the man who invented basketball, on the faculty at the YMCA School for Christain Workers in Springfield, Massachusetts, in 1891. Stagg even played in the first hoops game that year, a contest pitting the faculty against the students.

By 1894, Stagg had moved to the newly formed University of Chicago, where he founded a basketball team that played a seven-game schedule against local athletic clubs. In 1896,

Mickey Rottner of the Chicago Stags drive against the Knicks in 1946.

Stagg's University of Chicago team defeated a YMCA club made up of University of Iowa students in what historians believe was the first five-man basketball game, one of the sport's key innovations.

In another important development, the University of Chicago's turn-of-the-century star, Hall of Fame center John Schommer, is credited with inventing the modern backboard.

Chicago's many other contributions include:

• The first widely integrated pro team, the Chicago Studebakers, playing only the 1942-43 season in the old National Basketball League.

• Pro basketball's first dominant big man, George Mikan out of DePaul, who played for the Chicago American Gears in the old National League, and then for the Minneapolis Lakers.

• The Chicago Herald American's "World Tournament," played from 1938-48, the first national pro championship, and the first competition that featured the best all-black teams playing against all-white teams.

• The oldest running pro team in the world, the Harlem Globetrotters, which got its start in Chicago in the 1920s.

> **The NBA back then was a very small business, like a neighborhood grocery store compared to the supermarket it is today.**
>
> **–Dick Klein**

Most historians agree that pro basketball came to life in 1896 with the formation of the Trenton New Jersey Basket Ball Team, leading to an explosion of leagues across the Northeast. Chicago, however, didn't get its first prominent pro team until 1925 when Bears maestro George Halas founded the Bruins to play in the American Basketball League. Both the Bruins and the league folded in early 1931, just as the Great Depression settled over much of the country.

Next came the Chicago Duffy Florals, who won the 1935 championship of the Midwest Basketball Conference, the forerunner of the National Basketball League, which was a forerunner of the NBA. The Duffy Florals folded after a second season, and Chicago was again without a team until Halas briefly revived the Bruins during the turbulent 1940s. And the Studebakers and the American Gears also operated during World War II, a time when pro hoops showed a faint pulse.

Finally the war ended, and in its aftermath came a new exhuberance for pro sports. In 1946, a group of hockey arena owners founded the Basketball Association of America, another forerunner of the NBA. Chicago's entry was the Stags, set to compete for fans with the American Gears in the rival National League. The Gears and Stags both challenged for the championships in their respective leagues, but they still didn't draw much fan interest (although the Stags gave away an incredible 80,000 free tickets one season). Chicago just didn't respond. By 1950, all of the city's pro hoops teams were dead.

Although the Globetrotters regularly played the Minneapolis Lakers from 1948 to 1952 in games that would attract 20,000 fans to Chicago Stadium, Chicago itself had no regular pro basketball team until the NBA granted expansion rights to the Chicago Packers for 1961-62 season.

The Packers got the first pick of the 1961 draft and took Walt Bellamy, the 6-11 center out of the University of Indiana. For a coach, they hired former Laker great Jim Pollard and arranged a deal to play in the Amphitheatre. Bellamy went on to win Rookie-of-the-Year honors by averaging 31.6 points and 19 rebounds, but the team finished 18-62 and found quick financial trouble.

"People weren't coming out," said longtime Chicago scorekeeper Bob Rosenberg, who kept stats for the Packers. "They weren't a winning team."

The NBA itself was barely surviving. The expansion to Chicago had made a nine-team circuit, but that hardly generated enough viewership for NBC. The network notified the league that it would not carry NBA games for the 1962-63 season.

With both his team and the league seemingly on the brink of failure, Dave Trager, the managing owner of the Packers, began looking around for an exit, which the city of Baltimore and a group of Maryland business interests were willing to provide. They offered to guarantee the Packers 1,000 season tickets and a $1.4 million buyout if he would move the team to Baltimore.

The Packers agreed, only they would have to remain in Chicago for one more season because the arena under construction in Baltimore wouldn't be ready until the 1963-64 season.

As a lame duck franchise, the Chicago team renamed itself the Zephyrs and moved to the Coliseum. "It was a bad building in a bad neighborhood," Rosenberg said.

The franchise produced yet another Rookie of the Year, Terry Dischinger, a 6-7 forward from Purdue who averaged 25.5 points. The second-year team with two high-scoring young stars (Bellamy averaged 27.9 points) finished 25-55. In the aftermath, the team packed up and moved to Baltimore to become the Bullets, a club that would make the playoffs in two more seasons and compete for the league championship in 1970.

"Trager said he gave Chicago a fair chance, which I don't think he did," Rosenberg said. "Had he waited one more year they would have become a winner."

The experience was enough to finish Chicago as a pro hoops town in the eyes of incoming NBA commissioner Walter Kennedy. Dick Klein, of course, was watching from the wings and had other ideas. He just needed money, lots of it, which would have put off most people. But where others saw a graveyard, he saw a gold mine.

Getting Started

IF YOU DIDN'T HAVE BIG MONEY, YOU needed a tremendous amount of blarney to talk your way into an NBA franchise in 1963. Particularly in Chicago, which was the last place the league wanted to be. By all accounts, Dick Klein had blarney to spare. How appropriate that when he finally got a team, he named it the Bulls.

"He was a P.T. Barnum-type guy," said Johnny "Red" Kerr, the Bulls' first coach. "He could sell anything to anybody."

"Dick was a fun guy," recalled Chicago sportswriter Bob Logan. "He had all these pretensions about being a great basketball mind. But what he was, was a guy you'd just like to sit down with and talk and drink and have fun.

"He got a bad rap in Chicago. He was the guy who put it all together. Without him, there wouldn't have been a Chicago Bulls. Dick, more than anything else, loved the sound of his own voice. Basketball was something he could be a thundering expert in."

Klein once told Logan that he would do anything, even jump out a window, to get attention. In many ways, his attempt to start the Bulls was more than a figurative leap.

A native of Fort Madison, Iowa, Klein attended Northwestern on a baseball scholarship. Basketball, however, proved to be his ticket. In 1941, he finished his sophomore season as the Big 10's second leading scorer and earned a spot on the All-Conference team. His big loss, however, was a flunked chemistry course that cost him his eligibility.

He knocked around in baseball briefly before entering the Navy and playing service ball during World War II. After the conflict he played pro basketball briefly for the American Gears before settling into a career in sales promotions.

By 1962, he was a 42-year-old ex-jock with 250 pounds spread over his 6-3 frame. He had a solid sales promotion business, a nice house in Kenilworth and a strange burning desire to prove that pro basketball could work in Chicago if you just made sure to put the fans first.

That November of 1962, as the Zephyrs were finalizing their deal with Baltimore, Klein secured a handshake agreement to buy the team for somewhere between $250,000 and $600,000 (depending on which account you believe) and keep it in Chicago. But in reality he didn't have the cash for that kind of deal. Every time he ran into somebody who appeared wealthy, Klein would pitch his idea. But no one wanted to throw away good money on yet another Chicago pro basketball venture.

So the Zephyrs packed up for Baltimore, leaving Klein with a substantial case of basketball blues.

The only cure, he decided, was to bring yet another NBA expansion team to the city, an undertaking that would require far more money

The Bulls were the NBA's first expansion team since another Chicago franchise had failed in 1963.

than Klein had. Undeterred, he founded the Chicago Professional Basketball Corporation that January of 1963 and began the hunt for investors.

The NBA told him it wasn't interested in Chicago, but when Klein persisted the expansion committee indicated that a new franchise could be had for $600,000. Klein thought he had the interest of an investor with $200,000, but no sooner had he begun talking with the league than the investor backed out.

Suddenly, he was back to zero funding. Regardless, he mailed a letter of application to the league on April 11. "I later learned the league ignored it because I hadn't included the required $100,000 deposit," he once told the Chicago Tribune. "Then I told a big lie."

He wired the NBA that the death of a partner's mother had placed his firm in probate. "I said the check would be forthcoming," Klein said. "Later, much later, I learned my telegram had been filed in the wastebasket."

Klein renewed his search for investors, looking high and low. His ally in this effort was John Yachim, a friend and investment banker who belonged to the prestigious Chicago Club, where the city's rich and powerful rubbed shoulders.

"I wanted a breed of cat that had enough muscle," Klein recalled, "that if we ever did get into a position of fruition, we'd have a strong argument with the league."

The Chicago Club was just the lair for this sort of animal. "Lots of brass, lots of leather, lots of thick carpets," Klein said. "The Chicago Club was a tight little island, and I got all of my investors there."

Not right away, of course. Pulling together the pieces would take nearly three years. And with each passing week, Klein's gamble would grow, because the more work he did to create a team, the less he did with his business, D. O. Klein and Associates, which hawked sales promotional items to banks and other businesses. Even when he eventually found investors, they would put up no cash. Instead, they signed agreements to provide cash if and when he secured an NBA franchise. So all of the costs of the venture came from his own pocket.

While his wife had some family money and his business was successful, Klein was far from wealthy.

So the tension of his loony dream kept building. In that sense, the Bulls were born of desperation.

In early 1964, Yachim directed Klein to his first big cat, Chicago industrialist Dan Searle, a pharmaceutical magnate who also had invested in pro baseball. Searle told Klein he was interested because running a pro sports team was fun and the tax incentives were nice.

"He committed to the program if I had the right kind of people to go along with it," Klein said. "There's a pedigree in a certain league. Nobody wants to be associated with people who don't have that pedigree."

Searle's commitment was a big step, but for months it was Klein's only success. Next he approached Ed Higgins, chairman of Pepsi-Cola bottlers in Chicago. "Higgins was interested, but he thought it was just a pipe dream," Klein said. "'You'll never get the right kind of guys,' he said. I said, 'Yes, I will, Eddie.'"

Chuck Comiskey, who had sold his share of the White Sox, gave Klein's hoops venture a gander, then passed. Next up was A. G. Atwater, Klein recalled. "A. G. told me that if I was trying to buy a boat marina, he'd be interested. He added, 'If you want to buy a basketball team, here's a stick of gum.'"

A break, of sorts, came in 1964 when league commissioner Maurice Podoloff, who had been against expansion, resigned and was replaced by Walter Kennedy, who favored expansion as long as it wasn't in Chicago.

"Dick, don't waste my time," Kennedy said when Klein approached him.

The NBA, however, announced that it wanted to add a tenth team, which generated interest from more than a half dozen groups across the country, including Texas oilman Lamar Hunt. On the heels of that came Klein's big break. The NBA was trying to renegotiate a network television contract. ABC Sports executive Roone Arledge told the league that the network wanted a team in Chicago to guarantee the interest of the nation's second largest city.

Suddenly, Klein's talk about a team in Chicago didn't seem so loony any more. In fact, several expansion groups, including Hunt's, shifted their location to Chicago to fit the league's new needs. But Hunt wanted to start his team in 1965, and the league wasn't ready.

With the NBA's changed stance, Higgins and others began to take Klein more seriously. "Everybody had a different reason, like tax shelters or equity gains, but suddenly we had the money," Klein said.

Or at least he thought he did.

But when he phoned Kennedy to say he had the money Klein learned the price had jumped to $750,000 because of the various groups now competing for a team.

That blow cost Klein two of his investors, but Searle stayed with him, as did Higgins. To raise more money, Klein scurried around and even tried to join forces with Lamar Hunt, but was rebuffed.

Finally, Klein recruited Elmer Rich, Jr., Phil Frye, Harold Mayer (of the Oscar Mayer family), and Hugh Knowles (of the Zenith electronics fortune), all of them with the pedigree of wealth that Searle required. Klein then took his $750,000 to the league, only to learn that Kennedy had raised the ante yet again to $1 million.

"They flipflopped so many times, in so many different ways," Klein said of the league's owners.

Two weeks before Klein was to make his presentation before the NBA, the league jacked the price one more time, to $1.25 million. "I felt like a guy who had been put against the wall and shot at dawn," Klein later told the Chicago Tribune. "My backers were ready to abandon ship, but I persuaded Elmer Rich and Harold Mayer to come to New York with me to see Kennedy. There we saw 17,000 raving maniacs in Madison Square Garden watching a violent game between the Knicks and the Lakers. That wrapped up my battle. It crystallized my backing. 'If New York can do this, so can Chicago,' Mayer said."

He raised the ante, and, miraculously, everyone stayed put.

Klein had put together what was perhaps the wealthiest group of owners ever to back a pro franchise. All of the groups trying to secure a franchise were invited to New York to make presentations on January 26, 1966. "We each had an hour before the NBA's Board of Governors," Klein recalled. "When I made the presentation, they asked me what single thing made my group stand out. I said, 'I have approximately a half dozen partners, and any one of them could buy the whole league. So we have financial stability, and we're in it for the long pull.'

"Then I sat in my hotel room waiting for the other seven or eight presentations. I was summoned back, and they all rose and applauded and congratulated me on getting the new franchise in Chicago. Needless to say, I was pleased as punch.

"Later, Lamar Hunt, who had the hotel room next door to me, knocked on my door and said, 'This is the first time in my life I've ever lost to anyone on a thing like this.' He asked, 'Have you got any more room in your group?' I said, 'I got one piece left.' He's still an owner of the Chicago Bulls to this day."

Although Klein's group paid $1.25 million for the franchise, the league announced the price as $1.6 million, Klein said. "They wanted to make the value of a franchise worth something. The next year they put a hard figure of $1.8 million for San Diego and Seattle. Then it went to $2 million for Phoenix and Milwaukee. The owners were living off of expansion money."

In announcing the move, Sun Times columnist Dick Hackenburg declared, "Basketball is not dead in Chicago, it's just in a state of D. Klein."

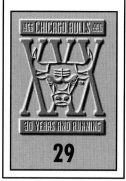

Coach Johnny Kerr's notes from the 1966 expansion draft.

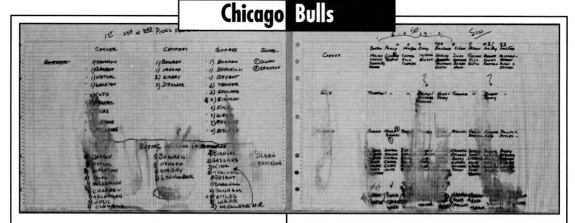

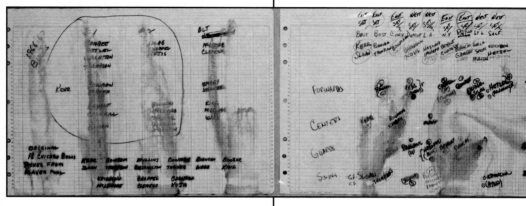

Syllables Count

HAVING SECURED AN NBA FRANCHISE, Klein now needed a name for his new team. A press conference was scheduled to announce the name, and each passing day brought added pressure to come up with something catchy.

"We were going to be playing in the Amphitheatre, which is near the stockyards," he recalled. "Chicago has historically been a meat-packing center, and I wanted something that would indicate that Chicago is the city of steel and meat and might, which it is. It's a hard-working, hard-hitting city. Always has been.

"So I started thinking of names like Matadors and Conquistadors. I finally thought Matadors would be pretty good, but that was three syllables. The only other multiple syllable name that had had any success in pro sports was the Canadiens in hockey. Chicago had the Bears and Sox and the Cubs and the Hawks, all single syllables.

"My sons and me are all in this meeting with Momma, trying to decide. Anyway, when I said, 'It's gonna have to be Matadors,' my baby son, Mark, said. 'Dad, that's a bunch of bull!'

"'That's it,' I shouted. 'Bull! Of course. That's what it is.' And there was instant approval in the family."

Having found a name, Klein next turned his attention to designing a logo and uniforms. "Dean Wessel did the logo," Klein said. "He almost gave up on me. He submitted about 40 things before I accepted one. My request was that I wanted the Bull to be a true bull, in a bull fight. You know, he's a big and black thing with long horns and red eyes and mean. I wanted a mean looking Bull. Most of the eary submissions were of full bodies. The Bull with his head down, that sorta thing. I said, 'I want a face. Gimme a face.' Then Dean gave me a face that looked real good. Now, I said, 'All we have to do is make his eyes red. I want blood on his nose, or red nostrils, and blood on his horns.' Which Dean did. He did a beautiful job. That became our symbol.

"On the uniforms, I wanted something a little different. The first year we wore harlequin uniforms. The players hated them, but some of the teams wear 'em even now. I put the Bulls head on the pants. Nobody had ever dressed up their pants before."

Itchin'

IN EARLY 1966, THERE WERE NINE TEAMS in pro basketball with nine head coaches and no assistants. To say the least, jobs were tight. When the NBA announced that it was adding the Bulls as a tenth team, there was a virtual stampede to the coaching employment line.

"Everybody in the league had somebody I should hire," Klein recalled. "The applications came out of the woodwork, literally dozens a day. I interviewed a lot of guys."

For a time, it appeared that the Bulls were ready to hire DePaul coach Ray Meyer, but the priests at the school talked him into staying put. So Klein resumed his search for a coach.

Very quickly a group of local fans brought to his attention Johnny "Red" Kerr, the southside boy who had made good, first as a center at the University of Illinois, then during a long, distinguished run in the NBA. Kerr was 33 and finishing out his career with the Baltimore Bullets. He and Klein wrangled over money (Kerr wanted $30,000 and Klein only wanted to pay $15,000), but they reached a compromise of sorts when Klein agreed to hire Kerr's longtime pal, Al Bianchi, as assistant coach, the first assistant coach in league history.

Bianchi was finishing up his playing career with the Philadelphia 76ers, and Klein decided the fastest way to clear up any contract problems with the two was to take them as players in the expansion draft. They would make a great coaching tandem: Kerr, the easygoing head man, and Bianchi, the firebrand disciplinarian.

"It won't miss," Kerr told reporters when asked about the reprise of pro basketball in Chicago. "I'm so enthused about it, I... I just itch."

With the coaching picture set and the expansion draft nearing, Klein turned to an unusual source of advice. Boston Celtics coach Red Auerbach wanted assurance that Klein wouldn't take guard K. C. Jones, who was nearing the end of his career, in the expansion draft. In exchange for Klein's promise not to take Jones, Auerbach agreed to meet in a New York hotel room to offer a private evaluation of every player in the league.

Klein was allowed to tape record the session, but he agreed to destroy it after he listened to it. Some observers snickered that Auerbach was hoodooing Klein just as he had hoodooed every other executive in the league over the years. But Klein insisted the information had great value. "Red lived up to his end of the bargain," he said. "We spend a solid 24 hours reviewing every player in the league."

Another of Klein's highly criticized moves was agreement to give up the first pick in the 1966 draft. Michigan All-American Cazzie Russell, who had grown up in Chicago, was the obvious prize. Instead of drafting first, Klein got the other owners to agree to protect only eight, not nine, players.

"That meant I could draft two players from each team," he explained. "I was castrated in Chicago on that one, because Cazzie Russell

Bob Boozer came to the Bulls from the Los Angeles Lakers in the expansion draft. He led the Bulls in scoring over their first three seasons and averaged better than 21 points per game from 1967 to 1968. In his second season in Chicago, he was named a starter for the All-Star game.

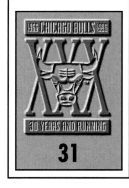

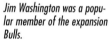

Jim Washington was a popular member of the expansion Bulls.

Dave Schellhase of Purdue was the Bulls' first pick in the 1966 college draft.

was a local product and a big hero at Michigan. He was an excellent player, but I felt we were better off doubling the talent pool."

After all, Klein pointed out, there were already 84 All-Americans in the nine-team league, and the broadened expansion draft would give him a shot at many of them.

On expansion draft day, the Bulls made the following picks:

- John Kerr and Jerry Sloan from the Baltimore Bullets

- Ron Bonham and John Thompson from Boston

- Nate Bowman and Tom Thacker from the Cincinnati Royals

- Len Chappell and Barry Clemens from New York

- Al Bianchi and Gerry Ward from the 76ers

- Jim King and Bob Boozer from the Lakers

- Jim Washington and Jeff Mullins from the St. Louis Hawks

- Keith Erickson and McCoy McLemore from the San Francisco Warriors

- John Barnhill and Don Kojis from the Detroit Pistons.

Klein told reporters he was particularly happy to get Washington and Boozer, two athletic forwards. Because centers were scarce, Kerr was intrigued by 6-10 John Thompson, who had spent two seasons in Boston as the backup center to Bill Russell. But Thompson decided to retire as a player rather than report to Chicago. He needed to search for something more "meaningful," Thompson recalled. "I had been on two championship teams and that was meaningful. But I didn't feel I wanted to spend the rest of my life as a basketball player." Instead, Thompson went back to his Washington, D.C. home and eventually became the well-known coach at Georgetown University.

In the college draft that May of 1966, the Bulls took nine players including first pick Dave Schellhase, a bulky guard out of Purdue

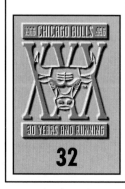

To kick off their ticket sales in May 1966, the Bulls posed two models with a caged Bull down on State Street.

who had led the nation in scoring, and second pick Irwin Mueller, a 6-8 center/forward from the University of San Francisco.

Once he got into the basketball business full time, Klein hoped that Jerry Colangelo, one of his bright young employees, would manage D. O. Klein and Associates. "He had been in the premium supply business with me," Klein said of Colangelo. "I wanted him to take it over, because he had a real knack for marketing. But when I went into basketball, he said he wanted to go, too. So he came in as marketing director."

It wasn't Colangelo's first hoops experience. He had been a hot-shooting team captain at the University of Illinois. "He was a left-handed bomber," Klein recalled with a chuckle, "with the attitude, 'Throw me the ball, fellas, and follow in.'"

Not only could Colangelo do the marketing, he scouted, too. "He had a good eye for talent, and an instinct," Klein said.

So good, in fact, that he only worked a season and a half for the Bulls before the expansion Phoenix Suns made him their general manager. Within time, he would come to own a major portion of the Suns and would enjoy a position as one of the most powerful figures in the league. Colangelo was the first of several Bulls staff members to move on to prominent positions in pro basketball.

"Jerry was a very confident and intelligent and self-assured young man who knew what he wanted and was willing to pay the price to get it," sportswriter Bob Logan observed. "I don't think he ever figured he'd wind up as the emperor of Arizona."

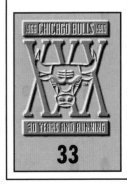

33

Keith Erickson was just one of the talents the Bulls found in the expansion draft.

On Pins and Parades

WITH THE PLAYERS AND COACHES SET, the next order of business was promotions. Klein, Colangelo and the small staff went to work trying to turn Klein's ideas into a product the city would buy.

"We had T-shirts and gold pins and jewelry," Klein recalled, "and passed them out by the thousands.

"We had a parade. We got a great big longhorn from down at the stockyards and put it on a flatbed truck. The parade was two trucks, that's all we could get together. Even if we'd had every season ticket holder in the parade, it wouldn't have been that impressive. We only had 176 season ticket holders that first year. The press that came to the parade might have been giggling, but at least they were talking about us."

"We took the trucks down State Street, and the big wigs were in a car behind us," remembered Ben Bentley, the team's first public relations director. "We sat in the trucks and we waved, and as we passed by, people said, 'Who's that?' They didn't know who the Bulls were. People were stopping and hollering at us. They were holding up their kids and showing them the bull and saying, 'They're gonna play basketball here. Basketball!'"

"In many ways, Dick Klein was ahead of his time," recalled sportswriter Bob Logan. "He wanted a total basketball experience for the fans."

Klein's goal was to create ambience in the Amphitheatre, the team's arena. "I have a menu from that first season," Logan said, "where Klein had all these ambitions to have things like they have now in the modern NBA. They had waiters to bring you a Chicago Bulls sandwich right in your seat."

"Klein used to sell 'Corrals' at the Amphitheatre," Johnny Kerr recalled. "Those were the box seats. You'd get four or five seats in a Corral, and the waitress would come over and wait on you, take your drink and sandwich orders, store your coat and galoshes."

Unfortunately, the Bulls would need more than customer service to ride out the coming storm. The trouble on the horizon was the formation of the American Basketball Association. Competing for talent, the new league would soon drive player salaries through the roof, making pro hoops even more of a high-stakes gamble.

The result was turmoil and financial peril in both leagues, as teams struggled to find the cash to operate. "Look at the Boston Celtics," Klein said. "They were sold five times in 10 years. After I got in the league, the Celtics were sold three times in seven years. The money got to be such a vital part of a franchise, you couldn't be the old-fashioned, seat-of-the-pants entrepreneur. You couldn't run your team like a showboat, even if you won championships."

Indeed, the most vulnerable teams were the youngest. For the Bulls, the landscape changed overnight. Chicago's new owner had put together a team whose symbol was blood on the horns of a bull. In a very short time, it would become apparent to Dick Klein that that blood might very well be his own.

Profile/Simply Red

*J*OHNNY "RED" KERR WAS THE FIRST coach of the Chicago Bulls. As Kerr has said many times over the years, someone must have called central casting to find him. It was a perfect fit. In addition to his sense of humor and his south Chicago neighborhood ties, Kerr brought with him something no one else in the franchise had: loads of NBA experience. An All-American out of the University of Illinois, he became an immediate starter at center as a rookie for the old Syracuse Nationals in 1954-55 and played a key role in their winning the league championship that year. He went on to average about 14 points and 10 rebounds over his 12-year career, most of which was spent in Syracuse.

But he was proudest by far of his consecutive-games-played streak. The 6-9 Kerr broke the 706-game streak of former teammate Dolph Schayes and went on to set a record of 844 straight games played (actually 917 including playoffs), a mark that stood for nearly two decades until Randy Smith ran up a 906-game streak that ended in 1983.

As coach of the Bulls, Kerr got results. Not only did he drive the expansion team to the playoffs during its first two difficult seasons of operation, he was named NBA Coach of the Year in 1966-67.

Bill Gleason: One morning there was a knock at the front door of my home. It was a Chicago city fireman named Reggie Fryer, who was one of Johnny "Red" Kerr's childhood buddies. He said, "There's gonna be this pro basketball team here. Red oughta be the coach."

I publicized his idea in my *Sun Times* column, and Fryer went around and people literally signed petitions like they used to do for the All-Star baseball game. He got something like 2,000 signatures of people promising to buy tickets if Johnny Kerr got hired. They just stormed Klein, and he had to say, "This is the most logical thing; this is the guy everybody wants." When Red would come into Chicago during his days as a player with the old Syracuse Nationals to play in the Stadium, there'd be probably 2,000 people out there just to see Red. And

most of them were his friends, either from the old neighborhood—he's a very strong neighborhood guy from Orchard Park on the south side—or from the University of Illinois. So John was a natural as coach of the Bulls.

Johnny Kerr: They had something like 1,600 names, but I'm not sure all of them were real. I was named coach, but I don't know if all of those people bought season tickets. It's a little bit like how they used to register people for voting in Cook County. You sort of had to weigh the votes.

Bob Logan: The guy was perfect as the first coach of the Bulls. A Chicago guy. A personality. He just made those first two seasons fun. I've said many times that I looked all over the NBA trying to find somebody who didn't like Johnny Kerr, and I never succeeded.

Johnny Kerr: In the interview, Jerry Colangelo and Dick Klein asked me what kind of team I wanted, and I said I wanted a club that ran the fast break and played defense. I knew I wasn't their first choice to coach. But Ray Meyer had turned down their job offer. I asked Alex Hannum, my coach in Philadelphia and a very smart man, what he thought about me taking the job. He said that expansion coaches always

Johnny Kerr watches maintenance workers adjust the height of the basket before a 1967 game in the Amphitheatre.

35

get fired. But I wanted to be a part of pro basketball in Chicago. I wasn't that concerned about the circumstances. One thing I wanted was Al Bianchi as my assistant coach, which Dick Klein agreed to do.

Bob Logan: Kerr always had the right one-liners or put the right spin on a loss, making it sound like, "Well, maybe it was a loss, but we sure had a lot of fun." Al Bianchi was a no-nonsense, tough basketball guy. He came from the playground, where if somebody was in your way, you elbowed 'em out of the way and went to the hoop.

Johnny Kerr: Al knew defense. He had a great feel for the game, and the players respected him. He was my drill sergeant. My main problem, outside of the fact that we didn't have a center, was Dick Klein. His first pick in the draft was a 6-foot-3 forward, Dave Schellhase, who had been a nice player at Perdue but didn't have the size to be a pro forward or the quickness to be a guard. Klein thought he would be a local favorite to help at the gate and gave him a $35,000 contract, which was big money back then. Schellhase came to training camp about 20 pounds overweight and was eaten up by our veterans.

Klein had other brainstorms, too. Like open tryouts. He put an ad in the papers, and about 180 guys showed up. Fat guys, little guys, guys with tatoos that said "Mom," guys who kinda looked like Mom. I told Al to line them all up against a wall and have them count off by twos, then have the twos go home. We did that, and later on we sent all the ones home, too.

Not too much later I had a deal set up to trade a second-round draft pick to St. Louis for a fine young player named Paul Silas, who went on to play key roles in championship teams for the Celtics and Sonics.

But Klein wouldn't let me do the deal. Instead, he sold the second-round draft pick to the Lakers. The league had given us that pick for not taking Cazzie Russell in the first round of the draft. L. A. used the pick to take Henry Finkel, a seven-footer who was a solid backup center for years in the league. Klein got $25,000 for the pick. He said we needed the money.

Another time, Klein brought a hypnotist to training camp, saying he had cured cancer. The hypnotist promised that he could take any five guys and work with them and they would be able to beat any other five guys. Of course that was a joke. He even claimed he could cure the stuttering of Barry Clemens, one of our players. We called the hypnotist the "Mojo man."

There was always something like that happening. I got a call from St. Cloud College in Minnesota asking me if I wanted to give their leading rebounder a tryout. His name was Izzy Schmissing. No joke.

I had them send Izzy over to us. He couldn't play and we had to cut him. Bob Logan of the *Tribune* wrote, "When the Bulls got ready for the exhibition opener, Izzy was among the missing."

Kerr left after two years to become head coach of another expansion team, the Phoenix Suns. Later he served as general manager of the Virginia Squires in the American Basketball Association. Then, in 1973, he returned to the Bulls as their business manager, a position he held for two seasons until part-owner Jonathan Kovler decided to take over as managing partner. Kerr then moved into broadcasting Bulls games, a position he still holds today. His insight and humor have helped to interpret game action for millions of Bulls fans over the past two decades.

Part Two

Blood on the Horns

Bulls Basketball, 1966-84

THERE WERE SPARKS APLENTY IN THE early years of the Chicago Bulls, and there was more than a bit of bloodletting, too.

Just months after pulling all the parts together to form the team, Dick Klein found himself in a fierce power struggle among the big cats who had invested in the franchise. "I rubbed a couple of furs the wrong way," he explained.

Did he ever.

Those early conflicts seemed to set off a run of bad karma for the organization. Underhanded dealings and goofy management became the order of business.

In the beginning, the Bulls played well despite the front office turmoil. For an expansion team, their showing was unfathomable—they made the playoffs in eight of their first nine seasons and ran up a string of four 50-win campaigns. They began life as a mildly amusing newcomer on the Chicago sports scene but soon developed into a cult that could fill the Stadium with 15,000 to 20,000 bug-eyed, screaming fans. The attraction was the gutty, hard-nosed style of coach Dick Motta's teams.

"We had a real team," said Bob Love, who led the Bulls in scoring for seven straight seasons. "I loved that team. I used to dream about us sometimes. I could see us out there running through the cuts, running through the picks. Those Bulls teams during the time I was there, we didn't win the championship. But our starting five as a team was just as good as any starting five. We could play anybody. Anybody. I don't care who it was. And we'd beat you. In the fourth quarter, if we were within 10 or 12 points of you, we were gonna catch you and beat you."

'66 '67 CHICAGO BULLS MEDIA GUIDE

Ultimately, however, the franchise couldn't overcome the turmoil of the constant personality conflicts. The Bulls ran through eight coaches in the nine seasons from 1975 to 1984, and by the late '70s the team was a picture of chaos. Futility was the dominant mood, and there was regular speculation that the Bulls would desert Chicago.

It seems the only thing that kept the club in place were the hopes of a small cadre of loyal fans.

"From a basketball standpoint, if you don't win a championship, you're a failure in a lot of peoples' eyes," Jerry Sloan said of the early Bulls. "The thing I really feel a little bit of pride in, is the fact that we kept the franchise here…. Otherwise the franchise would have been gone. You look at everything the Bulls have accomplished here now and how big it has become. We were able to keep it at a certain level, and the Jordan teams were able to take it from there.

"I've always felt after having played and lived much of my basketball life in Chicago that these fans here deserved that, because of the price they've paid to endure some of the things we had to go through."

As you look over the history of the Bulls, there's nothing like it in all of pro basketball, maybe in all of pro sports. That's because of the personalities. The franchise was really built around some very highly opinionated people. There was conflict almost at every level. And when you have conflict, you have sparks flying, and when you've got sparks flying, you've got fascinating material.

–Pat Williams

The Bulls' first training camp was a scramble.

Slaughterhouse Five, 1966-67

*I*N 1965, THE PROSPECTS WERE LEAN FOR *making a living playing pro basketball. For nearly a decade, the NBA had consisted of just eight or nine teams. The old pros who played back then like to say the talent was compressed to a very hard core of players, dense as matter in a black hole. For most players, each training camp meant a fight for their professional lives. Probably no training camp was ever so competitive as that first Bulls camp, which opened on September 10, 1966 at North Central College gym. Eighteen players had come to the team in the expansion draft, plus another half dozen rookies from the college draft. "Because most of them are kids, they're hungry," Johnny Kerr told reporters. "Maybe that's a good thing."*

Jeff Mullins: I don't think there's ever been a training camp like that first Bulls camp. That was a tough team to make. You had guys like Jerry Sloan and Keith Erickson and Jim Washington and me all fighting for a spot on the roster. It was the most competitive situation I've ever been in.

Jerry Sloan: We had all been put out on the street, so to speak, by our former teams. Everybody was fighting for a job.

During training camp, the Bulls traded Jeff Mullins, Jim King and cash for San Franciso Warriors point guard Guy Rodgers.

Dick Klein: The Jeff Mullins deal was the worst I ever made. We had a young team that could run and jump and really fly without the ball. But we had to have somebody to deliver the ball, and Guy Rodgers was that person.

I originally made the deal for Jerry Ward and Jimmy King. But Al and John were very upset about the inclusion of Ward in the deal and insisted it be Jeff Mullins. I said Jeff was a player we should keep. We argued about eight hours on a Labor Day, all day long.

Johnny Kerr: We needed Guy Rodgers to handle the ball for us. But Al Bianchi and I didn't want to trade Jeff Mullins. We told

Klein to trade Gerry Ward and King for Rodgers. But Klein said he had already given his word on the trade, and he didn't want to back out. So, the trade went through. Mullins went to the Warriors and became a star.

Bob Boozer: Guy was a good quarterback in that he could be outspoken. He'd let you know. He was a competitor from Philly, from Temple. He was a good man in the middle of the fastbreak, and we ran some pretty ones. When you got open, he got you the ball, and you got it where you could do something with it.

Bob Rosenberg: Guy Rodgers was a great passer and a deadly shooter. He had 908 assists, which broke Oscar Robertson's single-season record. He did what they wanted him to do that year, which was make them an exciting team. Both Guy Rodgers and Jerry Sloan made the All-Star team that year. Who could imagine an expansion team placing two players on the All-Star team?

Dick Klein: Before we played our first game I was on a radio show in New York with Howard Cosell, and I casually said I thought we'd make the playoffs. Howard ridiculed me and made a little feature out of it for broadcast that night on his national radio show, that the stupid new owner of the Chicago Bulls had the audacity to think his team would make the NBA playoffs in its first season. A friend of mine sent me a taped copy of the show. After we made the playoffs that year, I sent it to Howard with a couple of choice comments.

Courtside seats that first season cost $4. The schedule included five games in Evansville, Indiana, to capitalize on Jerry Sloan's popularity there. All of the Bulls' 36 home games were broadcast on WGN radio, and WGN-TV aired a dozen contests with the action called by Jack Brickhouse. The team's first media guide was 12 pages with a Xeroxed cover.

Irwin Mueller, the Bulls' second-round draft pick in 1966, proved to be a player.

39

Chicago's Guy Rodgers set the NBA single-season assist record in 1966-67.

40

The Bulls ran up a 6-3 record in exhibition season and notched their first regular-season victory in their first game, against the St. Louis Hawks in St. Louis, 104-97, on October 15, 1966. Their opening night lineup was Rodgers and Jerry Sloan at guards, Bob Boozer and Don Kojis at forwards and Len Chappell at center (later to be replaced by 6-foot-7 rookie Irwin Mueller). It was Chappell who scored the first basket in Bulls history, 11 seconds into that first game.

St. Louis coach Richie Guerin had predicted before the season that the Bulls wouldn't win 10 games. Then, three nights later in their first home game, the Bulls defeated the San Francisco Warriors, 119-116, with Jerry Sloan scoring 26 points. The Warriors had held a 13-point lead going into the fourth quarter, but Rodgers scored 14 points in the final period and finished the game with 20 assists. Newspapers said the official gate, 4,200, was "padded by about 1,000."

Ben Bentley: I sat on press row for the first home game, and I was getting rumblings. "It ain't gonna be here long," they said. "They'll be like the Zephyrs." George Strickler, the assistant editor of the *Tribune*, didn't want to see a game, but I got him to come out that first night. He told me, "We can't get too excited about it. We don't know how long they're gonna be here."

After three wins, the Bulls' first loss came against the Warriors, Rodgers' old team, and

produced the first bench-clearing brawl in team history. It was set off by a fight between Rodgers and former teammate Paul Neumann. The officials ejected both players, then allowed both to return later in the game.

Jerry Sloan: We won four out of the first five games, and people were excited in Chicago. We had to play the Knicks at the Amphitheatre. They got people who can't get into the game. It's sold out. I thought, "My goodness, we're not that good, are we?" We certainly found out that night. The Knicks waxed us pretty good, and reality started to set in. But we didn't lose sight of the fact that if we kept working we were gonna win some games.

Dick Klein: We could have sold 30,000 seats that night in a 7,000-seat arena. We let 9,000 in and the fire marshal came to me and said, "Dick, you gotta close the doors."

Bob Logan: People broke down the door and were storming the place. There was a sign that said, "We Believe." It was an unreal atmosphere, but everybody knew the euphoria wouldn't last.

"They're fighting to get in," Amphitheatre general manager Mert Thayer told a reporter. *"I've never seen anything like it."*

"I just hope they come back," Klein remarked.

Jerry Sloan: It was a unique group of guys. We all got along well together and had a lot of fun. Of course Johnny and Al really helped us in that category. They were fun guys to be around.

Bob Boozer: Back then we were more like family. Today, there's just too much money in the game. At the time, I was pretty much a no-nonsense guy. I wanted to play ball. But Johnny Kerr was humorous. He'd keep us laughing. We had a lot of fun. It was not the same as being with a veteran team. Keith Erickson was a prankster. Irwin Mueller used to drink like a case of beer after every game. We couldn't understand how he could drink like he did and continue to play at the level he did. Johnny could drink some beer, too. They'd be popping caps all night long and talking basketball.

Chicago's Keith Erickson battled for a rebound against the Warriors in November 1966.

1966 CHICAGO BULLS 1996
XXX
30 YEARS AND RUNNING

41

The Bulls' first game, played in the Amphitheatre.

Sometimes that was the only way to get by. We lived on those red-eye specials in and out of Chicago. Late at night and early in the morning, there we'd be, trudging in and out of those airports and hotels.

In early November, the Bulls improved their record to 7-6, good enough for first place in the Western Division. Then, 7,000 fans showed up at the Amphitheatre to see them play the Celtics. The Bulls lost, and the officials needed a police escort away from the building. The defeat started a nine game losing streak. Before long, the Bulls had fallen to 8-15 and last place in the division. To make matters worse, a harsh winter had descended upon the city and deposited the Great Snow of `67.

Bob Logan: I remember how cold it was that first winter and how small the crowds were.

Dick Klein: One time we played a game when 26 inches of snow fell. The Lakers were snowed in, but Johnny Kerr told me we could not cancel a game for any reason. Anyway, the Lakers got there, and I think they beat us by something like 45 points. The body count in the Stadium, including security guards, was something like 72 people.

On Sunday January 29th, the Lakers won 142-122, and the "announced" attendance was 1,077. Afterward, the losers treated the

winners to a steak dinner. By the end of February, they had fallen to 25-44 and last place, three games behind Detroit for the final playoff spot. As the losses mounted, the Bulls quit keeping statistics on turnovers. "We gamble a lot," Kerr explained to reporters.

Ben Bentley: Klein was the owner and general manager, and he wanted to be the coach, too. Klein would always have a little something to say to the coaches if they lost a game.

Bob Logan: Bianchi was infuriated by Klein's practice of sending notes to the bench during games saying to put Dave Schellhase in. Dave Schellhase couldn't play, but Klein had to go down with the ship because he was the guy Klein had wanted in the draft. Dave was a real nice person. He was just out of his league in the NBA, even in those days when guys like Bill Buntin could stand there and take up space.

Johnny Kerr: Klein always wanted to run plays and tinker with the game plan. He'd call Al and me up and he'd give us two lineups. He'd say, "Whaddya think of these lineups?" I'd say, "Why? What's the deal?" "Well," he'd say, "they weigh exactly the same and are exactly the same in height." Al and I would look at each other and say, "That doesn't win any ball games for you.

Bob Boozer boxes out the Warriors' Al Attles.

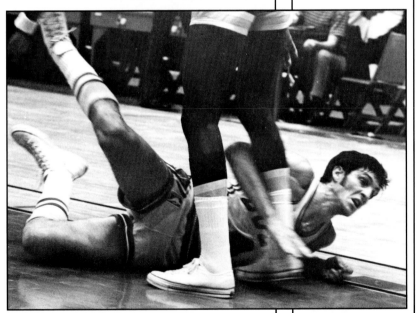

Don Kojis was on the finishing end of the Bulls' first alley oop slam dunk play.

You gotta match up."

On March 1 in Evansville, 11,274 fans turned out to see the Bulls take on Wilt Chamberlain and the Philadelphia 76ers, who were marching to a 68-13 record and an NBA championship. That 'Sixers club is often cited as the greatest in league history, but the Bulls upset them, 129-122, starting a playoff drive of their own that ran through March and allowed them to overtake Detroit.

The Bulls lost their first playoff game to the Hawks in St. Louis, which left Kerr complaining. "This has got to be the roughest series I've ever seen," Kerr told reporters. The Bulls returned to Chicago to lose their first home playoff game, before a crowd of 3,739 at the Coliseum (at 15th and Wabash) because a boat show had created a scheduling conflict at the Amphitheatre. Hustling as usual, PR director Ben Bentley got the Mayor's office to send a telegram to the team in St. Louis before Game 3. It read:

"Win or lose tonight, the Bulls have found a place in the hearts of all Chicagoans. They are Chicago's kind of team. It took the Blackhawks

Jerry Sloan's bruising style made him a starter from his first days as a Bull.

40 years to win—I'm sure the Bulls will do it in five." Richard J. Daley, Mayor

They lost the third game in St. Louis, 119-106. "If they hadn't made that trade for Rodgers, they wouldn't have won 20 games," Hawks coach Richie Guerin said afterward.

43

Ben Bentley, right, presents the 1967 NBA Coach of the Year award to Johnny Kerr, center, as Dolph Schayes, left, comments on his years playing with Kerr.

1966-67 COACH OF THE YEAR
Dolph Schayes, John Kerr, and Ben Bentley

Profile/
Benny the Burglar

TODAY'S FANS MIGHT NOT REALIZE IT, but before there was "Benny the Bull," there was "Benny the Burglar," the nickname affectionately given to Ben Bentley, the team's first public relations director. Broadcaster Jack Brickhouse first recommended that Dick Klein hire Bentley, a former boxing promoter. He served the club from 1966 until 1973, when he resigned after witnessing a rather messy power struggle between coach Dick Motta and General Manager Pat Williams. Many observers suggest that Dick Klein's best move was hiring Bentley, whose personal charm and press contacts were vital to the Bulls' survival during the early years. Bentley also served as the team's public address announcer and became known for drawing out the players' names in introduction. Stooormin' Norman Van Lier!

Bill Gleason: The International Boxing Club had folded, and Ben was scuffling. He was a natural, because Ben was welcome in every newspaper office in the city, and he knew how to promote. Ben was a perfect foil for Klein, just as he had been a perfect foil for Rocky Marciano and those people because Ben is very resilient. He absorbs things and they bounce off of him, and he

just goes on. But the fascinating thing about those early Bulls is that they had four people running the whole operation: Klein, Kerr, Colangelo and Bentley. Those four people did everything.

Ben Bentley: Pat Williams named Benny the Bull after me... He came to me one day, he said, "You know what? I've got this idea for a bull mascot, and I've got a guy who might be the bull. I've been thinking of a name. It's an ideal name. Benny the Bull. The words are great." Then he said, "Maybe one of these days you'll want to be the..." I said, "No, no. Take my name for Benny the Bull. But I'm not running around in a suit."

Tom Boerwinkle: After they drafted me, the Bulls brought me into Chicago, and I'd never been in Chicago in my life. My plane arrived at 10:30 at night. They said, "We'll have someone meet you out the plane. We'll recognize you." I get off the plane and this short, stout, very-promoter-looking guy with a big cigar gets up and says, "You must be Boerwinkle."... I'm this young rawboned kid out of Tennessee, and Benny is giving me this line: "Big Boy you're going to own this town in five years. I'll get ahold of you. You stick with me, do what I tell you to do and we'll go all the way." Cigar ashes were going every which way, and he started singing "Chicago! Chicago!" and the whole bit. I'm saying to myself, "Holy Mackerel, the circus has come to town."

Jerry Sloan: I'll never forget the first night we played in the Amphitheatre, and Benny announced us coming out on the floor. That was the greatest thing I ever heard in the world. I thought we were coming out for round one of a boxing match.

Ben Bentley: I visited the newspapers every single day. By 10:30 or 11:00, I was on my way. One thing the Bulls did for me, they allowed me to take the newspaper people to lunch, to a nice lunch. Even if it wasn't a sportswriter, I'd talk to somebody.

Bob Logan: I wrote the story when Benny left the Bulls to go to work for the Chicago park system. I said, "Benny usually announces what he had for breakfast." If

1966 CHICAGO BULLS 1996
XXX
30 YEARS AND RUNNING

Guy Rodgers, Keith Erickson and Jim Washington at practice in 1967.

Chicago Bulls

OFFICIAL SOUVENIR YEARBOOK
FOR FANS, RADIO-TV AND PRESS

1967-68 $1⁰⁰

Second Year Blues, 1967-68

ASSISTANT COACH AL BIANCHI HAD *grown increasingly irritated with Dick Klein over the course of the Bulls' first season. When the playoffs ended, Bianchi promptly accepted a job to coach the Seattle SuperSonics, an expansion team.*

Johnny Kerr: Right in the middle of the playoffs that first year, Klein had demanded that Al leave the team and go scout a college game. We ignored the demand, but that was like the last straw for Al. He told me he couldn't stand working for Klein.

Dick Klein: I wanted Johnny to hire another assistant. He thought we could get along without somebody. We struggled that second year.

In January of 1967, McCormick Place burned in Chicago, creating a shortage of exhibition space in the city, which meant that the Bulls had to move out of the Amphitheatre for their second season and into the Stadium. The Stadium was owned by Blackhawks owner Arthur Wirtz. Klein immediately worried that the larger building would swallow the team's meager fan following.

Bob Logan: The fire hurt 'em, but it probably assured the Bulls' survival because it allowed Arthur Wirtz to get his hooks in the team.

Dick Klein: I went to Arthur Wirtz and said, "I'm selling 3,000 to 4,000 seats, and you got 18,000. We'll rattle around in the Stadium like a Ping-Pong ball on a brick street. But I gotta have a place to play, and I can't afford your normal rent." Arthur was extremely generous with his concept. He said, "I'll start you on a low-ball basis, and as you grow, I'll expect to get paid more and more. In other words, you produce a crowd, and I'll get some revenue."

One of the most entertaining developments of the Bulls' first season had been the "Kangaroo Kram," an alley-oop play that developed between point guard Guy Rodgers and high-flying forward Don Kojis. Johnny Kerr recalled it as being the first alley-oop he had ever seen.

you wanted to pick out one guy who epitomized Chicago, it would be Ben Bentley. Benny had this whole schtick he went through, this whole routine. When he told a story, he played all the parts in it. It was just like street theatre with Bentley.

Jerry Krause: Without Benny, this team never would have had a chance to succeed in the city of Chicago. He didn't know the basketball was round. But he got people to pay attention to the team. And he smoothed over a lot of messes. Many a time Motta would tell a writer to go to hell or do something stupid, and Benny would go straighten things out.

Norm Van Lier: When you think of the Stadium, you think of Benny. He was great. Benny didn't get a lot of calls for black players to do promotional things, but Benny got me out there to meet people. He had me over to his house for dinner several times. He was very special.

"It was a variation on a back door play," Kojis once explained. "At first, Guy would feed me a bounce pass for a layup. Then other teams started looking for it, so I told him if my man turned away, anticipating the pass, I'd roll to the basket and take off. Usually he put the ball right on the money, and we pulled it occasionally to keep the defense honest and to stir up the fans."

Strangely, Dick Klein decided to leave Kojis unprotected in the expansion draft that spring of 1967, and he was lost to the San Diego Rockets.

The loss of Kojis likewise reduced Rodgers' effectiveness, and when the Bulls opened with a losing streak that fall, Klein shipped the league-assists leader to Cincinnati for Flynn Robinson and two draft choices. Known as "Flingin' Flynn" for his heave-and-go offense, Robinson moved into the starting lineup. The loss of Rodgers and Kojis meant that Kerr had to abandon the team's entertaining running game for something more plodding. Also, center Erwin Mueller grew disenchanted with Bulls management and briefly jumped to the ABA. The shortage of players figured heavily in the team's terrible start the second year.

Bob Boozer: It was discouraging to see Guy go. It was discouraging to see Klein selling and trading players to keep the cash flowing. Losing Kojis hurt, too. Not only was he a leaper, but he was quick and had a nice jumper. Without the players we had a rough go that second season.

The Bulls lost their first nine games in the fall of 1967, won one in Seattle, then lost another six. Desperate to shore up their weakness at center, the Bulls had pulled in 6-foot-11 Reggie Harding from the Detroit Pistons. One of the first players to move directly from high school to the pros, Harding had been suspended for the 1965-66 season. Sadly, Harding had been raised on Detroit's mean streets and could never overcome his gangster background. (He would be shot to death in 1972.) He was known for finishing practice and leaving without showering, pausing only to towel off and spin the cylinder on his revolver. Once while playing in Detroit, Harding apparently began shooting at teammate Terry Dischinger's feet to make him "dance."

One night teammate Flynn Robinson awakened in the dark, turned on the light and found Reggie pointing a gun at him. Legend has it that Harding robbed the same gas station three times in his own Detroit neighborhood. According to Kareem Abdul-Jabbar, the third time Harding robbed the place, the attendant said, "I know that's you, Reggie."

"No, man, it ain't me," Reg was said to have replied. "Shut up and give me the money!"

Johnny Kerr: I got a chance to get Reggie Harding. We needed a big center. I had heard about his pistol. Rumor had it that he carried it in his gym bag… He'd play one-on-one with Flynn Robinson. Flynn would beat him, and Reggie would say, "Get out of here Flynn before I pistol whip you." Everybody figured he might have it with him.

When we were in the midst of that losing streak in '68, we played the Lakers in Los

Clem Haskins, a point guard out of Western Kentucky, came to the Bulls in the 1967 draft.

Angeles. We needed a win in the worst way, and we had a one-point lead with just a few seconds left on the clock. The Lakers got the ball at half court, and I put Reggie in to guard Mel Counts, their big guy. I didn't want them getting an alley-oop. Counts set up out near the free throw line, but Walt Hazzard, who was taking the ball out of bounds, threw the ball over the backboard and the buzzer sounded. I was jumping around and screaming because we had finally won a game. I looked up, and Reggie had decked Mel Counts. He got up and shot two free throws and beat us.

During that West Coast road trip, Harding was called home for his mother's funeral. For the next 10 days, the Bulls didn't hear from him. Finally he returned, saying that he had been appointed executor of his mother's estate and needed the extra time away. A few days later, the Bulls placed Reggie Harding on waivers.

Jerry Sloan: In the second year, we had to open the season on the road because the Stadium wasn't available because the Ice Capades were there. We started off losing nine games. It was horrible. Finally we played Seattle in Seattle and won a game. Ben Bentley, the director of PR, had the Salvation Army band waiting for us at four in the morning at the airport. Standing out there were about three guys with a guitar and a fiddle or something. We were waiting to throw quarters in a cup because we'd finally won a game.

Dick Klein: We lost 15 of the first 17 games we played that second year, so our fans really lost interest. Playing in the Stadium, we were like a cannon shooting in an empty hall. Ben Bentley always wanted me to announce big numbers. So one time I went along with it. Bob Logan of the *Tribune* wrote, "The announced attendance, which is highly fictional, is..."

Ben Bentley: We were doing nothing at the gate. I remember we played Seattle, and the next morning the *Tribune* led off by saying only 650 had watched Seattle beat the Bulls. Walter Kennedy called me up and asked, "How could you allow that?" I said, "They're newspaper people. I can't control what they write."

Finally, it got to the point, when they'd ask me for the gate, I'd say, "Well, the crowd is small tonight, but we're sold out New Year's."

The plummeting attendance figures angered several in the ownership group who wanted to sell the team. Klein, however, refused, creating factions among the owners: those who wanted to dump the Bulls and those who didn't. Klein's primary backers were Lamar Hunt and Dan Searle, giving him enough to hold off Rich, Frye and others who wanted to sell.

Bob Logan: Klein was suffering. All he wanted was to have the Bulls win and have himself acknowledged as the genius he knew he was.

Although the Bulls struggled to a 29-53 season, they only had to outdistance expansion teams in San Diego and Seattle to make the playoffs, which they did. In the first round, they fell behind the Lakers 0-2, but Flingin' Flynn Robinson scored 41 points in Game 3 in Chicago to give the Bulls their first playoff victory, 104-98. But from there the Lakers shifted guard Jerry West to shut down Robinson, and the Bulls fell four games to one.

Down the stretch of the season, Klein had been openly critical of Kerr. At season's end, Kerr accepted Jerry Colangelo's offer to become head coach of the brand new Phoenix Suns.

Bill Gleason: To think of this guy making the playoffs with the team they gave him. He was also NBA Coach of the Year. Then after his second year he's gone, which wasn't a very bright thing for Dick Klein to do.

Here Comes Dick, 1968-69

To REPLACE KERR, DICK KLEIN HIRED *Dick Motta, an unknown coach out of Weber State whom Jerry Colangelo had discovered during a scouting trip.*

Dick Klein: The three guys I zeroed in on were Roy Skinner at Vanderbilt, Vic Bubas at Duquesne and Dick Motta. Skinner actually said yes to the job until his wife came to Chicago and saw the real estate prices. So I hired Dick Motta. He was a winner and a teacher. I had a young team. I wanted a coach who coached. Dick was a great motivator and a great teacher. He was hard-nosed. The press immediately wanted to know why I didn't get somebody more important.

Bob Logan: Dick Motta arrived the day George Halas announced his retirement from the Bears. So there was very little coverage of this new coach in town. That was typical of the Bulls. They couldn't catch a break in those days.

Jerry Sloan: I was back at Evansville working on a master's degree when Motta came to Chicago and started with a camp for the rookies. Our trainer, Bob Biel, called me and said, "You better get your butt back up here. This guy's gonna kill you." When I got here, Tom Boerwinkle looked like he'd been run over by a car. He had a pair of loafers that looked like he'd had 'em for about 10 years. He couldn't bend over to tie his shoes so he'd just slide those loafers on his feet. He was worn out already, and I thought, "Gosh, we gotta start our season here in a few weeks, and this guy's supposed to be our first-round draft choice, and he won't be able to find the arena he's so tired."

I walked in and met Motta. I just told him I thought we could win. I've always felt that way wherever I was playing. You always have a chance to win if you're willing to work at it.

After I'd worked out a while with the team that night, I had a long conversation with Dick, and I felt like this is gonna be the guy to help us get better.

The Bulls lost McCoy McLemore, Dave Schellhase and Craig Spitzer in the 1968 expansion draft when Phoenix and Milwaukee came into the league. During the previous season, Klein had traded Mueller to Los Angeles. But that September, the owner/manager traded back for him, giving up versatile Keith Erickson in the process. "I never trusted him after that," Motta would later explain. By opening day, the

The Bulls hired Dick Motta, an unknown out of Weber State, after Johnny Kerr left for Phoenix.

Tom Boerwinkle was the Bulls' first pick in the 1968 draft.

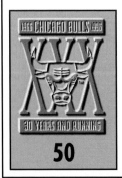

owner and his new coach were hardly speaking to each other. The opening day lineup consisted of Boozer and Jim Washington at forwards, Flynn Robinson and Jerry Sloan at guards, and rookie Tom Boerwinkle at center.

Bob Logan: They had no players that season. They were working on a shoestring, and Motta was constantly at Klein's throat about getting some players in there.

Pat Williams: Motta turned on Klein early. I think Dick had no respect for Klein. He didn't think Klein knew what he was doing. Klein wanted this center from Italy. He told Motta, "Coach, we're gonna have 21 feet of front line." Dick said, "Yeah, and they won't be able to guard anybody."

In January, Klein sold Mueller to Seattle for $75,000, prompting an outburst from Motta, who threw a dollar bill on the Stadium floor and told reporters, "Money won't play." At the time, the Bulls were trying to cactch San Diego for the final playoff spot.

Dick Motta: Klein sold Irwin Mueller to Seattle, and that's when I said, "You can't play money. Money won't play." If we hadn't had to worry about the bottom line... We were broke. The owners weren't broke, but we were. We were running to the bank to see if our checks were gonna bounce.

We had four people in the front office. Gladys answered the phone and did the books. We had a coach and no assistant. When we first started there were no newspaper people following us on the road. We didn't do radio on the road. We didn't do any TV on the road. They sold, I think, 38 season tickets that year. Elmer Rich and the board tried to sell the team five or six times. They were all very wealthy men. But we did things bottom dollar.

We were gonna be the St. Louis Bulls, the Toronto Bulls. We were gonna be someplace else. Peter Graham was thinking of buying us and moving us to San Diego.

The owners approached Ben Kerner in St. Louis. He had just sold the Hawks. The owners offered him the Bulls for $600,000. He turned it down after looking into the feasibility of moving the Bulls to St. Louis.

Dick Klein: The only losses we had were tax losses. I ran a nickel-dime operation. I was the biggest cheapskate in the world. There was always cash flow. In fact, I never called the last $50,000 pledged by the owners.

Sloan scored a career-high 43 points in a March 5th win over Milwaukee, which helped push the Bulls a half game ahead of the San Diego Rockets in the playoff race with only nine games left. But Motta's first team struggled down the stretch and failed to make the playoffs despite an improved 33-49 record.

Move: The Love/Weiss Deal

ON NOVEMBER 7, 1968, THE BULLS traded Flynn Robinson to Milwaukee for Bob Love and Bob Weiss, unwittingly finding in Love a major talent at forward. The deal was precipitated by a flare-up between Dick Motta and Robinson, who had been removed from the starting lineup.

Bob Weiss: They were at practice. Flynn throws up a half-court shot, and Dick says, "Flynn, why don't you practice the shots you're gonna take in the game?" Flynn says, "Why don't you practice your coaching?"

Dick went home that night and called Dick Klein and said, "If Flynn's there tomorrow, I'm gone."

Dick told me that later that night Klein called him up and said, "Well, I got a trade. I traded for Bob Weiss and Bob Love, and it's the worst trade I've ever made. You boob," he said and slammed the phone down.

Dick Klein: Motta called me one night and said, "If Flynn Robinson is on this roster tomorrow, I'm quitting." I said, "Dick, I'm sorry I have to accept your resignation. Flynn has to be on this roster another 36 hours by league rules." He said, "What do you mean?" I said, "I just traded him to Milwaukee for Bob Love and Bob Weiss." He said, "Oh."

I said, "Don't give me an ultimatum like that. It's not good business." He was young and aggressive. He was being recognized by the press as a coaching genius, and he was feeling his oats. Motta was now gonna tell me how to run the team. He told Frank DeFord a bunch of crap for a *Sports Illustrated* article, how he throws me out of the locker room and won't talk to me unless he feels like it. That was a bunch of crap, but it was all in print and ran all over the nation. I started getting letters from old friends, people I hadn't seen in years. They asked me, "What kind of team are you running? Are you just a figurehead?"

Bob Weiss: Motta had no idea who we were, and Klein did not like the deal. Klein just had to do it. It was just one of those things that worked out. I played for years as the sixth man, and Bob Love went on to become an All Star. But it was a deal that they were forced into.

Jerry Krause: The Bob Love trade was a stroke of luck. We tried to get somebody else, but they insisted on giving us Love. After we got him we tried to get rid of him twice and couldn't do it. Nobody wanted him.

Dick Motta: We got Love and Weiss on the same day for Flynn Robinson, and that was the major turning point of the franchise. Then we got Chet Walker for Jim Washington, and that was the final piece.

OFFICIAL PROGRAM

Bob Love (10) and Bob Weiss (8) were the prizes in a trade that sent Flynn Robinson to Milwaukee.

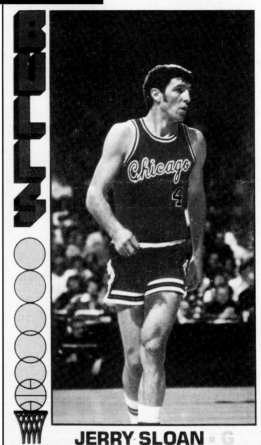

JERRY SLOAN • G

Sloan's play was 90 percent determination, 10 percent talent.

COURTSIDE
CHICAGO BULLS
OFFICIAL PROGRAM

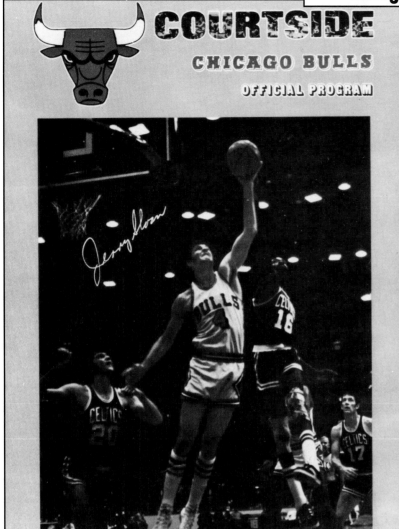

Jerry Sloan was Mr. Chicago Bull.

Profile/ Mr. Chicago Bull

BEFORE MICHAEL JORDAN arrived, Jerry Sloan was known as Mr. Chicago Bull. At 6-6, he was a big guard, known for his defense and rebounding. Born and raised on a farm in the hardscrabble oil fields of southern Illinois, he played briefly at the University of Illinois and at Southern Illinois before transferring to Evansville, where he led the team to two NCAA Division II championships. Drafted by Baltimore in the second round of the 1965 NBA draft, he played one season with the Bullets before being selected by Chicago in the 1966 expansion draft. Just a few games into his first season, the Bullets approached Chicago about trading Sloan back to Baltimore. "No, a thousand times no," Dick Klein told them. "We're going to keep Jerry. I knock on wood every time I see him."

Over an 11-year NBA career, he averaged 14 points and 7.4 rebounds, but his real contribution, his intense defense, escaped statistical analysis. His playing career ended with a knee injury during the 1975-76 season. He was a two-time All Star and four times was named to the league's All-Defensive first team and twice to the All-Defensive second team. After his playing days, he accepted the job as head coach at Evansville, his alma mater, only to change his mind and resign five days later. That fall of 1977, just months after his resignation, the Evansville team and coaching staff were killed in a plane crash. Sloan became an assistant, then head coach of the Bulls. Today, he coaches the Utah Jazz, and star forward Karl Malone says that Sloan is still so intense most nights you can't touch him in the huddle. Sloan's number 4 was retired by the Bulls in 1977, and for years it was the team's only retired number.

Jerry Sloan: I grew up in southern Illinois, a small farm, 16 miles out in the country. My father passed away when I was four, and there were 10 kids in the family. Everybody else around us was in the same boat. We were fortunate to survive.

Johnny Kerr: Jerry was always an excitable person. I roomed with him in Baltimore on occasion. We'd play a game, and I'd go out for a couple of drinks and a sandwich. I'd come back at maybe one, two o'clock in the morning. I'd have the light off and be taking off my jacket. I'd see this glow of a cigarette in the dark. Jerry would be sitting up on the other bed, and he'd say, "Red, remember that play in the third quarter?" I'd be getting ready for bed. I'd already had a couple of beers, and I'd forgotten about what happened in the third quarter because there was another game tomorrow. But he was so intense he wanted to know why we did certain things in certain situations. That really impressed me, and when I learned I was coming to Chicago as the coach I knew he was gonna be one of the players I'd take in the expansion draft. He didn't get a lot of playing time with the Bullets, but I saw him every day in practice. Nobody wanted any part of him. I knew the intensity he had.

Jerry Sloan: When I was coming to Chicago, Johnny Kerr told me, "You're kind of like a spring that's wound too tight. You might just fly all over the place. You don't want to get that wound up."

I worked hard on trying not to get that way. But I had those tendencies. That's the only way I could compete. I wasn't good enough, in my mind, unless I maintained a high level of intensity.

When I left Baltimore, I didn't know if I'd be able to play in this league or not. I was drafted fairly high, but I didn't play much in Baltimore and started to have doubts.

Two weeks before I went to Chicago, my brother shot himself. I had gotten myself mentally ready to play. But I was concerned because I hadn't worked out for a week because of my brother's funeral. Fortunately,

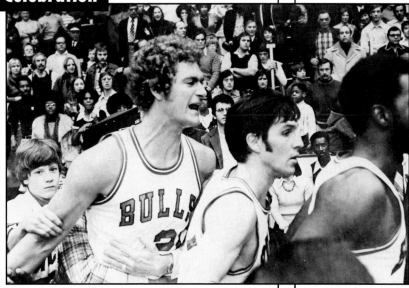

Sloan, pictured here with Dennis Awtrey, was a leader

Jerry Sloan.

I was in great shape. I could play hard every minute in training camp, and I got a little confidence. From that point, Johnny Kerr gave me more confidence by allowing me to play.

The arrival of Dick Motta as Bulls coach in Sloan's third season in Chicago created a perfect match of competitive attitudes.

Dick Motta: When we had our first training camp, it took about 10 minutes to recognize that he was very special. There weren't many players that had his intensity.

I began to depend on him more out of necessity than anything. It was a natural evolution. He approached his play like he was desperate. One time at a clinic I heard him say, "When I put the shoes on I get nervous because it might be the last time I'll ever get to put 'em on. So I want to play the best game I've ever played or have the best practice I've had." He typified that his whole career.

Bob Love: Jerry was gonna give you a day's work every day he came into the gym. As hard as he was, when he was on the floor, if you blew on him he would fall back and grab you on the way down to take the charge.

The game I remember about Sloan, we were playing New York in Chicago Stadium. The Knicks had Willis Reed and Earl Monroe and Walt Frazier and those guys. Willis Reed got a rebound and threw it out and was gonna beat Boerwinkle down the floor. He was hauling it down the floor. He had his head down, and when he looked up, Jerry Sloan was right there, man. He ran over Sloan. Charge! Willis fell on the floor and hurt his knee. He already had a bad knee. He looked at Jerry and said, "Mother———, don't get in front of me again. You made me hurt my knee." You know how guys talk. Sloan said, "I ain't afraid of you."

Later in the game, Willis Reed got another rebound. He hauled off down the sideline again. This time he saw Jerry. Willis didn't go right, and he didn't go left. He ran over Jerry. When he hit Jerry, he walked all up to his head and scraped him and left Converse marks, from his forehead all the way down to his ear, man. All you saw was a red mark. And there was Willis saying, "I told you not to get in front of me!" Sloan said, "Mother———, I still ain't scared of you."

And the rest of the game, every time Willis got a rebound, he looked. He looked for Jerry. Jerry would have guys zigzagging down the floor, because you couldn't touch him. He was the greatest charge taker that I have ever seen in my life. You couldn't touch him, because he'd just fall back. Unbelievable.

Jerry would make guys so mad. Right now he would be considered the all-time greatest defensive player the game has ever known if he was playing on TV. He would have every kid in America copying that style. I loved the way the guy played. I was so happy I played with him and Norm Van Lier, because they made other guys so angry the way they played. The two best defensive guards in the history of the game, and they played on the same team. The best.

Norm and Jerry were out there like two rats, and if the ball fell on the floor, it was like a piece of cheese. Those guys would undercut you, overcut you, clip you, do anything they could to get that ball. And they would get it, boy. And Dick Motta just loved it. He loved those guys. They really kept us pumped up.

Matt Guokas: Jerry and I used to have our battles when we played against each other. Jerry is a unique defender in that he did not get up and put a lot of pressure on you, but he played angles, played position very well. He would make you do a lot of things you didn't want to do, but he didn't do it with pressure. Jerry was an excellent team defensive player and rebounder. When I played against him, we would get tangled up underneath the basket. There would be some elbow throwing, and we got in each other's face a couple of times. I was very happy to be on the same team with him. He was very demanding that you did certain things defensively, that you played hard, and that you got on the floor for loose balls and stepped up and took charges.

That, of course, was the other thing about playing against Jerry. He used to flop. He'd pull you on top of him and get you in foul trouble with a lot of charges. You wouldn't get away with that in today's game. There's still a lot of flopping that goes on, but you couldn't put your arms around a guy and pull him down. Let me put it this way:

They got away with it when I was on the other team, but when I was on the Bulls it seems they got called for it.

Jerry was the consummate team player. Everyone that played with Jerry respected him. He was always in pain with a very bad groin injury. He would not get it stretched out before practice, yet he would go out and practice very hard for about an hour, which was all you could get out of anybody.

Bob Weiss: Jerry and Norm Van Lier would just jump in front of you. Jerry would take the hit. His weight would be on his heels, so it didn't take a whole lot to knock him over. But a charge is a charge. I think the term "flopping" was basically an excuse for these guys they were drawing the fouls from. Jerry and Van Lier were very, very good at it. Jerry mostly. He was always getting in somebody's way and taking the punishment.

Pat Williams: Nobody could quite figure out why we were so successful. Dick Motta used to say, "When people look at this team, they forget the one key ingredient—the size of Jerry Sloan's heart."

Jerry Sloan was just fearless. His body would take such a pounding. In all my 28 years in the league, the player I most admire is Sloan. I've never been around a greater competitor, a more focused guy, a guy who cared as much…

He's the only guy I've ever seen who played with his fists. He had huge hands. When he'd go for the ball on a steal, he'd punch it. He'd punch the ball right out of your hands. There's never been another Sloan. Never will be.

Dick Motta: My second year in Chicago we had to make up a game. We had a game snowed out, and the league put it right at the end of the season. We had to play five games in five nights, and we needed to win four of them to make the playoffs. We beat Boston and Detroit in Chicago, then beat Milwaukee in a game played at Madison, Wisconsin. But with about a minute to go in the game, Alcindor came out from behind a screen and knocked Jerry down. Jerry broke two ribs and separated his ster-

num. We had to bus down from Madison to O'Hare after that Sunday afternoon game to catch a flight to Omaha to play Cincinnati for a game Monday night. So we had a doctor meet us at the airport. He basically told us that Sloan shouldn't go, that he should stay home. But Jerry insisted on going just to be with the team. We just needed one more win.

The next day I went to the arena, and Sloan was there. He said, "I couldn't sleep. I've been walking around. I've found this little corset thing. Let me warm up."

I said, "No, I'm not gonna let you." He said, "Coach, you gotta let me warm up." So he warmed up and I went back to the locker room. Later, I came out a little early, and he came up to me and said, "You know I've never asked you to do one thing. I've never told you to do one thing. I'm gonna ask one favor now."

I said, "What's that, Jerry?"

He said, "If I were you, I'd start me."

I started him, and he couldn't raise his arm. Chet Walker and I had to stretch the uniform to get him in it. His ribs were broken, but he just wouldn't quit.

Sloan takes another charge.

56

Johnny Kerr and Sloan at Sloan's 1978 jersey retirement.

OFFICIAL PROGRAM

Sloan was an excellent rebounding guard.

We were down three early in the second half, and Cincinnati called a quick time-out. In the huddle, Jerry said, "C'mon guys, let's go. We've come from 33 down before."

I looked up at the clock and said, "Jerry, what's wrong?"

He said, "Oh, I thought we were down 33."

The pain was so excruciating he was incoherent. He was going on an empty tank. We won the game in overtime, and made the playoffs. I was able to rest Jerry the last four games, and he played in the playoffs.

So it was easy to build a team around that type of performance. He had a bad game once. I think his sister-in-law had died, and he went down to Evansville to the funeral and wasn't going to make it back. But he rented a small plane and got there about three minutes before tip-off. Chet Walker looked at him and said, "I thought you weren't gonna play tonight."

He said, "I couldn't miss it."

Chet said, "You're a hell of a guy, Jerry."

And that's how everyone perceived Jerry. No coach and player had a relationship like Jerry and I had. It was very special. He was my sounding board, my assistant coach the first four years when I didn't have an assistant coach. So I would bounce trades off of him. I bounced all of our deals off of Jerry. I felt it was more his team than it was mine. He was an incredible guy. He still is.

Gar Heard: Sloan and Dick were like brothers. It was like blood. They had such a great love for each other. Even now. I don't think anything could come between them. Sloan was the one guy who would play every night. On some nights I didn't see how he walked out on the floor. He was so banged up with his knees and stuff. But every night he came on the floor you knew he was gonna get it on.

Dick Motta: They retired Sloan's number 4 in Chicago. I don't know if he'll ever be in the Hall of Fame, but he should be.

Profile/
The Raging Bull

ICK MOTTA NEVER PLAYED HIGH
school or college basketball. And, at 37, he had never seen an NBA game when Dick Klein hired him out of Weber State in 1968 to coach the Bulls. His first two teams struggled, but then the Bulls had four straight 50-win seasons under his guidance. In 1974, his team dipped to 47 wins, but that year the Bulls won a divisional championship. One of the early proponents of set offenses in pro basketball, Motta was named NBA Coach of the Year for 1970-71. He was an intensely competitive man during his days with the Bulls, the kind who generated a storm of controversy at every turn.

Bob Rosenberg: He used to kick the sign in front of the scorer's table and put dents in it. One time Jack Madden gave him two technicals, then gave him a third for spitting on the ball and handing it back to him. He ended up that game with four technicals, but that's when they changed the rule. In those days, you could get three or four technicals and still not get kicked out. So they changed the rule. Motta did not like to lose.

Matt Guokas: Jerry Sloan was arguing with Jack Madden. We were going to a time out, and the ball was rolling toward Dick. Dick has gigantic hands. He was able to palm it. He picked the ball up with his left hand. He was kind of looking at the ball and feeling it and he was walking out to Jack Madden. Right before he handed it to him, he laid a big one on the ball and Jack didn't really see him spit on the ball. But when he had it in his hands, Jack knew Dick had spit on it.

Jerry Sloan: He spit on it and gave it back to Jack Madden. That cost him $1,500, I believe.

Norm Van Lier: Motta led the league in technicals. But he didn't like it when a player got one. We were supposed to settle down, but he was still going off.

COURTSIDE

DETROIT PISTONS   VS. Apr. 13   1974 PLAYOFFS CHICAGO BULLS

Gar Heard: Dick and Norm Van Lier and Jerry Sloan, I think they had a thing going. Every time one would get a technical the others would get one, too. It was amazing. You could count on one coming right after the other, no matter who got one first. We were guaranteed at least three technicals a night. Dick would get furious with them for getting technicals, but I think he enjoyed it. Those were two guys that he really loved, and they really played hard for him. Those guys fed off of Motta's antics. Jerry and Van Lier were kind of like the emotional leaders, and everybody else followed suit. Dick was right in that. He knew he could get those two guys fired up and everybody else would come along.

Bob Logan: When Motta went into this other dimension, he was liable to do anything. I remember the night he drop-kicked the ball into the upper deck at Cobo Arena.

Motta's style was confrontational.

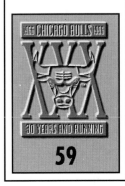

Motta was ejected for throwing his jacket at an official during a nationally televised game in 1974.

Bob Weiss: The play happened right in front of our bench. Dick just caught the ball and took two steps like a punter and kicked the ball into the upper deck and sat down. One referee was breaking up a skirmish, and the other one was telling the scorer's table who the foul was on. So neither of them saw the kick. And now Dick Motta is sitting down and the refs are looking for the ball. And Van Breda Kolff comes storming down the court yelling, "He kicked the ball!!! He kicked the ball!!!" The officials don't know what the heck he's saying, so they gave him a technical. I think Van Breda Kolff got two technicals and was kicked out of the game. Meanwhile, there's two guys playing catch with the ball in the balcony. They finally got it down.

Jerry Sloan: Van Breda Kolff got kicked out of the game for being upset because the officials didn't know who did it. Meanwhile, Motta's sitting there on the bench like nothing ever happened.

Bob Logan: It was just Dick's personality. He was a confrontational sort. That's part of his makeup. It's what made him a great coach. If there wasn't some enemy there, he would find one some way or another. And that's the attitude he instilled in the Bulls. That's why Chicago fans loved them. The fans were out there to see this confrontation between Dick Motta and the world, which is what it was.

Bob Love: Dick Motta really kept us motivated, really kept us playing hard. Before every game, he would come into the locker room and tell us what the other team was saying about us. "They're saying that you guys can't play. They're gonna run you off the basketball court. All the reporters are saying that, too. I heard this guy on the radio saying the Bulls don't have a chance tonight." Motta would tell us that stuff. Boy, we'd get in the dressing room, and you'd see smoke coming out of guys' ears. Norm Van Lier would start kicking over the trash can. Jerry Sloan would push over a table and hit the wall. I was always kind of a calm guy. I kept my feelings in. I would sit over in the corner and I would start think-ing what I was gonna do to the guy I was guarding. Dick knew we were all striving for recognition. He was, too.

Norm Van Lier: Dick Motta's whole approach was, "We work the ball, we work the ball, we play defense, we wear you out." If we were within five points going down the stretch, we were gonna beat you… because we were in better shape. We physically wore you out. Motta believed if you make an opponent go through pick after pick after pick on the defensive end, eventually his offense will suffer.

Bob Rosenberg: When they drafted Kevin Kunnert from Iowa, he came in and put his feet on Motta's desk. Motta said, "Get out." Motta didn't like that kind of stuff. They traded Kevin Kunnert. He never played for the Bulls.

Norm Van Lier: Motta will not take blame for anything on the negative side, but he surely will take credit for everything on the positive side. Besides all that, I loved playing for the man. He's a great coach. Well-prepared. No-nonsense. We need more coaches like him from a pure basketball standpoint. But there are some other areas, the human side, he's got a side that's very weird. He was definitely a strange character. He didn't want anyone to figure him out.

Ben Bentley: You never knew where you

Dick Motta.

Motta knew what he wanted from his teams.

Motta's Bulls mastered the set offense.

OFFICIAL PROGRAM

Motta was named NBA Coach of the Year in 1971.

stood with Dick Motta. One day he's friendly with you, the next day he's cold, especially when I was on the road with him. He was tough on the players. I lived with them so I could sense it. They were very unhappy, especially the players he'd pull out. He'd pull them out of a game and say, "Sit at the end of the bench. Don't sit near me. Sit way back there. Where'd you go last night?" Even some of the players' wives would say, "Did you see what he did yesterday? He tried to make a fool out of my husband!" I know it was not a healthy relationship between Dick Motta and the team. I was in a situation where I had to be on my toes all of the time. The players would tell me stories, and I'd say, "For chrissakes, don't go saying that to the press." And he was hard on the press. An argument broke out in the locker room between Motta and Lacy Banks, the *Sun Times* basketball writer. They almost came to blows, and I had to step in between them.

Bob Logan: Dick was always looking for some other meaning in what people said and what they wrote. He would try to get on the press. There were some Chicago guys who got back in his face and told him to stuff it.

Jerry Sloan: Dick would get very down. I spent a lot of time with him when he got in those situations. It affected me and a lot of the other players.

Pat Williams: Motta was a man with no self esteem who had come up from nothing. He never realized how talented he was. He still viewed himself as the little scrub from back in Midvale, or wherever he was from in Utah. He had never really gotten over that. His parents were from Italy. They were dirt farmers. He grew up in the fields harvesting vegetables.

Kip Motta: My grandparents grew hot chile peppers and squash and all kinds of vegetables. They used to hoe them by hand. They'd take all the produce to market once a week and sell it.

Jerry Sloan: Manic/depressive is the nature of the farming business. You depend on something you have no control over. Coaching is kind of like farming in that sense.

Clifford Ray: Chet Walker and Norm Van Lier always stood up for me if sometimes Motta got too crazy on me. He used me as the guy to whip when he wanted to fuss at everybody. They kept him in balance. I've always had a tremendous amount of respect for Coach Motta. I've always thought he was the ultimate pro coach. I loved the way he allowed his teams to learn half-court offensive sets. As far as the criticism of him, I look at it this way: He was a young coach back then.

Kip Motta: Dad had to have been scared back then. He was in a situation he had never been in before, and all he knew how to do was just coach basketball.

Profile/Boerwinkle

TOM BOERWINKLE'S BEST PASSING SEASON was 1970-71 when he averaged nearly five assists per game. A seven-foot, 265-pound center, he was the Bulls' 1968 first-round draft pick out of the University of Tennessee. Despite losing his father and grandather within a month of each other his rookie season, he adapted surprisingly well to the NBA. Although he suffered from several knee injuries, Boerwinkle played 10 NBA seasons and racked up more than 2,000 assists and 6,000 rebounds.

Bob Logan: I remember Boerwinkle got booed unmercifully in the Stadium. He was the fans' whipping boy… Every time Boerwinkle was introduced or did anything, they got on him bad.

Motta wanted the toughness out of him. He would have liked it if Tom went out there and knocked people down. That was never Boerwinkle's style.

Jerry Sloan: That's one of the sad things about Tom when he was a player. He was a guy who gave as much to the game as anybody could have given here in Chicago. But he was the least respected of any of the players who played here. We couldn't have succeeded without him, because of the kind of player he was. He really set the whole Motta program up because of his ability to pass the ball.

Motta was on him all the time, and Tom had a tough time understanding it. But all Dick was trying to do was make him a better player. I think he did. Tom kept working and kept working.

It's just unfortunate he didn't get the kind of respect he deserved until after he quit playing. Then people started respecting the fact that, "Hey, this guy was good…"

Tom Boerwinkle: I have tremendous respect and admiration for Dick Motta. I think what he has accomplished has been phenomenal. I think of what he did for me personally. He took a kid that most said didn't belong and made him fit.

Bob Love: We had that offense where we threw the ball into Boerwinkle. Let me tell you about Tom Boerwinkle. Name any center you want to name. Tom Boerwinkle was

the greatest passing center to ever play professional basketball. This guy was uncanny. He knew when to bounce it, he knew when to throw it hard, he knew when to lob it. Any way you name it, he could do it. I've never seen a guy who had that kind of ability who played the center position. I mean he could see.

Boerwinkle, who owns and operates an oil distributorship in Chicago, served as the Bulls' radio analyst during their championship seasons in the early 1990s.

Boerwinkle defends Wilt Chamberlain in 1971.

The early version of Benny the Bull had a strange countenance.

Saved By The Bull, 1969-70

*T**HE BULLS' ORGANIZATION WAS MARKED** by infighting during the summer of 1969. The team drafted Larry Cannon out of LaSalle and Simmie Hill out of West Texas State in the first two rounds of the 1969 draft, but Klein further angered and alienated his staff by refusing to bid for either player against offers by the American Basketball Association. Both top draft choices wound up playing in the other league. Chicago took Norm Van Lier out of St. Francis in the third round and traded him to Cincinnati.*

Dick Klein: By 1969, a couple of members of the board, notably Phil Frye and Elmer Rich, said, "Look, we're gonna sell the team. We're not getting any place holding on to it." The up-front tax shelter had been used up, and they were eager to get their money out. They said, "Dick, you promised we could all double our money in five years. It's been less than five years, and if we move now we can triple our money. Let's sell it." A Chrysler corporation executive in Detroit wanted to buy the team and indi-

cated he would pay us $2 million for it. But I had enough stock, more than 20 percent, to block the sale. Rich and Frye wanted out, and they thought I was being selfish. Motta, meanwhile, wanted control. He found out that he had friends on the board. They voted after the '69 season to move me out as managing partner. I still kept my stock, but they moved me out of there.

Acting on the recommendation of Bill Veeck, board member Phil Frye contacted Philadelphia 76ers business manager Pat Williams about becoming the Bulls' general manager. Williams said he jumped at the opportunity.

While they were signing Williams, the Bulls were also trying to work a trade with Philadelphia for forward Chet Walker, a star forward from the 'Sixers 1967 championship team. Dick Klein recalled that he first arranged a trade for Walker and Wally Jones just after the 1969 season, but Klein was forced out as managing partner before the deal could be consummated.

Jerry Krause: I knew Walker from when we had gone to school together at Bradley. Philadelphia had called and their general manager, Jack Ramsay, had talked about trading Walker and Shaler Halimon for Jimmy Washington. Pat Williams at the

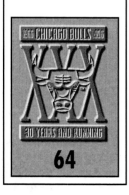

time was the business manager for the 76ers. Before Pat was ever brought in, we didn't think this deal would be done. Klein didn't want to make the deal. He loved Jimmy Washington. I was a little suspect because I couldn't figure out why Ramsay would want to make it. It was too good a deal for us. So I told Motta, "I'm going to go to Philadelphia on the excuse of seeing a Baker League game. I'm going to call Chet and have him meet me, and we'll have dinner together and go to the game. I'll find out what's going on with him and Ramsay."

I flew into Philadelphia and met Chet. I learned that he and Ramsay weren't getting along, but other than that there was no problem with Chet.

I called Motta from the airport that night and told him, "If we can do this, this is going to be one of the great trades of all times." The 'Sixers called later and said they definitely wanted to to make the trade. But there was a delay on our part, because our other owners were in the process of forcing Klein out.

In his book, The Gingerbread Man, *Pat Williams recalled that his becoming the Bulls' general manager was a strong factor in closing the Walker deal for Chicago.*

Jerry Krause: Strangely enough, our owners were in the process of hiring Pat Williams, the 'Sixers' business manager, as our general manager.

Finally, several days later Pat came on board as our general manager. So Pat comes in and says, "What's goin on? What do we want to do about this Chet Walker thing?" Motta and I told him, "The first thing you do is you get on the phone and you finish this deal we've already got going. You just call Ramsay and finish the deal." Pat was young and didn't even know how to do it. We told him what to do, and he finished the deal. But that's how the deal was made.

Unbelievably, the 'Sixers gave up Chet Walker and Shaler Halimon for Jimmy Washington, who was a good player. Ramsey just had a thing for Chet. They just weren't getting along, and Chet's easy to get along with.

Once the Bulls hired Williams, the deal bringing Walker and Shaler Halimon to Chicago was completed. All three—Walker, Williams and Halimon—played a role in the Bulls' amazing turnaround over the next two seasons. Walker, in particular, provided the firepower Dick Motta's offense needed at forward. And Pat Williams, a protégé of Bill Veeck, brought a promotional flair to the operation of the franchise.

Bob Logan: Pat Williams was as close to Bill Veeck as you could get, which was what the NBA badly needed. His strength was getting coverage and attention to the Bulls.

Pat Williams: Dick Klein was a visionary. Give him credit. He had the vision to start the Bulls in a city where pro basketball had failed repeatedly. But managing it on a day-to-day basis and dealing with the people problems, that was not Dick Klein's forte. He was a coach at heart. He could not divorce himself from the on-court activities. He wanted to be in the middle of that. Klein had been suspended basically as managing partner that summer of 1969. The other owners realized he could not stay in the operational role. There was supposed to be a buyout of his share, but the buyout didn't happen. Dick was there as the owner; he had tickets to the games; but he had no power. It was weird, strange.

One of Williams' first ideas was to establish a team mascot, Benny the Bull. In his memoir, Long Time Coming, *Chet Walker recalled seeing the mascot for the first time that fall of 1969 and thinking the creature had a "pitiful moth-eaten costume." Walker didn't know the outfit was brand new.*

Pat Williams: Not long after I got to Chicago, I met this young man who worked in real estate named Landey Patton. He was a Princeton graduate. He came to me and said if there was anything he could do to help, all I had to do was call. Not long after that I got the idea for Benny the Bull. I knew we needed something, a symbol, a mascot, something to attract the kids. I drew the name from Benny Bentley, our public relations man, but he didn't want to be the Bull. So I phoned Landey Patton and asked him, "Do you still want to help

COURTSIDE

OFFICIAL PROGRAM 50¢

Oct 16-70

LOS ANGELES vs. CHICAGO BULLS

66

By 1970, the Bulls had jelled into a solid nucleus.

out?" Believe it or not, he was willing to wear the Bull suit. I told him it would only be until I found somebody else. I think he wound up wearing the outfit three years. Benny the Bull became our shining symbol, something the kids could relate to.

My biggest job in Chicago was just getting the sport sold. There was no nucleus, no base. You had the huge overpowering presence of the Bears and the Blackhawks and the two baseball teams. We were the fifth sport in town and fifth by a mile.

The overwhelming job from the day I got there was to get people involved, get them introduced to pro basketball and get them to be willing to come to the Stadium. Remember, this wasn't long after the riots of '68. The word in town back then was, "It's a dump. You take your life in your hands if you go down there." For the Blackhawks, the fans didn't think they were taking their life in their hands. The answer: There was safety in numbers. For hockey games, there were 17,000 fans going in and out. Together they felt safe. But if there's only 3,000 going in and out, as there were for Bulls games, the fans felt they could get picked off too quickly. So our job was to create masses of numbers.

Boy, I hit every banquet, every circuit, every promotional idea. Anything you could do to whipsaw people in there, we were doing it.

Dick Motta: There was Victor the Wrestling Bear. Ben Bentley had to wrestle the bear. It was one of Williams' promotions to have the fans wrestle a bear. But Bentley put out a press release about a vicious, flesh-eating bear, and the Humane Society got ahold of it and protested. They wouldn't let anybody but our own staff wrestle the bear, so Ben Bentley had to wrestle this gentle old bear. I still have a picture of Ben Bentley down on his back, and the bear licking his face.

Tom Boerwinkle: Suddenly you bring in a circus act in to get people to come. Pat was a promoter; he certainly did a lot to bring the awareness of the team to the people in Chicago. I think it bothered Motta from

the standpoint that to some degree it deflected from the real event of the evening. I think Motta felt that his importance was somewhat equalized.

Dick Motta: We did all kinds of things like that to get fans. But then we started to play, to win. Then we went to sellouts. We did all the sellouts with a staff of five. We didn't have marketing, we didn't have assistant coaches. We had a trainer and a ticket man and a secretary and a comptroller, and that was the whole time I was there with the Bulls. We didn't have anyone, and now they have a staff of 50 or 60.

Bob Weiss: The first couple of years there'd be like 400 people in the stands. Some guy would be yelling, and you could hear him as plain as day. But we built it up from there to where there were 19,000 people in the stands for a playoff game against the Lakers.

Ben Bentley: One of the first times we drew people was when the popular Kareem Abdul-Jabbar came to Chicago with the Milwaukee Bucks. We drew about 13,000 that night. I went gaga when I saw the people flocking in. Dick Klein would always ask me for the ticket figures. That night I got them, and when I went to Klein, I said, "We're gonna be in big trouble. The number is 13,000 [actually 12,269], but no one's gonna believe it. They're gonna think we padded the numbers again." Klein said, "Forget about that. 13,000. I want that figure out."

Williams' efforts shot attendance figures beyond a 10,000 per game average for the season. Though it was obvious the crowds had grown substantially, reporters still speculated that the figures were padded.

Bob Logan: Pat Williams brought attention to the Bulls, but what really changed the atmosphere in the Stadium was Sloan and Van Lier knocking people down and starting fights and the Bulls winning with that explosive, combative style of Motta's.

Bob Weiss: We started to become a pretty good team in Motta's second year, after we traded and got Chet Walker, and Bob Love became a player. I started to fit in, and Boerwinkle had had a year of seasoning.

67

Walker and Love were incredible weapons… Not many teams had two great forwards like we did.

Jerry Sloan: The fans responded to the kind of team we were because the city is a blue-collar city, and the players were much the same way.

Bob Logan: Everything goes in cycles. Once they let Bobby Hull go, the Black Hawks' cycle was over, and the Bulls' cycle began. There was a vacuum there, and the Bulls filled it.

The Bulls' motto in the fall of 1969 was "Look Out Above." The opening night lineup included Clem Haskins, the first-round draft pick in 1967, at point guard, with Sloan at off guard, Boerwinkle at center, and new forwards Bob Kaufman and Chet Walker. Before long, however, Love had taken Kaufman's starting role and would lead the team in scoring with 21 points per game. He scored 47 in March against Milwaukee to tighten his grip on the starting job.

The season unfolded in series of entertaining events. In November, Boerwinkle hit a shot at the buzzer to tie the Hawks 124-124, but the officials ruled it late. It was actually hard to tell from the old hockey clock way up in the Stadium rafters. The Bulls protested, and, surprisingly, the league agreed, ruling that the game, tied at 124, should be resumed the next time the teams played with one second placed on the clock. This gave the Bulls' publicists an opportunity to hype the "One-Second Game." Completed in the Stadium in February, the game was won by the Hawks in overtime.

The Bulls had depth problems at guard. Sloan suffered a serious groin injury in December and missed 29 games, which brought more playing time for Halimon, a smooth ballhandler given to scoring outbursts. Haskins played well enough to keep his starting job (and he made a club record 11 straight field goals against Detroit in February), but Motta continued to express his dissatifaction with Haskins' play.

Boerwinkle, meanwhile, led the team in rebounding at 12.5 per game. On January 8, he had a Bulls' single-game record 37 rebounds in a 152-123 win over the Suns in the Stadium.

Bob Weiss: We had had about 10 days of below zero weather, and the heater broke in the Stadium. You could see your breath. The people in the stands were all wearing their coats. Of all the teams to play, Phoenix comes in that night, and it was so cold they couldn't do a thing. Tom Boerwinkle had 37 rebounds that night. We just killed 'em.

Later that month against Milwaukee, Halimon produced what was considered for years the most amazing finish in team history (until Michael made them seem almost routine during his Air Show era). With two minutes remaining in a January 17 game in Milwaukee, the Bulls were down 13. They cut the lead to eight with a minute to go, then to four with one second left.

Tom Boerwinkle: Halimon hit a shot, stole the inbounds pass and hit another shot on the next inbound pass. On the next inbounds pass the Milwaukee player throwing it in bounds hit the back of the backboard. We got the ball back and Halimon hit another shot. I think if you look at the records, we were down 6 with seven seconds to go and we tied it. He hit it all three times, which was an amazing comeback, and we won in overtime.

The Bulls finished 39-43, good enough for third place in their division and a playoff matchup with Atlanta. But Walker was hampered by a groin injury right before the playoffs. The Bulls managed a win in Chicago when Haskins set a team playoff record with 13 assists, but otherwise the Hawks controlled and eliminated Chicago, 4-1. "I wish the season started all over again tomorrow," Motta said after it was over.

Chet Walker.

Profile/Chet the Jet

CHET WALKER AVERAGED 18.2 POINTS over his 13-year NBA career. He spent his final six years playing in Chicago, and although he retired in a bitter dispute with Arthur Wirtz, Walker was held in great esteem by Dick Motta, his teammates and the fans.

Bob Rosenberg: Chet was the best one-on-one player from the baseline in the league. The moves he had were unbelievable. If he didn't make the basket, they'd foul him, and he was very good from the line.

Norm Van Lier: Chet, as far as I'm concerned, is one of the classiest human beings I've ever run into. And you talk about a go-to guy. I'm talking about delivery. You can run plays all day, but when it's time to break down in the last two to three minutes of a game, Chet was gonna get a bucket or get to the foul line and get two points.

Bob Weiss: Chet wasn't real gifted athletically. He wasn't a leaper, but he was just so smooth and knew how to play. And he was very smart. Defensively, again he wasn't a gifted athlete, so he wasn't a stopper. But he was very smart about it. He was like Larry Bird, you just didn't beat him much.

Gar Heard: Chet is probably the one guy on that team that I respected more than anybody else. He was a true professional. No matter what he did. He went out every night and gave it his all. He was a great guy to learn from. He was very patient. He never got in a rush to do anything. He knew what he was capable of doing, and he was the one guy, when we needed a basket, we could go to.

Walker was the master of the pump fake.

Chet Walker on the drive.

70

Walker worked the lane.

make you jump anyway. Chet would get those guys and shake 'em and pump fake 'em and draw the foul. And he shot 85 percent from the line when he played with us. He was a tremendous player.

Matt Guokas: For all the years that he was in the league, Chet was a great clutch player…. When teams stopped our offense, we needed good one-on-one players to finish it off. Chet was the guy.

Clifford Ray: I really think it's embarrassing that a guy of Chet's stature isn't in the Hall of Fame. Chet saved the Bulls franchise. Coach Motta and Phil Johnson, his assistant, were young coaches at the time. Chet Walker was the guy who made them look good, because when the game got tough they put it in Chet's hands to take over.

I remember many times he'd come inside and pump fake three or four times to get the defender off his feet and draw a foul. He was that smart. He never took a bad shot. He was the guy who helped Dick Motta mentally become a veteran coach.

Jerry Sloan: I say to this day Chet Walker is one of the greatest clutch players to play the game and has never gotten the recognition he deserves.

Walker today is a movie producer in Los Angeles.

Chet's short jumper was deadly.

Bob Love: Chet is probably the most underrated forward to ever play the game. I've never seen a guy who could do the same thing, the same way, and get you off your feet each and every time. The best ball faker, besides Oscar Robertson, that I've ever seen. Pump fake. He would make you jump, boy. And if you didn't jump, he'd

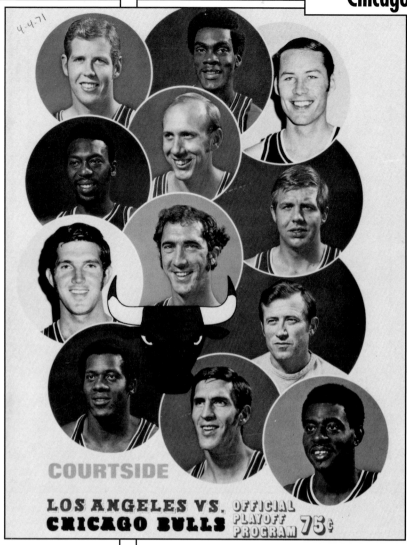

COURTSIDE

LOS ANGELES VS. OFFICIAL
CHICAGO BULLS PLAYOFF PROGRAM 75¢

The Lakers were the challenge in the '71 playoffs.

1965 CHICAGO BULLS 1995
XXV
30 YEARS AND RUNNING
72

Fifty Wins! 1970-71

I N 1970, THE BULLS, DRAFTING LATE IN the first round, picked Jimmy Collins out of New Mexico State, thus bypassing Nate "Tiny" Archibald and Calvin Murphy, two future Hall of Fame guards selected in the second round.

Pat Williams: Jerry Krause bought into Jimmy Collins early. Krause had seen Tiny Archibald play at Texas Western, but it was a slowdown game and Jerry was not impressed. Then late in the year, right after the draft, Motta saw Archibald play. He came back and said Archibald was a great player. But it was right after the draft. We went with Collins, and Archibald is now a Hall of Famer. Collins never had an impact on a single NBA game.

Jerry Krause: I really screwed up on that one.

Dick Klein: Jerry Krause shouldn't take the fall for the Jimmy Collins draft. A lot of people were impressed with Jimmy Collins. He was a good little college guard.

Jerry Krause: Archibald was so small we didn't take him. I had seen Jimmy play against Nate twice, and Jimmy killed him both times. Beat him to death. Years later, after Archiblad became a star, Motta used to say, "That frickin' Krause, he made me take Collins over Archibald." Motta never admitted he was at the game that Jimmy played super at the point, and he never admitted that we'd called Don Haskins, Archibald's coach at Texas-El Paso. But nobody, not even Haskins, had a clue that Archibald was the big-time scorer that he was. He averaged about 15 points a game in college. Haskins later told me, "Don't you think I'd of let the son of a gun score if I'd thought he could.?" Here Archibald turned out to be a Hall of Famer, so Motta tells everyone I'm the guy who missed him. After that, Dick and I were on the outs. Dick was hard to live with.

In fact, after I left the Bulls, Dick and I didn't speak for many, many years.

Collins was signed to a $250,000, no-cut contract. Motta put Collins through a rough training camp that fall. Motta often turned Jerry Sloan loose on first year players, and Collins underwent a brutal introduction to pro basketball, one from which he never recovered. During his second season in Chicago, the Bulls released him and paid up the rest of his contract.

After the 1970 season, the Bulls had traded guard Clem Haskins to Phoenix for center Jim Fox. With Love playing so well, they shipped forward Bob Kaufman to Philadelphia.

The NBA was realigned into four divisions. Chicago inhabited the Midwest Division with Phoenix, Milwaukee and Detroit. The season also brought the appearance of a pair of new, basketball-style scoreboards to replace the old hockey clock in the Stadium rafters. The team also got new offices, moving from North LaSalle Street to 505 Michigan Avenue.

Pat Williams: We had just traded Clem Haskins for Jim Fox, and our guard line was weak. We started that year and we were in trouble because Jimmy Collins couldn't play. So Bobby Weiss had to go into the starting lineup, which was too much for him. On opening day in Philly, the Philly guards just killed us. It was a disaster, and Motta, in a state of deep depression, calls me at 2 a.m. and says, "I need a guard. Get me Savulich." I said, "Dick, who is Savulich?" He said, "Mike Savulich. He played for me at Weber. He can at least get the ball up the floor."

Dick would get into periods of huge despondency. I'd come away saying, "It can't be this bleak."

Matt Guokas was holding out in Philly… We thought maybe we could get him. Sure enough, we quickly made the deal and felt very good. Matty immediately joined the club in New York and met with Motta that afternoon before the game and played that night.

Dick said, "He picked up my offense quicker than any player I've ever had."

With the deeper lineup, the Bulls charged out to their first 50-win season. On defense, they gave up 105.3 points per game, second lowest in the league.

Tom Boerwinkle: Walker and Love were the forwards. I was in the middle, and Jerry and Bobby Weiss and Matty Guokas were the guards. I think two things happened. We became believers in what Dick Motta was trying to do, which was somewhat unconventional at that time because the league had been dominated by Boston. The Celtics had won the championship 11 out of 13 seasons, and they did it by open-court, up-and-down basketball. And here comes Dick Motta, saying, "We're going to play a different type of a game." That was hard to sell to the players and hard to sell to the fans. But he became a coach who stuck with what he believed in, and he convinced his players that if they did it right, it would work.

Despite their progress, the Bulls found themselves in a late-season battle with Phoenix for the final playoff spot in the West and secured it with a late-March, two-game showdown with the Suns, in which Walker and Love combined

for a 113 points. *Earlier in the season, the Stadium fans had roundly booed Boerwinkle in a loss to Milwaukee and Abdul-Jabbar. But during the March playoff run, Boerwinkle grabbed 33 rebounds against Kareem to forge a Bulls' win. The 51-31 finish earned Motta Coach-of-the-Year honors.*

Love set club records in minutes played, a whopping 3,482, and points scored, 2,043. Walker led the league in free-throw percentage at .859.

The combined performances earned the Bulls a first-round matchup against the Lakers. They battled back and forth with Los Angeles and tied the series a three apiece after Weiss scored 25 points in the Stadium to give the Bulls a 113-99 win in Game 6. The Lakers, however, controlled the seventh game in the Forum and advanced.

Tom Boerwinkle: We always struggled to win in the Forum. I'll remember till the day I die Gale Goodrich dribbling off the clock in the seventh game and me trying to chase him around trying to steal the ball.

Clifford Ray, Walker, Sloan and Love collapse around the Bullets' Wes Unseld.

73

Howard Porter's draft came to haunt the Bulls.

Move/The Howard Porter Draft

THE BULLS TOOK HOWARD PORTER IN *the second round of the 1971 draft at the height of the player wars between the* NBA *and the* ABA.

Pat Williams: That winter of 1971, Dick Motta had gone to see Porter play when Villanova played Notre Dame at the Palestra. Dick came back and told me, "I've seen three great college forwards in my day—Elgin Baylor, Gus Johnson and Howard Porter."

Dick Motta: We never could get the third forward we needed. We drafted Kennedy McIntosh. Howard Porter we stole from the ABA.

Pat Williams: Porter had secretly signed with the ABA in December of his senior year at Villanova and later was assigned to Pittsburgh. The ABA was doing all sorts of wacky things back then to stay in existence, but Porter's contract was solid and at first he was pleased with it. Then Villanova caught fire at the end of the year and wound up going to the Final Four. They got to the final game and lost, but that run made Howard Porter the most visible player in the college game.

His name was on everybody's lips, and all these rumors were circulating about his signing secretly. But we drafted him in the second round anyway. Everybody else stayed away from him with the reports that he was going to the ABA. But we had an extra second pick so we took him. Boy, was it instant fireworks. We got the rights to this phenomenal player. Could we get him? It became a huge story in Chicago. Just a mega-story.

Dick Motta: We made a trade from the NBA to the ABA. We sent Paul Ruffner to the Pittsburgh Condors. It was a cross-league trade, the only one in history. And nobody said anything. We never asked anyone in our league office. We just traded him over there. We even gave them two exhibition games in the deal.

Pat Williams: We had a settlement with Pittsburgh, and you know the sad thing was—I don't believe this ever came out—we were doing everything we could to cover for Howard, to keep the story of his

illegal signing from coming out. The Pittsburgh Condors at that point didn't care. They were getting blown away and were going to file a big lawsuit. I remember this vividly. We had to meet Pittsburgh's price, and they would let the story slip away. There was a $25,000 difference, and our owners would not do it. As a result, Pittsburgh filed the lawsuit, and that's when the NCAA found out Porter was ineligible and Villanova got screwed. For another $25,000 Pittsburgh would have gone away quietly. But our owners would not bend. It was heartbreaking because I knew what was coming. It was going to be an ugly story.

The NCAA stripped Villanova of its 1971 tournament victories and second-place finish because Porter was ineligible.

Dick Motta: Porter had signed, I think, three contracts. We sorted out all the agents. We paid him big money. And there was a question about the military draft. You had to be 6-8 or 6-9 to be exempt from the military draft. I remember the day we went to the doctor. We stretched him that day. A 6-6 forward turned out to be 6-8. So we get his medical deferment and go through all of this.

Pat Williams: That fall in training camp at Wheaton College, we'd gone through all these huge problems and tied up a ton of money in Porter. The legal problems and the Villanova thing had been ugly. We finally got to training camp. On the first day, we ran through all the drills, passing and dribbling and this and that.

When the morning session ended, Motta and I got together. I'll never forget Dick, because he always spoke so slowly and deliberately. He said, "Howard Porter can't play."

Dick Motta: All Pat said was, "Tell me it isn't so. Tell me he can play." I said, "Pat, the guy can't play."

Pat Williams: They'd have passing drills and he couldn't pass from here to there. Porter could run and jump and shoot. But his defense and ballhandling were very robotic, very rigid. It was impossible. He couldn't run a play. It was just painful.

HOWARD PORTER FORWARD

Bob Logan: If only Motta hadn't fancied himself such a general managing genius and insisted on signing Howard Porter and insisted he was the next Gus Johnson. They paid Howard Porter almost as much as they paid for the franchise.

Howard Porter signed a $1.5 million contract, a substantial contract in that era, and played three seasons with the Bulls, averaging between five and nine points in each of them. In all, he played seven NBA seasons and averaged 9.2 points.

Pat Williams: Dick later blamed it on Jerry Krause. But if you read his scouting reports, Krause was not a huge Howard Porter fan. Dick was the type of guy, whatever went well, he was the architect... . Dick would not take responsiblity for any screwups.

75

Van Lier and Bobby Weiss trap Bullet Mike Riordan.

A Matter of Trust, 1971-72

ALTHOUGH HOWARD PORTER struggled, *Jerry Krause had found another solid rookie in the '71 draft, 6-foot-9 center Clifford Ray, a third rounder out of the University of Oklahoma who earned a spot on the All-Rookie team. Ray and Boerwinkle split time at center, and both averaged seven points and better than 11 rebounds per game.*

The other big addition was Norm Van Lier, who returned to the club in a November trade after playing two seasons in Cincinnati. The new lineup boosted the Bulls to a 57-25 season.

Off the court, the franchise had been rattled by another power struggle that stretched across the spring and summer of 1971.

Jerry Krause: Motta was gonna get me nailed if he possibly could, but he was threatening to go to the ABA. I told Pat Williams, "Let Motta go to the ABA. Let's go down to Norman, Oklahoma, and get this young college coach nobody has heard of named John McLeod." Pat couldn't do that. Pat was basically a very good human being, but I told him Motta was gonna stick a knife in his back.

Pat Williams: Motta got this huge offer to go to Dallas of the ABA, and it just jarred us. We'd just had the Howard Porter draft. We'd had a good year. I talked to Krause, and Krause said, "Let him go. Get John McLeod from Oklahoma." The owners said, "We can't do that." Motta was popular; Motta was successful. He had just been named Coach of the Year. Things were going well. Jerry said Dick would end up

The Lakers hammered Chicago in the '72 playoffs.

1966 CHICAGO BULLS 1996
XXX
30 YEARS AND RUNNING

Van Lier in traffic.

Bog Logan: Krause and Motta are obsessed people, but in totally different ways. They couldn't stand each other. So it was interesting to watch 'em go at each other. There's no question that from a pure basketball standpoint, Krause is a much better judge of talent than Dick Motta ever was. If Motta had just stuck to coaching and left the general manager aspects of it alone, both he and the Bulls would have been infinitely better off. Motta wanted to call all of the shots because he didn't trust other people. He thought the writers, the players, the fans all had a hidden agenda that would be used against him.

Jerry Krause: The early history of this franchise is a psychiatrist's delight.

Forced out of a job, Krause left to become a Phoenix Suns' scout. The Bulls, meanwhile, got off to a great start. In a December 29th game against Kareem and Milwaukee in the Stadium, they drew a record crowd of 19,497 who saw Bob Love score 41 points in an upset win. "Nobody in the league can get the shot away just over your hands the way he does," Milwaukee's John Block said of Love. "There's nothing you can do to stop him."

Love was named to the West All-Star team, but Chet Walker was overlooked. To remind the voters of their mistake, he scored 56 points against Cincinnati the week before the All-Star game.

Although the Bulls were the league's best defensive team, giving up only 102.9 points per game, a series of March injuries drained their momentum. Boerwinkle was lost for the season with a knee injury. Love sprained an ankle, and Walker pulled a hamstring, leaving the Bulls limping for their first-round playoff matchup with the Lakers, who had finished 69-13 and were finally on their way to a title. Chicago's season ended with a 4-0 sweep. Despite that, Motta seemed satisfied. "We did our best," he told reporters.

getting me. As it turned out, Motta ended up getting us both, because part of his deal to stay in Chicago was that he was gonna bring Phil Johnson in as an assistant and Krause had to go.

Motta hated Krause, just hated him. He had no respect for Krause; he couldn't stand him. I walked right into that in '69 when I arrived. Dick does not mask his feelings very well. He had been there one year, and he and Krause were like oil and water. Krause was younger than Dick. He was just hanging on, just a guy out on the road scouting.

Clifford Ray rebounds against the Lakers.

Norm Van Lier: The Lakers were always in our way. They were a better basketball team. Simple as that.

Profile/ Butterbean

ONE OF BOB LOVE'S PROUDEST *accomplishments is the fact that he led the Bulls in scoring for seven straight seasons. He was also an excellent defensive player. Three times he was named to the All-Star team. In 1989, Love's number 10 was retired by the team, although B. J. Armstrong continued to wear 10 until he was lost in the 1995 expansion draft. During his playing days, Love's public exposure was limited because of a severe stutter.*

Bob Love: I used to eat a lot of butterbeans as a little boy growing up down in Bastrop, Louisiana. My family and friends knew that and started calling me "Butterbean." It wasn't a name that I minded. We had 14 kids in a two-bedroom house. There were only two beds, which meant there was a scramble every night for the bed. Because I was one of the smallest, I usually slept under the bed. My first hoop was a coathanger. My first ball was my grandfather's smelly old socks. My Grandmother always told me, "Never be ashamed of who you are, or where you came from, but always be proud of where you're going."

… Back in those days, we didn't know anything about speech therapy. Every Sunday she would stick three marbles under my tongue, and I had to read from my Sunday school book. Every Sunday I swallowed two marbles when I'd get thirsty and ask for a drink of water. I would stutter asking for the water, and my Grandmother would say, "Spit it out, Robert Earl!" I never learned to spit it out, but I learned to stop asking my grandmother for that water. Every night I would get down on my knees and pray to the Lord to please help me find a way to speak… .

A lot of times when I was a little boy, I'd come home crying from school. Kids would laugh at me because I couldn't talk. They'd make fun of me, but I never held anything against them. They were just kids. All of them were my friends. But they could be cruel. You know how kids are. I'd come home crying lots of times, and my Grandmother would always tell me, "Robert Earl, let me tell you something. When you pray for something to happen and it doesn't happen, it's not time for it to happen. All you got to do is hold on. Only the Lord knows when it's time for something to happen. When it does happen, it's right on time." My Grandmother was the wisest woman in the world.

The 6-foot-8, 215-pound Love attended Southern University, an all-black school, where he became a basketball star in the early 1960s.

Bob Love: Back then black players were not allowed to go to white schools, and all the talent was basically concentrated in the black schools. I played against all those guys and I held my own and beat just about everybody I played against in college. I surprised a lot of people, but I didn't surprise myself. My last year of school I averaged 31 points and 18 rebounds. I could play the game.

The Cincinnati Royals selected Love in the fourth round of the 1965 draft. He played well at their camp but was sent to the Trenton Colonials of the Eastern League, where he played his first pro season and earned Rookie-of-the-Year honors. For the 1966-67 season, Love returned to the Royals.

Love launches against the Celtics.

Bob Love.

Love had the size, determination and quickness to be a versatile defender.

Bob Love: Oscar Robertson and I just kind of hit it off. I was his first roommate. Oscar really didn't want a roommate till I came along. I would just keep him laughing all day because I stuttered really, really bad. He used to call me Bayou Beans. We'd tell jokes, and he'd tell me how to play guys and what he did. He would show me how to get open…. Oscar and I loved to spend hours after practice; he would show me how to shoot. I kind of copied my shot off of him. I already had the behind-the-head shot, but I really didn't have the fake.

Oscar Robertson: Bean credits me with helping him, but he already had it in him.

Bob Love: On the basketball court I feared no one. I didn't care who it was. I could jump just as high as anybody. I could shoot. I could run just as fast as anybody.

I had two good years in Cincinnati, but at the end of the 1967-68 season, the league had the expansion draft for the Milwaukee Bucks. We had a general manager named Pepper Wilson. Oscar told him, "You gotta protect Butter from the draft. Bean is going to be a great player." But the people in Cincinnati said, "Bob can't talk. He's a stutterer and he's never going to be any use to the organization because he can't talk." So they put me in the expansion draft, and Milwaukee took me.

Oscar Robertson: Because Bob had a speech impediment, they figured that affected his game. In those days, managers thought a lot of dumb things like that.

Bob Love: I led Milwaukee in scoring during the exhibition season with something like 18 points a game. But I was unable to give interviews or talk on the radio. The

Bucks management told Wayne Embry, who was on the team: "Go to Bob Love's place and tell him we're gonna cut him. He can't talk." Wayne said, "Hey, man, I'm not going over there and tell him nothing. The damn guy just led us in scoring. He's a hell of a player." Wayne had seen me in college and knew that I could play. But the general manager at Milwaukee said, "Bob stutters. He can't talk. We got to get rid of him." Wayne came over to my house and told me what they said. Man, it really, really hurt my feelings. I always thought that being a basketball player was playing basketball, not talking. This was the second time in a year this had happened to me. Somehow they worked out a deal with the Bulls. Me and Bobby Weiss for Flynn Robinson.

Just hours after his trade to the Bulls on November 7, 1968, Love sustained severe back injuries in an auto wreck on State Street. As a result, he missed a major portion of the 1968-69 season.

Bob Love: Later, after the trade, I learned that the Bulls really didn't want me. They wanted Bob Weiss. I couldn't understand that. I looked at the stats. I was averaging more points than Bobby. I was a better defensive player. I thought I was one of the top defensive players in the league. I could never understand their thinking. I still can't today.

But I didn't let it interfere with me. I kept my head up. When I came back from the wreck injuries, I practiced harder than anybody. I'd stay around afterward and shoot. I'd run. I had made up my mind, "If all these people think that because I can't talk it interferes with my basketball playing, if I ever get a chance, I'm gonna show 'em."

That next year, the Bulls were gonna bring in a guy named Bob Kauffman. They got him in a trade from Seattle. This guy was gonna be the savior of the Bulls. Bob was 6-9 and weighed about 250. Dick Motta virtually gave him the starting job. But all during camp I played well, and all of a sudden there was a real competition. Kauffman couldn't guard guys, and he couldn't score in Motta's offense. I just blossomed. I just started killing these guys scoring, and I

Butterbean worked the boards.

could always move without the ball. I could always get my shot. I knew how to post up guys and I could always run. A quarter of the 1969-70 season passed before Dick Motta inserted me into the starting lineup. But I never looked back.

For six straight seasons, Love scored better than 21 points per game for the Bulls.

Norm Van Lier: Love was a great scorer, and we went to him enough. But more than that, Bob Love played defense and was physical. Because he was a scorer, people forget he was a defender. But he stopped all the big-name forwards in the league, shut 'em down, night after night after night. I'm talking about the Connie Hawkins, the Spencer Haywoods, the Dave DeBusscheres, the Rick Barrys. Bob Love shut 'em down.

Bob Love: As great as Dr. J. was, Doc never dunked on me. I played him straight up. I wanted no help from nobody. I had pride in my game, I had pride in myself. I guess I had something to prove. Doc would swirl around and dunk on other guys. He never dunked on me. Never.

Norm Van Lier: I'll never say Bob was a great shooter. He was a scorer. There's a big difference. But when it counted, he was there. He really didn't have a jumper. It was more of a line-drive, tiptoe shot. Bob's about 6-9, with long arms. He'd bring the ball back behind his head like Oscar Robertson used to do. It was effective as long as you had wrist, and Bob had plenty.

After leaving the game in 1977, Love found himself faced with financial and marital problems and back surgery. He tried to get coaching jobs but was rebuffed. One former teammate told him he wasn't qualified.

Bob Love: All of the stuff I had to go through when I retired, you would not believe how humiliating it was. But I never blamed anybody. But it seemed like people always tried to make me feel like "Bob Love can't talk."

I'll never forget in 1984, when I was married for the second time, I came home from the doctor one day. I came in my house and looked around. Everything I owned—my furniture, my money, my car—everything I had was gone. I looked there and saw a note from my wife. Basically she said she didn't want to be married to a guy who couldn't talk, who was gonna be crippled for the rest of his life.

I had just had two back operations. I wasn't able to work or anything. I was left with nothing. I sat there, and I got scared. I got angry. I had all kinds of thoughts. You can imagine. I decided that night to get on my knees and ask the Lord for strength and courage to go on.

The next morning I got up. I was walking with a cane and a crutch. I started walking. I walked about a mile the first day. Then I did the same thing the next day. After a while, I was able to walk pretty well. I went downtown to Nordstrom's and asked for a job. They told me they would hire me, but I'd have to start at the bottom. They made me start with busing tables and washing dishes. Oh, man, I had some embarrassing moments, let me tell you. NBA players would come in there with their kids and see me in my little white hat and apron. I had to go in and wipe their tables. It was embarrassing, but I didn't quit. Like I tell the kids today, the easiest thing in the world would have been for me to quit, to take off that hat, throw it down and walk out the door. But I didn't do that.

I took all those looks and stares, and I turned them into an opportunity. I became the best busboy/dishwasher in the world. I wasn't gonna let what anybody thought or anybody said keep me from reaching my goals. I was just gonna do what I had to do to make it. And it all paid off.

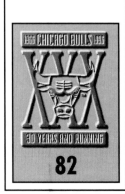

All the time I was struggling, not one time did Dick Motta call me. He retired from the Dallas Mavericks, and then he came back and got a job coaching the Sacramento Kings. One night, while I was with Nordstrom's, I went to see his team play in Seattle. I told him, "Dick, you should hire me as an assistant coach." He said, "Butter, I'll hire you. I'll call." He never called me. I guess it was because I couldn't talk, or he thought I wasn't qualified.

Over 40 years I had prayed to be able to get up in front of a crowd of people and talk. I mean I prayed every night, to be able to speak. I never once thought it wasn't going to happen. In 1974, I suffered one of the most embarrassing moments of my life. I was a big scorer that season, but I didn't talk much to the media because I couldn't. But I was invited to be honored at a Boy Scouts luncheon. Over 3,000 kids were there. They promised me there would be no speeches. I met parents and shook their hands. During the meal, they introduced me and suddenly the crowd started chanting, "Speech! Speech! Speech!" My heart was beating. I stood there three minutes and couldn't utter a single word, not a single word. When I left, I couldn't hold my head up. In the car, I cried. I said, "Lord, please help me find a way to speak."

I didn't get that opportunity until the people at Nordstrom's paid for my speech therapy.

The first person I called when I learned how talk was Dick Motta. He was down in Florida, at his home there. I said, "Coach, the reason I'm calling you, I just want to thank you for all the help that you gave me, for allowing me to play in Chicago when nobody else wanted me, for all the encouragement that you gave me through the years that I played for you. I just want to tell you, Coach, that I love you." And Dick said, "Is this the same Bob Love that I know?" I said, "This is Butter." He said, "You don't sound like the Bob Love that I know." I said, "Coach, this is me."

We talked and we talked. Finally Dick told me, "Butter, you don't know how I appreci-

ate this. Out of all the guys I coached, you're the only guy who has ever called me and thanked me."

Just last year, I saw Dick at the pre-draft camp in Chicago. He was back coaching in Dallas. He said, "Butter, what I'm gonna do, I'm gonna bring you down to Dallas and let you show these guys how to run this offense during training camp." It would have been fun to do that. I said, "Fine, Dick. You know how to call me." He never called me. But that doesn't matter. Dick knew that when I played for him that I gave him 100 percent. When I see him today, I hug him and we talk like nothing has happened. I don't want to hold the hard feelings in my heart. I've got to move on.

Today Bob Love is director of community services for the Chicago Bulls, making several hundred speeches a year to school children and student groups in the Chicago area.

Bob Love: When I go around to the schools and talk to kids, they look at me and ask, "How did you do all of that?" I tell them, "A lot of times life is not fair. It's not meant to be fair. But you've got to have a dream, and you've got to hold onto it." It wasn't meant for me to speak back then, but it's meant for me to go to the schools now and tell the kids about hope, to tell them about life. And that's the greatest feeling in the world.

BOB LOVE   FORWARD

Van Lier's attitude eptiomized the feisty Bulls.

Profile/ Stormin' Norman

*T*HE BULLS *picked Norm Van Lier, the son of a Pennsylvania coal miner, out of little St. Francis College in the third round of the 1970 draft and promptly traded him to Cincinnati. In November 1971, they traded back for him. In high school, he had been a stand-out football player, and that showed in his style of play. A three-time All-Star, he played seven seasons for Chicago and teamed with Jerry Sloan in the NBA's most intimidating backcourt.*

Norm Van Lier: Jerry Krause put a pro career in my mind when I was a junior. He said, "Hey, kid, you can play in this league." He's the only scout who ever talked to me.

Jerry Krause: Van Lier was a tough kid. The best thing about Norman, he's a mean son of a bitch.

Jerry Sloan: When Norm played for Cincinnati, we got in a fight down in Northern Illinois in a preseason game. There was about eight guys who ran us right through the door. It was a glass door at the end of the gym. Their bench was right next to it. The next thing I know I'm lying flat on my back with about 10 guys on tops of me. Fortunately, I was still alive.

Dick Motta: A lot of people say that getting Norm Van Lier was the final piece to our team... but with Matt Goukas, Bob Weiss and Jerry Sloan we had already had a 50-win season before Van Lier got there.

Jerry Sloan: The first game he played for us was in Baltimore.... It was like automatic once he stepped on the floor with me. There was nothing said. Knowing what we had to do defensively was instantly communicated.

Norm Van Lier: I was called Stormin' Norman through college, but Ben Bentley really stretched it. He was the best in the business. When he introduced me as "Storrr-man Norrr-man," it really got 'em in a frenzy in the Stadium.

Jeff Mullins: There were no two tougher guards in basketball than Sloan and Van Lier. They were extremely competitive, very physical guys, the kind who would knock you down, then pick you up. They were always trying to draw the charge. I'll never forget. We had a rookie from North Carolina named Bobby Lewis. When we played the Bulls, I told him, "Bobby, you gotta watch Sloan and Van Lier because when you give the ball up and cut through, they'll sorta get you by the jersey and pull you down with them." Lewis sort of half-listened to me and went in the game. Sure enough, he comes down the first time, and Jerry pulled him right over. Charge. The next time Lewis came down the other side and cut through. Norm Van Lier stepped in front. Another charge. A few minutes later Sloan got him again. Lewis got three straight charges without the ball and went bananas and had to sit down.

Jerry Sloan: Norm and I were very similar. We were both crazy when it came to playing.

Norm Van Lier: A lot of those charges were legit. A lot of people didn't have the guts to do it. A lot of those charges were hard, sure-enough, red-dog hits. But I took charges. I didn't pull you down. I wasn't strong enough to do that.

Jerry Sloan: Your hands have gotta be faster than the eye. We always had to have some means of taking people's minds off the game when they were on offense. Otherwise, they'd have just run by us like a layup drill if we'd let them play.

Nate 'Tiny' Archibald: I got a chance to play with Norm two years in Cincinnati. He was just a great leader. He didn't score a lot of points, but Norm brought a different attitude, a different demeanor to any team he played on. His hustle. He taught me a lot about how to prepare to go out and do battle with all of those bigger guys we faced. Then Norm got traded, and I had the misfortune of having to play against Norm and Jerry Sloan. That was the toughest team to prepare for. We had some duels. They always outdid us. I remember we called our division the Black-and-Blue Division, mainly because we played against Chicago. I really didn't want them to physically beat me up, so I had to outrun those guys.

A lot of people said they flopped on defense, but they were just guys that were glued to people.... I'd get past Norm. The next thing I knew, Jerry Sloan was in my face. They had that great mentality about guarding people. They had pride.

Norm Van Lier: I started to get physically beat up in Chicago. I'd never had that in Cincinnati. I wanted to run and shoot like everybody else. We had run under Bob Cousy in Cincinnati, and I had led the league in assists. It took me a year and a half to adjust to Motta's slowdown style. I had to come to Chicago and walk the ball up, small as I was, and set picks for forwards. I was picking forwards, somebody 6-8. That's the duty I had. That's why Jerry was such a valuable piece. He was 6-5 and 200 pounds; he could set those picks.

In Motta's offense, the guards gave the ball to Tom Boerwinkle, who was a great passer. Then we'd set picks while the center ran the half-court offense. It was all timing. Our forwards did all the scoring.

Clifford Ray: Norm had energy to burn. Constant motion. He loved the Allman Brothers. He was big time into southern rock. But when the game started, he was the most competitive guy that I ever ran into. He always spoke his mind, too. It hurt him sometimes. But I respected him for that.

Matt Guokas: I had a tremendous amout of respect for Norm. He played so hard and played his role with that team so well. Just a gritty defender, a clutch player. Norm, like a lot of players today, would kind of fly off at the handle at whatever. Not so much at Dick Motta but at referees. He would get into these battles with referees and it would affect his play. He got thrown out of a lot of games because of it.

Norm Van Lier made his first All-Star appearance in 1974 and was named to the All-Defensive first team and to the All-NBA second team. He repeated as an All-Star in 1976 and '77.

Norm Van Lier: I liked being named an All-Star. But I hated the All-Star festivities themselves. I didn't fit the All-Star mode. The game is just a show. I can't do there what I did to make me an All-Star. I'm gonna take charges in the All-Star game? I'm gonna dive for loose balls? Instinctively I'm gonna do it. It was very hard for me to even play in the All-Star game.

NORM VAN LIER • G

New York's Phil Jackson grabs Chicago's Gar Heard.

New Bosses, 1972-73

DICK KLEIN'S PROTRACTED WAR WITH HIS co-owners came to a conclusion before the 1972-73 season. For almost three years, Klein had maintained enough of a faction to hold onto a chunk of Bulls stock, but his group of supporters finally dissolved in 1972. Lamar Hunt had been firmly in his camp, until Klein produced San Diego businessman Peter Graham to purchase the team. Little did Klein know that Graham and Hunt had bumped heads over a pro football franchise.

Rather than join forces with Graham and Klein, Hunt pulled his support away, and Graham's bid was declined. Faced with the ultimatum to buy out the other owners or agree to sell his shares, Klein reluctantly sold for a nice profit.

Bob Logan: Klein had struggled from day one. He sold his shares, and it made him a millionaire. But he'd have given up every penny of that just to hang around the team.

Milwaukee realtor Marv Fishman signed an agreement to purchase the team, but the NBA owners rejected Fishman's ownership. Fishman in turn filed suit against Arthur Wirtz and the Bulls, and it would take more than a decade for the litigation to be resolved.

In 1972, Arthur Wirtz then purchased the Bulls with a group that included Lester Crown, George Steinbrenner, and Phil Klutznick. Jonathan Kovler, who had bought 10 percent of the team from Klein in early 1972, and Hunt remained on board as owners.

Dick Klein: The Wirtz/Klutznick bunch bought it for $3.5 million. My mistake was having partners who weren't in it for the long pull.

Pat Williams: We began to have some success in the early '70s. You began to feel basketball's presence in Chicago. Good things were beginning to happen. I think Wirtz realized that, so it made good sense for him to own the team. We were successful. We were just getting it turned around.

Meanwhile, Howard Porter's big contract only served to make several starters angry because he was being paid so well to sit on the bench.

The Bulls were set to go to Hawaii for an exhibition tour in September of 1972. At first, Bob Love declined to go, saying he wanted to be paid better. Finally, he made the trip. Boerwinkle reinjured his knee during a drill and wound up playing only eight games the entire season. To replace him, Chicago acquired Dennis Awtrey from Philadelphia.

Despite these setbacks, Motta's system was now a picture of execution.

Tom Boerwinkle: Our pre-game meetings lasted about 30 seconds. We never put plays on the board. Never watched a film. Never went over scouting reports. Dick Motta's philosophy was, "We're not going to do a whole lot of things, but what we do, we're going to do right. And we're not going to change things for different teams. We're going to do the same thing whether we're playing against the Boston Celtics or the last team in the league."... We kept it simple, but we executed.

The highlights of the year included back-to-back 49-point performances by Bob Love. The

Pat Williams graced the cover of the 1973 playoff program.

Norm was a fan favorite.

CHICAGO BULLS 1972-73 PRESS GUIDE and yearbook

The 1972-73 season brought a power struggle.

1973 PLAYOFFS

LOS ANGELES LAKERS VS. CHICAGO BULLS

OFFICIAL PROGRAM $1.00

Motta and Pat Williams were at odds during the 1973 playoffs.

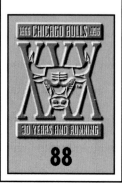

Bulls finished 51-31, good enough for second place in the division.

Motta had figured his team would meet Milwaukee in the first round of the play-offs, but the Bucks closed the season with a 14-game win streak and tied the Lakers with a 60-22 record. The Bucks won a coin flip to get the top seed, and suddenly the league informed the Bulls they had to fly to Los Angeles on short notice to play the Lakers. Motta was furious, both with the league and with Pat Williams for not finding a way to get the schedule changed.

Ben Bentley: There was a big fight that broke out between Motta and Pat Williams over flying out of Chicago after one game to meet L.A. the next night. Motta said he did it for the team. He blamed Pat for not asking the league for another day.

Pat Williams: Dick turned on me. The league had scheduled the play-offs. I'll never forget his statement to me. "You don't have a gut in your body," he said as we head-ed out to play the Lakers. Like I could determine the playoff schedule. What Dick wanted to do is not show up. "We won't show up," he said. "Well, Dick," I said. "It's gonna be a forfeit then." In many ways, Dick was like a 3-year-old. He was amazing.

The Bulls fought the Lakers to a 3-3 tie in the series, then took a big lead in the closing min-utes in Game 7 in Los Angeles. With 2:58 to go, Chicago led 90-83, but the Lakers went on a 12-2 run to claim the series.

Gar Heard: We had a lead with about 45 seconds to go in the game. Rowland Garrett and I were sitting on the bench talking about how the lead was slipping away. Being young kids like that, we talked about how the playoff money was slipping out of our pockets. I remember one great play Wilt made. He blocked a Norm Van Lier layup that really turned the whole game around.

Norm Van Lier: We just absolutely blew it. Turnovers. Missed shots. And they just came storming back. They had all but given up. That one was hard to take, because of the rivalry we had developed with the Lakers.

In the locker room after the loss, the team was racked with dissension.

Jerry Sloan: Some guys said Boerwinkle didn't deserve a full playoff share because he had been out injured. I said, "Well, if you're gonna be that way about it, then pro-rate my money based on the number of games that I played. I think I missed four or five games myself."

That July of 1973, Williams was forced out and quickly took a job as general manager of the Atlanta Hawks.

Bob Logan: Motta and Williams got along for a while because Williams did what Motta asked him to do. When Williams wanted to do something different, the con-flicts arose. It got to be a me-or-him situa-tion. Motta went to the owners, and they sided with him. It came down to Williams or Motta, and the owners knew who the most valuable man was. That was the end of Williams.

Jerry Krause: I told Pat that Motta was gonna get him. And he did.

Profile/Arthur Wirtz

IT WAS IN 1935, A TIME OF DEPRESSION *disaster sales, that Arthur Wirtz teamed with the James Norrises junior and senior to purchase Chicago Stadium at a bargain. Over the ensuing four decades, Wirtz came to own the Blackhawks and numerous other entertainment ventures, although he never claimed to love or care about sports, especially basketball. But in 1972, the Bulls interested Wirtz because they had found a home in Chicago, and more important, they could be counted on to fill his Stadium for as many as 50 nights a year.*

Not long after buying the Bulls, Wirtz teamed with three other investors—Phillip Klutznick, Lester Crown and Jonathan Kovler—to form a four-man executive committee to run the team. Over the next dozen years this group would draw much criticism for its management-by-committee style. Yet throughout this period, Wirtz's reputation remained intact: He was a tough business guy, and he kept the building clean.

Johnny Kerr: Wirtz was a big showman, and I loved him. He was 6-4 or 6-5 and weighed well over 300 pounds. I'd go to see him in his office over on the twentieth floor at the Furniture Mart. We'd always be interrupted by phone calls, from Mayor Daley, from all kinds of important people. He was in on everything.

Ben Bentley: Wirtz was as stern and as sharp a businessman as you'll ever meet. Before coming to the Bulls, I had worked for him on the old Wednesday night and Friday night fights at the Stadium. Even when he joked at you, he joked in a stern way. You had to pause for a minute to see if he was kidding. You became subservient to him when you talked to him. He had a way of talking where immediately he became the warlord and you became the peon and you were nodding to what he said. He put you on the defensive right away.

Irwin Mandel: Arthur Wirtz was a most charming man, but the toughest negotiator I have ever dealt with. He was very imposing physically, too. He had so much money and such thick skin that it gave him leverage in negotiations. If a deal fell through, or he couldn't sign you, so be it. It just wasn't as important to him as it was to anybody else. He didn't need the money as much as the other person, so he rarely gave in. He was a self-made man. He made money in the Depression by buying properties that had gone under… Arthur was the son of a policeman. I don't think he had any advanced

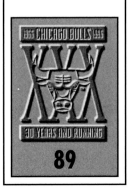

degrees. He was a street-smart man. He didn't go to that many games. He would go count the house, and sometimes in the middle of the game he would come up and make bets with me on what the attendance was. He did this after he had just found out from the box office. After a while I caught on.

Pat Williams: Arthur Wirtz was great at never taking any direct heat. He was just an overwhelming presence. He was a hockey man through and through. He had lost some money on basketball back in the '40s. He was a hard-core businessman. He knew how to be profitable. And the Blackhawks? You couldn't get a ticket. It was just a dominating sport in Chicago. They ruled with an iron fist. I guess it was Chicago at its best, the whole patronage system, and Arthur Wirtz was Da Boss.

Irwin Mandel: He molded every meeting to how he wanted it to go... Agents were scared of him. They went along with what he said and almost always he got the better of the deal. In my opinion he could get an agent to agree to terms that he would have not agreed to with anybody else.

He was passionate about being a good businessman when it came to the Bulls and everything else. The Bulls, the Blackhawks, the Stadium, the Bismark Hotel, a lot of real estate. He owned a liquor company and a bank, too. And later on he bought some racing horses, including a horse called Governor Skipper, who was very successful. Arthur Wirtz made a lot of money.

Rod Thorn: Mr. Wirtz was tough. He wasn't giving anything away. He came from the school where you had to work for what you got. He wanted to win at whatever he did, whether it was buying more buildings or whatever.

Irwin Mandel: Not long after I went to work for the Bulls in 1973, Arthur Wirtz said we should get new offices, and I said, "Great. I'll look into it." And he said, "No, you won't look into it. I have just the place for us. It's at 333 North Michigan." I said, "Shouldn't I look into different places?" He said, "333

North Michigan is where we should go." As it turned out—I'm sure it was a coincidence—it was a building that he owned.

A few years later I was looking into liability insurance. I had a few agencies that I was looking into, and I had each of them bid on that insurance. One of the agencies was owned by Arthur Wirtz, and he called me and said, "I understand you're bidding this insurance. I have a suggestion. You place this insurance with my agency. Otherwise, I'm going to bid your job." So it didn't take me to long to conclude that his agency was the one that we should go with.

Johnny Kerr: Wirtz always told me, "If you ever get in a situation where it's an unfavorable light, blame me. I got big shoulders." He didn't care, really.

Irwin Mandel: He did not believe in marketing. He felt that how good the team or product was, was what sold it. If he was living today I think he would modify that view. I agree with him a hundred percent in the importance of the team. That is by far the most important factor. But he went further and placed very little in marketing. In the NBA today, you can see that the best teams usually have the best marketing. I feel that he didn't put enough importance into the marketing.

Jerry Sloan: The owners were all looking for ways to make money without spending any. That's the bottom line, and that's what's so frustrating from a player's and coach's perspective. You gotta spend money to make money.

Arthur Wirtz died in 1983. In writing his obituary, Chicago sportswriter Bill Gleason said: "The Stadium was warm in wintertime and clean at all times. Art Wirtz insisted that his employees work hard, and he paid them with something in addition to money, something that can neither be taught nor learned in the universities' business schools—fierce loyalty.

"He was one of the last of the German-American barons. His rule was autocratic. He hid his benevolence. He was one big, tough, old guy. You say you didn't like him? He didn't care. He didn't give a damn."

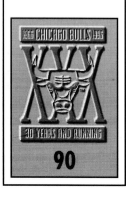

CHICAGO BULLS

1973-74
PRESS GUIDE
and yearbook

Giving The Hoof, 1973-74

Against the Bucks, even Benny got the heave.

THE BULLS HAD ARRANGED TO TRADE Bob Weiss and Clifford Ray to Philadelphia for rookie Doug Collins, the top pick in the '73 draft. But the deal fell through when Ray's knee failed to pass a physical. Then Motta, who was eager to ditch top pick Kevin Kunnert, sent Gar Heard and Kunnert to Buffalo for forward John Hummer, a move that critics called one of the worst trades in NBA history. Motta himself seemed to agree months later, when he abruptly sent Hummer to Seattle for a draft pick. Motta stopped Hummer in a parking lot and told him not to get on the team bus because he'd been traded. "It's not the right way to treat human beings," Hummer said bitterly.

In the other big move, Johnny Kerr was brought in to serve as the Bulls' business manager in the wake of Pat Williams' firing. He worked under the direction of new owner Arthur Wirtz, who headed up the team's executive committee.

Johnny Kerr: Right after I became business manager, Arthur Wirtz told me to stop the free tickets. The Bulls had been throwing tickets all over Chicago. You'd come to the parking lot, and guys would be selling tickets three for a dollar, or a dollar apiece. I had to pull tickets from the Boy Scouts, from the safety patrols in the schools, from honor students. It was really not a favorable thing to do. But on opening night, Wirtz called me and said, "Congratulations. We had $8,000 in ticket sales in two hours tonight, and we've never had that before."

Assistant coach Phil Johnson was named head coach of the Kansas City-Omaha Kings, leav-

Boerwinkle returned from injury and found his way to the heart of controversy.

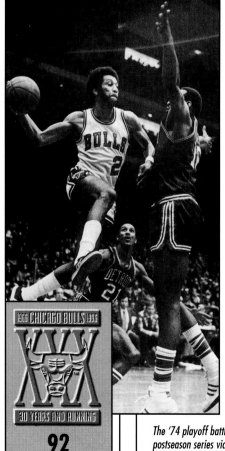

Ray slams on the Pistons.

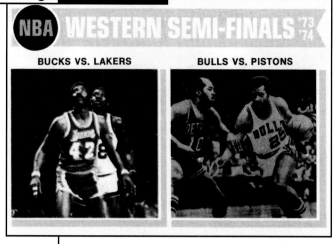

ing Motta alone to fill the jobs of general manager, head coach, assistant coach, and scout. Love missed all of training camp with yet another holdout. It didn't matter. With a 12-game winning streak, the Bulls got off to a 13-2 start, the best ever.

The lack of staffing, though, eventually caused problems. Furious about an overtime loss in Seattle, Motta shoved a referee and was suspended for a week and fined $2,000. With no assistant coaches, Motta was forced to leave the coaching to team trainer Bob Biel, a podiatrist. Motta asked junior college coach Ed Badger to help Biel, leading to Badger becoming Motta's assistant.

The Bulls defeated Cleveland in late March to give them 32 home victories, a team record. They finished the schedule at 54-28, their fourth straight 50-win season, good for another second place finish in the division. Their first round opponent was the Detroit Pistons.

Tom Boerwinkle: Detroit had Lanier, Dave Bing, Jimmy Walker. That was the first legendary Chicago-Detroit battle.

Norm Van Lier: Those were battles, man. Good old fashioned battles. We hated each other. But we'd put our arms around each other after the game. It was tough then, but we didn't have anywhere near the hate that Detroit

Bob Love
SCORING

Chet Walker
FREE THROWS

CHICAGO BULLS

BULLS TEAM leaders

Clifford Ray
REBOUNDS

Norm Van Lier
ASSISTS

and Chicago had in the '89 and '90 series.

The teams pushed the matchup to a 3-3 tie, but Jerry Sloan tore the plantar fascia in his foot and could not play in Game 7 in Chicago. The Stadium crowd, however, roared loud enough to spur Chet Walker and Bob Love to outstanding performances, and the Bulls claimed their first playoff series victory, 96-94.

Next came the Milwaukee Bucks and a 4-0 elimination. Kareem Abdul-Jabbar's performance convinced Dick Motta he needed a big powerful center to win a championship. Game 4 in Milwaukee brought the ejection of Motta, Sloan (who was on the bench injured) and even mascot Benny the Bull. News reports the next day noted that the mascot "gave the hoof" to the officials and the crowd as he left the arena.

The '74 playoff battle with the Pistons brought the Bulls their first postseason series victory.

1965 CHICAGO BULLS 1996

30 YEARS AND RUNNING

Move/Missing Maurice No.1

THE BULLS DRAFTED MAURICE LUCAS, who had played for Al McGuire at Marquette, and Cliff Pondexter, who had played for Jerry Tarkanian at Long Beach State, in the first round of the 1974 draft.

Dick Motta: We were always trying to get that third forward. We drafted Clifton Pondexter and Maurice Lucas at the same time. But Arthur Wirtz said we could only sign one of them. Ed Badger decided that Pondexter was a better talent. Lucas later became all-pro and was a big factor in Portland winning their championship. A rotation of Bob Love, Chet Walker and Maurice Lucas at forward, that would have brought us a championship. Instead, I had to play Jerry Sloan at forward. I had to move him down. That third forward was always a problem position for us. We traded for John Hummer; we traded for John Tresvant. It was like the Bermuda Triangle. No matter who we put at the third forward, they disappeared.

Johnny Kerr: They drafted Clifton Pondexter and Lucas. Lucas had left Marquette. When he came in for a visit, he had already fired one agent. Motta felt, "Here's a guy who can't make up his mind. How strong is he gonna be?" Lucas would have been perfect for Motta's tough team with Van Lier and Sloan and Love. It was a major miscalculation in talent, a little like Portland bypassing Michael for Sam Bowie in 1984.

The other kid, Pondexter, was just a kid. His agent came in. He had on a white suit, a white shirt, a white tie, white jacket, white pants, white socks and white shoes. Bob Logan said it looked like he had come over from a Charlie Chan movie.

Dick Motta: Pondexter's first injury was a forerunner of the stress fracture. They hadn't coined the phrase "stress fracture" then, but he had one. We could have wallpapered four buildings with his Xrays.

Signed to a major contract, Cliff Pondexter played three seasons for the Bulls and averaged 3.9 points. Maurice Lucas played a major role in Portland's 1977 NBA championship.

But the Bulls failed to sign their other number one pick, Maurice Lucas.

MAURICE LUCAS ▪ F

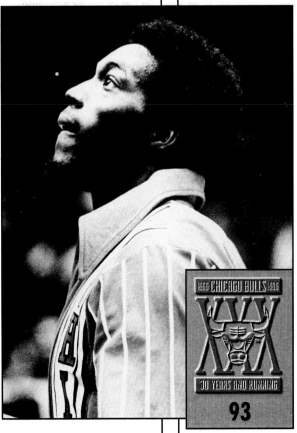

The Bulls signed Cliff Pondexter out of the '74 draft.

Super Fan in 1975.

Super Fan in leaner times.

Profile/Super Fan

IN THE 1970S, A SPORTING GOODS salesman named Jeff Platt gained wide recognition at Bulls games as Super Fan.

Bill Gleason: There was a guy named Super Fan, and this was strictly voluntary. He was a huge young fellow, probably weighed about 280 to 300 pounds and about 5-foot-9. He would run around the Stadium, and he would exhort the crowd to cheer. He was a tremendous favorite; he was a bigger drawing card than most of the players.

Tim Hallam: Tommy Edwards, our PA announcer back then, would start saying, "Where Are You Super Fan?" Edwards would do this two maybe three times a game, whenever the team needed a lift. Super Fan couldn't get his feet off the ground. He'd just sort of rumble around the Stadium while the organist played the *William Tell Overture*, and when he'd stop he'd pirouette. He wore like a bad, kind of soiled red Bulls T-shirt. It was too tight, stretched across his stomach and tight in

the armpits. He looked like a fan who went to the park and played football in the shirt, then slept in it, got up the next day and came to the Stadium. As he ran around the Stadium, he'd slap five with the media guys and little kids who came down to the railing. Then he'd be done and he'd be sweaty and he'd kneel down and bark something out. He was in his own world, and it was a Bulls' world.

Brian McIntyre: He was a fool, but he was a Bulls' fans' fool. One night our organist wasn't there, and her mother substituted. Her mother kept playing the *Overture*. Super Fan did one lap and stopped at the organ. She kept playing, so he did another lap. He comes back, and she's still playing. So he starts a third lap, but then he stopped and staggered over to a chair, just gasping. We had a doctor look at him just to make sure he was okay. He was so tired he had to miss the next game.

Tim Hallam: This was no show. The guy lived it 24 hours a day.

Bill Gleason: The ironic thing, and sort of typical of Bulls history, he was fat. When he was fat, he had about three bellies and four chins and everything would quiver. And then he made a terrible mistake. He lost weight and trimmed down, probably because he had become an idol, a fan favorite. As soon as he got slender he lost all of his appeal. Nobody cared for Super Fan anymore.

Move/The Ray-Thurmond Trade

*I*N THE WAKE OF HIS TEAM'S 1974 PLAYOFF *loss to the Milwaukee Bucks and Kareem Abdul-Jabbar, Dick Motta decided to go after a major power center, so the Bulls traded Clifford Ray to the Warriors for veteran Nate Thurmond. The move set up a terrible irony for the Bulls. The Warriors relied heavily on Ray to win the 1975 NBA title, and they narrowly beat the Bulls to do it!*

Johnny Kerr: When Dick Motta went over to talk to Arthur Wirtz about getting Nate Thurmond, he asked me to come along. Wirtz said, "Here now, Dick, who is this guy?" "Nate Thurmond," Dick said. Wirtz asked, "Where does he play?" Dick said, "San Francisco." Thurmond had spent 10 years in the league, and Wirtz didn't know who he was. "You're telling me he can help us win?" he said.

Motta said, "Yeah, but he's got a restaurant in San Francisco, and I don't know if he'll leave it to come to Chicago."

"What's the name of the restaurant?" Wirtz asked. Motta told him, and Wirtz said to hold on a minute. Then he phoned his secretary, Gertrude, and asked her to find out how much liquor Thurmond's restaurant was buying from his distributorship in San Francisco. About 15 minutes later Gertrude phoned back with the answer.

"Don't worry," Wirtz said. "He'll come."

Jeff Mullins: I thought we were crazy when we traded for Clifford. But Clifford was just like Nate. He was a center that made everybody better. He didn't do the same things that Nate did, but what he did, he did well.

Nate had a tougher adjustment because the Bulls never counted on their center for much other than passing to their forwards. Nate had been much more of a focal point in Golden State. But that's what happens when an aging player gets traded to a team late in his career. It's hard for the new team to build around him.

The Bulls finally got a big offensive center in Nate Thurmond.

Tom Boerwinkle: When Nate came here, it was a totally different style. One of the big theories was Chicago was a good ball team but it would never be a great ball team until they get a good center. They wanted a center that was in the mold of a Wilt or a Russell or a Nate Thurmond or Bob Lanier, a big dominant center. We played Atlanta on opening night, and Nate blocked 12 shots. He had a triple-double his first night. But it was a tough year for him. It didn't materialize like the Bulls had hoped.

Jerry Sloan: Nate was more of a scorer. We had all been molded around Boerwinkle in the high post as a passer.

Bob Logan: Thurmond couldn't play in Motta's system. That was the tragedy of it. Everybody thought they had finally gotten the big center they needed. Thurmond said, "I didn't realize how delicate this system was." It just called for a center to do things that an offensive center like Thurmond never considered doing. It was just too late

Clifford Ray: The Bulls were always thinking about the Milwaukee Bucks, because Kareem was right up the road. We always seemed to get by Detroit, but a lost of things would happen against Milwaukee.

Thurmond and Sloan work the boards against Portland's Bill Walton.

in his career to make that kind of transition, so Boerwinkle was back as the starter.

Norm Van Lier: Motta's biggest downfall was he never made adjustments to the type of talent he had coming in. Nate Thurmond was a classic example. Motta was into "I need a big center to win the championship," because Kareem or Wilt was always in our way. So we needed a center to negate them. Motta may have said he wanted a low-post center, but he didn't play

Thurmond in the low-post. He didn't change his system at all for Nate Thurmond, not at all. The irony is that Clifford Ray and George Johnson, two centers who weren't dominant, took away Motta's opportunity for a championship.

Bob Weiss: We always felt like second-class citizens because we didn't have the superstar center. We were pretty good. Maybe if we had just realized it, we might have gotten over the hump by ourselves.

The Last Shot, 1974-75

*T*HE 1974-75 *SEASON HELD GREAT promise for the Bulls, but that drifted away in the first two months. Love and Van Lier asked for a pay raise they had been promised by former general manager Pat Williams. But Dick Motta, now the general manager/coach, refused. So Love and Van Lier began a holdout that ran through all of training camp and into the first few weeks of the season.*

When the schedule opened, the starting lineup was Jerry Sloan, Matt Guokas, Rick Adelman, Chet Walker and newly acquired center Nate Thurmond. Guokas had come back to the Bulls in an offseason trade.

Norm Van Lier: I held out because Pat Williams had agreed to give me a new contract... But Dick Motta just took over. I guess he was gonna be a tough guy.

Bob Logan: It was just incredible pennypinching stupidity on Motta's part, but it was compounded by Love's greed.

Jerry Sloan: There was some selfishness on everybody's part. Had there not been some of that, I think this team would have had the chance to be in the Finals.

Kip Motta: I remember Norm's first game back after holding out was against Boston on the road. I didn't know what kind of shape he'd be in. It was a close game, and there was a loose ball on the floor. I remember him diving about 10 feet right between someone's legs and getting the ball and making a play.

There were a hundred plays like that. Every night. Taking charges. Diving on the floor and knocking people down, those types of things that he and Jerry did all the time.

Norm Van Lier: If I hadn't come back and played, that team would not have won a doggone thing, the way they started out.

Matt Guokas: It was an embattled year for Norm with the problems that he had with Dick Motta... They did not communicate very well. Nevertheless, Dick still in a very

Much of the offense went to Walker.

professional way did his job, as did Norm. He went out and played very hard. Night in and night out, he was the best guard in the league that year. And that was saying something because Walt Frazier and Earl Monroe were the competition.

Upon returning, Love led the team in scoring at 22.1 points per game, and Thurmond averaged 11.3 rebounds. Sloan was again named to the league's All-Defensive first team. Chicago was the NBA's best defensive team, giving up just 95 points a game.

The Bulls set a record by winning 12 straight home games over January and February and finished 47-35 to claim their first divisional title. In the first round of the playoffs, they defeated Kansas City, 4-2, then moved on to face Golden State, winners of the Pacific Division with a 48-37 record. The two teams had traded centers, with former Bull Clifford Ray now playing the post for the Warriors. Although they didn't have the home-court advantage, the Bulls won Game 5 in Oakland to take a 3-2 series lead.

Clifford Ray: The worst feeling I'd ever had in the world was playing against my former teammates for the Western Division championship. It was unbelievable.

Jerry Sloan: That was a great series against Golden State. We played about seven guys, but most of the starters played about 40 to

were playing as well as we could. I looked up, and we were only six ahead, and I knew we were in trouble.

Tom Boerwinkle: If I ever think of a moment in my career, it's when we came out for that sixth game. We were in a position to win the series and move on to the Finals for the first time in Chicago Bulls history. Nobody will know for sure, but I can't imagine that place ever being louder than it was that day. It was one of those times when the presence of the Stadium bored right into you. The anxiety level was extremely high. We played very well for most of that ball game. We had a healthy lead in the second half, 16 or 17 points, and all of a sudden it just kind of went away. I remember struggling desperately to make it come back. But all of a sudden Rick Barry, who had played a terrible series, got hot, and when Barry got hot . . .

Clifford Ray: I thought they lost the leads because we were a better team. We were a very good defensive team with a lot of speed, and they were an aging team.

The Bulls collapsed badly at the end of Game 6 and lost 86-72, sending the series back to Oakland for a seventh game.

Tom Boerwinkle: We had already won one game there, so we knew we could win Game 7. We got a big lead again, but Dick Motta made a decision that he was gonna go with his starters all the way. At the time, there was a lot of controversy about it… but I think Dick felt we'd already had one lead filter away from us. We saw the same thing happen again. We got a big lead, but down the stretch we couldn't buy a shot. Their coach, Al Attles, was a smart guy. He used 10 or 11 players, and he wanted to prevent us from passing the ball inside. For us to win, Bob Love and Chet Walker had to score. Attles used his shot-blocking centers, Clifford Ray and George Johnson, to make sure that didn't happen.

I remember having to take jump shots from outside the free throw line, which wasn't my game. But it became almost like a panic, because we couldn't get the ball inside. Nothing else was working. I figured

Mickey Johnson (8) and Thurmond helped close up the middle for Chicago. Matt Guokas is the Bull to the right.

45 minutes a night in the playoffs. That was the frustrating thing. People said we were too old. We were in our 30s. But I don't know if anybody 21 could have played as hard as we did, for the minutes that we played. Looking back on it, I think the excitement and the moment was something nobody had dealt with before. I think we probably got ourselves so high that we just couldn't get it done.

Dick Motta: We went to Golden State and won Game 5. Then we came home to play Game 6 on a Sunday afternoon on Mother's Day. There was great energy. We

I'd try to make something happen. Dick probably should have jerked me out then, because we got away from what we did best.

Matt Guokas: Rick Barry got off to a very poor start. He was a streak shooter, and he missed like seven or eight shots in a row. In frustration, Barry turned to the bench and said, "Get me out of here!" And they did take him out. He came back in a little later and got a hot hand. Then he went cold again and went out again. And then he came back in again. The key to that final game was George Johnson, the Warriors' backup center. He wound up blocking a lot of shots down the stretch. We couldn't make a shot. Love and Walker were driving to the basket, and he was just blocking their shots or changing them.

Ed Badger: Dick was conservative anyway, and we got real conservative in that last game. He thought we could get by.

Tom Boerwinkle: We were thinking, "If we could just get one shot we could stop their momentum and turn this thing around." We couldn't hit the one shot. We saw this golden moment in Chicago Bulls history slipping through our fingers.

The Warriors overcame another double-digit Bulls lead to win, 83-79, taking the series 4-3 and the Western Conference crown. From there, Golden State went on to sweep the Washington Bullets, 4-0, for the 1975 NBA title.

Jerry Sloan: That was a pretty sad day for me, because you're looking at the end of your career and wondering how many more opportunities you're going to get.

Norm Van Lier: Motta never said anything until the end of the season when we lost to Golden State. Then it was my fault because I had held out. He said it in the locker room after the seventh game. He said it to my face. It was my fault, it was Bob Love's fault, because we held out. He said we lost home-court advantage.

Dick Motta: Love and Van Lier held out for 10 games. We went 3-7, and lost the home-court advantage by one game. We had taken the regular season series from Golden State.

Johnson was a shotblocker.

Sloan scores against Golden State in the '75 playoffs.

99

Walker defends Rick Barry in the Western Finals.

Boerwinkle rebounds in the '75 playoffs against Kansas City.

Jerry Sloan: I think Dick had to speak his mind. That's who Dick Motta is, and that's why he's a great coach. A coach has to get those things off his chest if he's going to live with himself. He said what he felt.

Tom Boerwinkle: We'd been together seven years, which was unusual at the time and unthinkable today. There was a lot of fall-out, real strong disappointment, real deep emotion there because everybody knew, although nobody said it, that it had kind of come to an end.

Dick Motta: That was the final hurrah of the Chicago Bulls as we knew them. I stayed one more year.

Tom Boerwinkle: The greatest thrill I ever had in the game of basketball are in a string of numbers hanging on the wall in my office. Norm Van Lier was number 2; Jerry Sloan was 4; I was 18; Walker was 25; and Love was 10. And I have nothing in my house or my office that relates to basketball other than those five numbers. I cherish

those numbers because without them I would have never made it. And Motta belongs on that number list, too, because he's the guy who organized it all.

Kip Motta: I think Norm and Jerry and Dad were all the same type of personalities. They were gonna fight and claw and bite and kick until they won games. One of Dad's favorite things to say was, "We'll keep it close until there's four minutes to go. Then we got 'em right where we want 'em." They'd usually win every close game.

Tom Boerwinkle: I tell people, "If you were to take Sloan, Love, Walker, Van Lier, and myself and put us out there and give us individual skill tests, hell, any one of us had a hard time dunking the basketball, me included." For four or five years we had the third best record in the league. We just couldn't get by Milwaukee or L.A. If you want to rate it on talent or abilities, we were way down the list. But Dick Motta had that incredible ability to draw out our competitiveness and then to channel and control it.

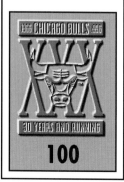

Profile/
Jonathan Kovler

*W*ITH THE BULLS' LOSS IN THE 1975 *playoffs, minority owner Jonathan Kovler moved in as the team's managing partner. In March 1972, he had purchased about 10 percent of the club from Dick Klein, who had needed the money to pay off a bank note. (The bank had called it in after hearing that Klein was feuding with the other owners.)*

Jonathan Kovler: I would have jumped out of a window to be involved in pro basketball. I was a Bulls season ticket holder and a serious fan.

Pat Williams: Kovler at that point was a young guy in his twenties, with family money from the Jim Beam distillery business. Kovler had his hair down to his shoulders and was dressed in blue jeans, really a bizarre character. He was the ultimate basketball junkie. He was one of these guys that just loved it and was really into it.

He bought a portion of Klein's ownership one morning and ended up that afternoon at practice at DePaul. He comes down right on the court. Motta knows nothing about him, never met the guy, and there he is. Motta ran him out, ran him right off the floor, just ran him right out of practice. Dick had no idea who he was. That's how the two of them started.

Jonathan Kovler: Motta was a confrontational fellow. He may have thrown a fit that day, but he never actually asked me to leave.

Bob Logan: Kovler was a very closed, private guy, an outsider trying to talk his way into the inner circles of basketball. He was never very accepted and respected by the other basketball executives, and certainly not by Motta.

Pat Williams: But Kovler just hung right in there and battled. That was part of my problem. Kovler wanted to run the thing day to day. He ended up getting what he wanted eventually.

Jonathan Kovler: After Crown and Wirtz and that group took over, they weren't actively involved. But we floundered through that first season with Williams and Motta fighting. So Wirtz took a more active role. I would phone Wirtz and ask him questions about the team. He eventually said, "Come on over and watch how we run things." I did, and we developed a working relationship. He finally asked me to get involved in 1975. The owners were becoming less satisfied with the structure of things, with Motta doing all three jobs. We determined early on that it was difficult to be the coach and to be in charge of the purse strings, too, as Motta was. Plus, player contracts were getting bigger and more complicated. There was a general feeling that we needed help, particularly after that playoff loss in '75.

Our main concern as owners wasn't making money. We wanted to run things on a reasonably businesslike basis and to be a winner. People have said we were wealthy men who kept the team poor, but that's not true. At the time, we had just stepped up and paid a lot of money for Nate Thurmond.

Rod Thorn: Jonathan tried to do what he could, given the parameters he had to work with.

He owned 10 percent or less of the team. Jon loved it, the trappings and authority and everything about it. As the mananging partner, Jon was the guy who took the hits for Wirtz. In fact, he took some hits for me, too.

Jonathan Kovler: That's true. I was the front man for the committee. I had to take the grief and the public criticism. I accepted that role and tried to mold the committee's judgment. Arthur Wirtz had a major influence on the committee's decisions, but I often agreed with Wirtz. Despite the criticism, it was a lot of fun. People now see that we, the Bulls, weren't the bad guys that the press made us out to be. The things we did never got translated properly. Now, the team has much better public relations. Back then we didn't care much about PR.

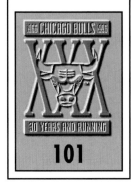

Free Fall, 1975-76

ANGERED DURING CONTRACT negotiations *with Arthur Wirtz, Chet Walker abruptly quit basketball in the fall of 1975 and embarked on an extended Caribbean vacation from which he refused to answer the Bulls' numerous calls. The franchise followed with a flurry of personnel moves, sending Nate Thurmond and Rowland Garrett to Cleveland for forward Eric Fernsten and center Steve Patterson and getting Jack Marin from Buffalo. From there the troubles piled up for Dick Motta's last Chicago team.*

Jerry Sloan: I hurt my knee during an exhibition game in Wisconsin. I just couldn't recover from it.

Jonathan Kovler: We went from the penthouse to the outhouse over the course of one season. There were a lot of headaches. Everybody was always disgruntled.

Tom Boerwinkle: There'd been a certain amount of bickering in the press after the Golden State loss. All of a sudden, we weren't winning the next season, and all of the bad things started to come out. All of the emotion that had been suppressed for the good of the organization now came to the surface.

Despite giving up a league-low 98 points per game, the Bulls finished 24-58, their worst season. In the aftermath, Dick Motta left to become the head coach of the Washington Bullets. Two years later, he would coach the Bullets to the NBA championship.

Jonathan Kovler: It was mutual. He was ready to leave, and we were ready for him to leave. We weren't happy, and I'm sure he wasn't.

Dick Motta: I asked Arthur Wirtz for permission to leave. First he said I couldn't, then he said, "Okay." So I interviewed with Washington and worked out the deal for the job there. When I took the job in Chicago, the team paid the premiums on a $200,000 life insurance policy. That was my only retirement. If I fulfilled my five-year

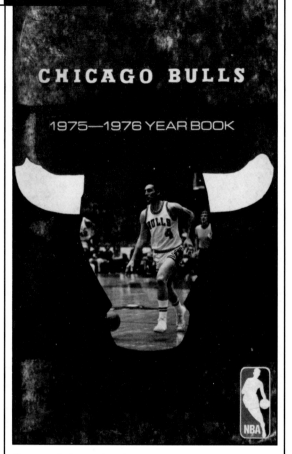

CHICAGO BULLS

1975—1976 YEAR BOOK

Sloan injured a knee early in the season.

contract in Chicago, they said they would pay the premiums for the rest of my life. When I told Wirtz I was taking the job in Washington, he said, "I gave you permission to talk to them, but I didn't give you permission to take the job." On the eve of the press conference announcing that I would be the coach in Washington, I went to Wirtz's house to talk about it. He said, "If we're gonna let you go, we need cash or a draft pick." Abe Pollin, the owner of the Bullets, said, "No." Wirtz said he had to have something, so he decided to let me go if they didn't have to pay the premium on my life insurance. I had stayed the five years in Chicago and earned it, but that was the way the Bulls did things.

Norm Van Lier: Just like that, Motta was up and gone. Didn't say good-bye or anything. The next thing I knew, Ed Badger was coach.

Miracle on Madison, 1976-77

WITH DICK MOTTA'S DEPARTURE hours after the 1976 season ended, the Bulls found themselves without a head coach or general manager. The draft loomed just days ahead, so Arthur Wirtz lured Phoenix Suns scout Jerry Krause back to Chicago to help make player personnel decisions.

Jerry Krause: Arthur Wirtz talked me into coming back to the Bulls as director of player personnel in 1976 after Motta left. I was only here four or five months. I wanted to draft Robert Parish in 1976. Wirtz wouldn't let me. Wirtz said Scott May had two lawyers who were bimbos, and he would be easy to sign. So we drafted Scott May.

Krause soon became involved in a public dispute with DePaul coach Ray Meyer, who told reporters that Krause had offered him the job of head coach. Krause flatly denied it, and privately phoned Meyer to ask why he would make such claims. The media interest in the story prompted Wirtz to fire Krause after just a few months on the job.

Jerry Krause: That was the worst part of my life. Arthur Wirtz was a very, very hard man to deal with.

Meanwhile, Wirtz had refused to allow assistant coach Ed Badger to follow Motta to Washington. Badger, who had coached Wright Junior College to a 66-0 record over two years while working for the Bulls part-time, resigned twice, only to have Wirtz refuse the resignation. Finally, with the season nearing, Wirtz offered Badger a one-year contract, but Badger refused to sign until Wirtz gave him a two-year deal. Wirtz reluctantly agreed, losing one of the few bargaining sessions in his tenure with the team.

The ABA's four strongest teams—the Denver Nuggets, the San Antonio Spurs, the Indiana Pacers and the New York Nets—merged with the NBA after the 1976 playoffs. The remaining ABA teams folded, and their players went into a special dispersal draft to NBA clubs. In that dispersal the Bulls paid $1 million to acquire center Artis Gilmore, who had led the Kentucky Colonels to the 1975 ABA title.

The presence of the 7-foot-2, 240-pound Gilmore created a rush of hope in Chicago, but

The offseason brought Artis Gilmore and John Mengelt.

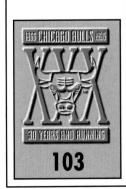

103

ADVANCE TICKET SALE ← 12 NOON to 6PM

Bulls fans line up for tickets for the '77 playoffs.

then the Bulls got off to a 4-15 start. Ten games into a losing streak, Chicago traded Bob Love to the New York Nets for a second-round pick and cash. From the core of Dick Motta's teams, only Van Lier, the Bulls' starting point guard, and Boerwinkle, now backup center, remained on the roster. Chicago signed free agent guard Wilbur Holland during the first week of the season and later acquired forward John Mengelt from Detroit. Holland was a consistent 15-points-per-game scorer, and Mengelt proved hard-nosed enough to deserve his "Crash" nickname. But the changes left Badger shuffling players around trying to find a chemistry.

Jonathan Kovler: Ed Badger's first year we started out with trouble but wound up being very successful. Scott May, our number one draft pick, ended up with mononucleosis. He later came back and made the All-Rookie team, but it took a while to get it rolling. Once we did we had a pretty good team.

Ed Badger: We start out with a 2-and-11 team, and boy, the media are trying to kill me. We lost to the Lakers in Los Angeles for our eleventh straight loss, and Dave Condon of the *Tribune* comes in the locker room and says, "How do you feel? Word around town is that you're going to get fired tomorrow." I said, "That has one redeeming fact." And he says, "What's that?" I said, "I won't have to talk to your fat ass again." That was the wrong thing to say. I never got a good writeup in the *Trib* after that.

In February, Van Lier was voted to the All-Star team. Shortly thereafter, the Bulls made a run that carried them from a 21-31 start and the bottom of the standings to a 44-38 finish, good enough for second place in the division and a trip to the playoffs. The run, dubbed the "Miracle On Madison" by the media, excited all of Chicago and brought a string of sellout crowds to the Stadium.

Ed Badger: We started plugging away and

Jonathan Kovler, (left to right) Arthur Wirtz, Scott May and coach Ed Badger at May's signing in 1976.

won 20 of our last 24 games. Nine out of our last 10 were sellouts. We had a good team. I ran a lot of Motta's offense, but Artis was a low-post center. So we put in plays for him. But if we hadn't had Tom Boerwinkle, we would have really been dead because he was playing better than Artis. I said, "I should start you." He said, "You can't do that to the big guy. I'm okay coming off the bench." Boerwinkle was a great guy.

One of the Bulls' stalwarts was 6-10, 190-pound Mickey Johnson, a leaper and shot-blocker out of little Aurora College who averaged better than 16 points and nearly 10 rebounds per game for Chicago from 1975-78.

Ed Badger: Crash Mengelt played hard, and Mickey Johnson was quite a character, a real intelligent kid. But he would always want to take the last shot, and he would never make it. We'd take a time-out, and we'd have Scott May, Artis and Wilbur Holland. None of those guys ever wanted to take the last shot. Mickey would say, "I'll take it." I'd say, "Keep quiet." He was like our power forward, but he was really a small forward. Scott May was our small forward, but if he played today he'd be a two guard. Wilbur Holland was small for a two guard. But back then we didn't worry about size as much as teams do now.

Once we started winning, the fans loved us. Mr. Wirtz would put about 25,000 people in the Stadium. Then he'd sit with the fire marshall. We got strict orders to say we never had more than 18,888.

With the Stadium's substantial standing-room capacity, the size of sellout crowds fluctuated. The Bulls actually reported four crowds in excess of 20,000 that spring, with 21,046, the largest in Bulls history, on hand March 22 to see Chicago beat Los Angeles.

The Bulls' first-round playoff opponent was the Portland Trail Blazers. Led by center Bill Walton and coached by Jack Ramsay, the Blazers were on their way to the 1977 NBA championship.

Jack Ramsay: The Bulls were our toughest series that year. They had a very good team. Artis Gilmore had probably his best season ever. Players like John Mengelt and Norm Van Lier and Jack Marin and Mickey Johnson—you didn't think of those guys as being stars, but that season Badger had them playing well together. In those days we played a three-game first round series. Fortunately, we had home court advantage over the Bulls.

Ed Badger: We could have won it all if we had gotten past Portland.

Jack Ramsay: We split the first two games, and the third and final game was in Portland. The referees were on strike then, and the game was officiated by substitutes, who didn't do a very good job. They were just incapable of calling an NBA game. Both teams were saddled with that. By the time we reached the closing minutes, several guys on each side had fouled out. We had a lead, but Chicago closed the gap. We got down to the nub of the game, and we were ahead by two.

With 15 seconds left, the Bulls had the ball trailing by two.

Ed Badger: We had a great play set up. Walton always fronted Artis. So we were going to throw it off the backboard. All Artis had to do was catch the ball and make the basket, which was legal. Mengelt was hot that day. He had something like 35 points. Mengelt was supposed to throw it in to Gilmore from out of bounds. Instead, he throws it in the basket. That was a violation. I could have killed him. He said, "I was so hot, Coach." I said, "You jerk."

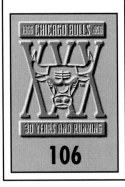

Profile/Gentle Artis

ARTIS GILMORE PLAYED PRO BASKETBALL for 17 seasons, five of them in the ABA with the Kentucky Colonels. He and Dan Issel led the Colonels to three ABA championship appearances and the 1975 title. Gilmore averaged 22.3 points during his ABA years and 17.1 points in a dozen NBA seasons. His two best seasons with the Bulls, 1977-78 and 1978-79, he averaged 23 points per game and totalled better than 1,000 rebounds each season. He had never missed a college or pro game when he came to the Bulls, and his Iron Man streak for pro games ran to 670, until he suffered a knee injury in his fourth season in Chicago. There was little talent around him most of his years with the Bulls, which left the fans, the media, and sometimes his teammates, complaining that Gilmore was a disappointment. One publication pointed out that with his multimillion dollar contract, he was being paid $60,000 per inch of his body. "It has been very tough on me in Chicago," Gilmore finally admitted in 1980. "I haven't been able to make the Bulls very successful."

Rod Thorn: Artis didn't like to be criticized. He was hurt a lot in Chicago. He wanted to prove that he was right up there among the best big men in the game. But it just wasn't in his personality to score a lot of points.

Reggie Theus: Artis was Artis. He was limited in his offensive repetoire. If you could just get him to catch the ball. Artis would tell me, "Reggie, don't throw me the ball when you're not looking at me. If you're looking over there, don't throw it over here."

Ronnie Lester: Artis was the elder statesman of the team. A great guy. With his size and his strength—he was one of the strongest guys in the league—a lot of guys thought he was too soft to be that big and that strong. They thought if he had had a mean streak or a nasty streak, he could have done anything he wanted to. But he was still a very good player.

Ed Badger: Artis always thought he was playing hard, but he wasn't.

CHICAGO BULLS ARTIS GILMORE

CTR

Said Gilmore in 1980, "I play against guys who are married and have families. I'm not going out to hurt anyone. But I do try to make my presence known. Using brute force against Darryl Dawkins or Wes Unseld is pointless. They're as strong as I am. I'm more effective when I keep my head, think about situations and take advantage of them."

He was named to the All-Star team 11 times, five in the ABA and six in the NBA, including three times as a Bull. Over his career, he scored better than 25,000 points and pulled down more than 16,300 rebounds

Spaced Out, 1977-78

*I*N 1977, THE BULLS SELECTED TATE *Armstrong out of Duke, Mike Glenn out of Southern Illinois and Steve Sheppard out of Maryland. Soon afterward, these selections were dubbed "the astronaut draft." Unfortunately, none of them ever really landed in Chicago.*

Jonathan Kovler: The "astronaut draft" was my line. Mike Glenn broke his neck in an auto accident. He later played in the league, but not for us. Tate Armstrong, our first round pick, never developed into the two guard we needed. And Steve Sheppard made the roster but only for one season and some games the next year.

Tim Hallam: I remember Tate Armstrong being drafted, holding out for more money. Here was this little golden-haired boy from Duke, Mr. All-American. He was coming in with Van Lier still around. When Tate came to his first practice, he was about a week late. Management thought he would be the answer to the problems at two guard. He held out, and the veterans were very pissed off about it. And they kicked his butt. Nicest guy in the world. But they treated him like dirt. Like, "Welcome, punk." They really treated him bad, but in a professional way. "Okay, kid, you wanted more money? Well now you're here with us." They physically abused him. I still see Tate every now and then. He's got five children and he's working down in North Carolina in banking. I think he was smaller than people thought. Scouting wasn't as proficient as it is today. Now they know the blood type and the family tree and the whole bit on every player. He was Duke's leading scorer, but they kicked his butt here. He got rattled. Who wouldn't be?

The enthusiasm from the '77 playoffs carried right into the next season. The biggest home-opener crowd in franchise history, 14,082, watched the Bulls begin the year with a win over Indiana. By the All-Star break, they owned the seventh best record in the league at

29-23 and seemed a lock for the playoffs. But from there, Scott May went down with injuries and things fell apart. The team had failed to re-sign the third forward, Jack Marin, and the thinned frontcourt simply wasn't strong enough.

Ed Badger: Tom Boerwinkle tore his knee up that season and ended his career. That killed us. Two things killed us. They wouldn't re-sign Marin for the same money. He had been a great third foward for us that first year. But we still won 40 games.

The Bulls finished 40-42 and failed to make the playoffs.

Tim Hallam: Badger didn't coach the last game of the season. He went on to coach the University of Cincinnati.

Ed Badger: I left before the last game. Jerry Sloan coached the last game. I had another year on my contract as an option, and Mr. Wirtz seemed fine with me. I went in to see him and said, "I've done a pretty good job here. I'd like to get another year on the contract, and I'd like to get more money." He says, "What more can you do for me?" I said, "I'd thought you'd appreciate what we accomplished." He and Kovler said, "It doesn't matter who coaches next year. This team will win 50 games." I said, "The way this team is constituted, it won't win 30."

Rod Thorn, a 37-year-old assistant coach with the New Jersey Nets, was hired as the Bulls' general manager shortly after the close of the

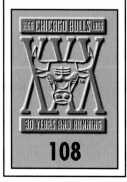

1978 season. The team's public relations office promptly touted him as "one of the youngest general managers in pro sports."

The second overall pick of the 1963 draft out of West Virginia University, Thorn had played for four teams and averaged 10.8 points over his eight-year NBA career. He had become an assistant coach in Seattle upon his retirement as a player at age 30 in 1971. He later moved to the ABA, where he served as head coach of the St. Louis Spirits until that franchise expired in 1976.

Jonathan Kovler: My first decision after Ed Badger bolted was that we needed a basketball person, someone to talk to the coaches and players, someone who could also deal with the owners. I interviewed several people. Identifying them now could reveal how stupid I was. I interviewed George Karl, Matt Guokas, Bill Melchionni and Rod.

Rod Thorn: When I got there, we were not very good. We were struggling all the time trying to get better. The executive committee was unwieldy. We had probably the richest ownership in professional sports, yet our team struggled in terms of operations. Jonathan Kovler was the managing partner, but he also had a full-time job managing his investments. It was tough getting things done when they needed to be done. But I knew exactly what the situation was when I went there.

Armstrong led the "astronaut draft" of Armstrong, Glenn and Sheppard.

General Manager Rod Thorn, Jerry Sloan and Jonathan Kovler at Sloan's hiring after the disastrous 1978-79 season.

Hitting The Skids, 1978-79

IN THE 1978 DRAFT, THE BULLS USED A second round pick to take Marvin Johnson out of the University of New Mexico and missed the opportunity to get either Maurice Cheeks or Michael Cooper, both of whom went on to long, distinguished pro careers. Marvin Johnson failed to catch on with the Bulls and never played an NBA game.

Rod Thorn: We held the draft at the Bismark Hotel, which Mr. Wirtz owned. He wanted it held on the stage there. We took Reggie Theus with the ninth pick in the first round. My big mistake that year was not drafting Maurice Cheeks in the second round. If we had drafted Maurice, we could have had a point guard and used Reggie at the two guard. Instead, Reggie was forced to play a lot of point, and that wasn't his natural position. We tried to make him into one, but that never worked.

Maurice Cheek's father was in the crowd at the Bismark that day, and when we didn't pick Maurice, he said, "You made a big mistake." And he was right.

Johnny Kerr: I always said we missed drafting Earvin Johnson by just one letter. We drafted Marvin Johnson. It was a shame we couldn't trade that "M" for an "E."

Ed Badger was close in his prediction. He said the 1978-79 Bulls wouldn't win 30 games. They won 31. But that was far short of the 50 games management had predicted—"no matter who coached the team.""

For the fourth head coach in Bulls' history, new General Manager Rod Thorn hired veteran Larry Costello, whose 1971 Milwaukee Bucks with Kareem Abdul-Jabbar and Oscar Robertson had won an NBA title. It wasn't a good fit.

But, in Costello's defense, the Bulls were clearly a team in transition. Gilmore led them in scoring (a 23.7 average) and rebounding (12.7). The season also marked the disappearance of the last holdovers from the Motta era. Norm Van Lier was waived, as were Tom Boerwinkle, who couldn't recover from a knee injury, and Cliff Pondexter. The new face of

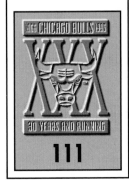

111

Scott May's career was hindered by injuries.

The Bulls wanted to make Theus a point guard.

the Bulls showed an opening night lineup of Mark Landsberger, Reggie Theus, Mickey Johnson, Artis Gilmore and Wilbur Holland.

Norm Van Lier: I don't remember my last game. It was such a down, depressed time of mental lapses and pain killers, I honestly don't remember the last part. All I know is, when it was time to let it go, I was happy to get away.

Rod Thorn: My reason for hiring Larry Costello was that he had coached a big low-post player in Kareem Abdul-Jabbar at Milwaukee. Larry had been very effective in getting Jabbar involved at the offensive end of the court. I thought we should involve Artis Gilmore more on the offensive end, and I thought Larry could do that. Later, I learned it was more a matter of Artis' personality. He wasn't suited to being more involved. Artis didn't want to take a lot of shots on a day-to-day basis. I think Artis got tired. We didn't have a strong backup, and he didn't want to play 40 minutes a game.

With the team's record at 20-36, Thorn fired Costello and turned the Bulls over to assistant coach Scotty Robertson.

Scotty Robertson: They told me, "I don't care if you win every game, you're not gonna be the coach next year. Jerry Sloan's gonna be the coach." They had passed him over when they hired Larry Costello, and all the media and the local people wanted Sloan.

The Bulls finished their season with 11 wins and 15 losses, and Robertson was replaced by Jerry Sloan.

Profile/ Rush Street Reggie

*T*HE BULLS SELECTED FLASHY UNLV *guard Reggie Theus with the ninth pick in the first round of the 1978 draft. Only 19, he moved into an apartment near Rush Street and quickly became a fan favorite.*

Reggie Theus: Chicago back then had a reputation of being very tough on rookies. So I went there with the frame of mind that I was probably going to get into a fight the very first day of practice. I figured the guy I was gonna have to fight first was Norm Van Lier, which didn't make me too happy. I was very aware of what had happened to Tate Armstrong the year before. He couldn't make the team they beat him up so bad. And Tate was a pretty decent player.

I don't think I slept the week before camp started. I was trembling I was so fired up. I

was ready to go. If Norm Van Lier had said hello, I'd have taken a swing at him. It turned out that Norm was the nicest guy on the whole team. He took me aside—and I'll always appreciate this—and told me, "They're moving me out and giving you my spot. You have guys on this team who already have a problem with you. Watch your back."

My biggest problem as a rookie was Larry Costello. He was a nightmare for me. I might have cause him some problems. That's because he asked me to do some things that to me were like speaking Greek.

I came to Chicago from a UNLV program that was all-out, fastbreak basketball. I came from a team that had just set eight NCAA scoring records. We ran a tremendous pressure defense. We were picking up full court from baseline to baseline, from tipoff to the final buzzer. I was actually drafted as a defensive player because I had played the

113

Reggie thrilled Chicago crowds.

point on Jerry Tarkanian's press. The Bulls saw my size, my quickness and my wingspan and figured I could be the next Jerry Sloan.

In those days my thing was passing the basketball, penetrating and dishing off. I wanted to thread the needle. I went from the UNLV big time to a pro situation where Larry Costello, my first coach, stopped practice one day and told me never, ever again to put the ball behind my back. They put me at point guard, then told me to walk the ball up the floor. Costello told me, "I don't want you to put that f—-ing ball behind your f—-ing back. I want you to be a f—-ing vision of me on the court!" I said, "Does that mean I have to wear that crew-cut, too?" He kicked me out of practice for that. Costello told people I was out of control. He really hurt my career in that sense. That stuff followed me for four or five years.

My education had come from growing up in Inglewood, California. I was 19 when I got to the NBA. The season started on my 20th birthday. I was a rookie with a team of old veterans. I took a lot of abuse. It made me very physically and mentally tough.

Johnny Kerr: Theus was one of the most exciting athletes the Bulls had had up to that point, I thought. You look at his career stats, he scored something like 16,000 points in the league. He was big-time excitement, but we just didn't have much talent to go with him.

Ronnie Lester: Reggie was into the NBA life, the big car, the wardrobe, that type of thing. I think some of the other players may have resented Reggie a little bit. He was probably our best player after Artis. After Artis started to get a little older, Reggie led us in scoring for four or five years.

Tim Hallam: Reggie was good looking. The women loved him. He was articulate, he

was flashy, he was a big deal at the time.

Reggie Theus: My second year in Chicago I went to a Michael Jackson concert. I was sitting in a semi-roped off area in the Stadium. I'll never forget, when the lights came up, a few people recognized me and started clapping. Then a few more joined in. Then it got a lot bigger. I got a standing ovation at a Jackson concert. I was very touched by that. I love Chicago people. They are the very finest. They know their sports there. Once you are accepted as a Chicagoan you are always a Chicagoan. They've always made me feel very special. I always thought the fans deserved more because the owners we had didn't seem to really care much about the team.

Jerry Sloan: The other players resented Reggie, because he was a star. He was well-liked by all the fans. But he was not a star specifically because of what he did on the floor. He had some success here. But what I think the players resented was that he got all the attention whether we won or lost.

Reggie Theus: I got the reputation of being Rush Street Reggie. I lived about a block and a half off Rush Street. It was amazing the contact I had with the people of Chicago, especially for a kid on a losing team. But after a while it got to be too much. In order for me to have any privacy at all I was gonna have to move. So I found a place in the suburbs.

Bob Rosenberg: It seemed to me that Reggie Theus was interested only in his scoring. He didn't seem to care if the team won or lost.

Reggie Theus: Unfortunately, in Chicago I had six coaches in my first five years as a pro. Playing basketball there was frustrating. The fact that it was impossible to win, the fact that we had nobody there, no players, no talent. I developed the idea that if I was a true pro, there are no circumstances that should ever stop me from doing what I do best. So I was able to accomplish certain things personally. Even though the crowds weren't very big, the fans really pushed my momentum. They kept me high and showed their support for me.

Flipping, 1979-80

IN APRIL 1979, THE BULLS HIRED JERRY Sloan as their head coach. To bolster the roster, they signed free agent big men Coby Dietrick and Dwight Jones. They also acquired guard Ricky Sobers from Indiana as compensation for losing Mickey Johnson to the Pacers.

The first pick of the 1979 draft came down to a coin flip between the Bulls and the Los Angeles Lakers. The prize was 19-year-old Earvin "Magic" Johnson, Jr., who as a college sophomore had just led Michigan State to the NCAA championship.

Commissioner Larry O'Brien made the flip at the NBA's New York offices while the Lakers and Bulls listened over the phone in a conference call. The Bulls asked to call the flip; the Lakers agreed. Heads, said Rod Thorn, following a suggestion based on fan polling.

Tails it was.

"I had hoped Chicago would win the coin flip because it was closer to home," Johnson later explained.

Jonathan Kovler: We did a promotion with fans at the end of the season. They phoned in and voted on whether to call heads or tails. We tried to generate as much interest as we could.

Rod Thorn: Johnny Kerr made a remark at the time. He said, "If you listen to the fans, you wind up sitting with them."

Jonathan Kovler: At the time, I jokingly said, "It's a $25-million coin flip." It turned out to be a $200-million coin flip.

The loss set up an immediate dilemma. Should the Bulls draft forward David Greenwood out of UCLA or Bill Cartwright out of the University of San Francisco?

Rod Thorn: We decided on a deal with Portland. Artis Gilmore for Maurice Lucas, Lionel Hollins and Tom Owens. Then we would draft Cartwright. Portland agreed to the deal, but then we had to get approval of the committee. When you traded a player of Gilmore's magnitude, you had to get everyone to sign off. But one member of

the committee was out of the country, so it took several days. The deal was hot, but then it got stale and Portland backed away. We already had a center in Artis, so we decided to take Greenwood.

Although he was troubled by injuries, David Greenwood played six solid seasons for the Bulls. He averaged about 14 points and eight rebounds over his first five seasons with the team. Those were good numbers for a power forward, but like just about every other player in the league, he simply could not compare to Magic Johnson, who led the Lakers to five NBA championships. For that reason, Greenwood's selection by the Bulls has always been viewed as a failed draft pick. The value of the Lakers during Magic Johnson's dozen years with the team jumped from about $30 million to $200 million, according to owner Jerry Buss.

Irwin Mandel: The committee, in my opinion, was a mistake the Bulls made. There were seven owners, and they were all very successful businessmen. They would all agree that the team was not run in the most efficient way possible. There was a four-person executive commitee—Arthur Wirtz, Lester Crown, Philip Klutznick, and Jon Kovler. Every decision had to go through them first, and those four were hardly ever all available. In sports you often need a fast decision, and that's too hard to do with four people.

On opening night, rookie David Greenwood and Scott May were the forwards, Sobers and Theus were the guards, and Artis Gilmore started at center. But the Bulls started in a hole at 5-15 and stayed there most of the year.

Mark Pfeil: David Greenwood tore cartilege in his knee and needed surgery. He asked how long it would take to recover. I said, 'That depends on whether I do the surgery or Dr. Noble does it.' David let it be known he didn't want me anywhere around. But I snuck into surgery and put a mask on. As he was going to sleep. I pulled my mask down and told him, 'Good night.' I thought he was gonna fight getting out of anesthesia.

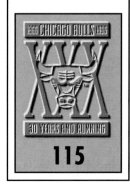

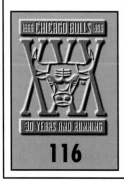

David Greenwood was the prize for losing the Magic Johnson coin flip.

Tim Hallam: There was a real sense of excitement with his hiring. They thought Jerry Sloan would be the one guy who could rectify this stuff. But they just kept bringing in young guys and draft picks, and none of them worked out.

Jerry Sloan: I wasn't ready to be a coach, obviously. But since I'd played here I figured if I had the right people around me to help me out, I had a better feeling for all the things that were going on here and some of the problems you were gonna have to deal with.

Mark Pfeil: Jerry was a wild man. His idea was, things don't have to be complicated if you lay your heart on the line every night. And that's the way he coached.

Reggie Theus: I thought Jerry Sloan had a lot of potential as a coach. The first year he

was Jerry Sloan, the player, coaching. You could see traits of him as a player trying to make you play defense like he did. Finally, I told him, "Jerry, I will never be the defensive player that you were, but you could never be the offensive player that I am."

Jerry Sloan: You have to have intensity to a certain point, but it can be very damaging to you. The intensity I had as a player, it was hard to put aside as a coach. Early in my career, any question from other people seemed to be more of a challenge than anything else. I probably took it that way. That was very difficult for me. I wanted everything to be perfect. I didn't realize that it wasn't going to be.

Sloan's first team finished 30-52, with the lone bright spot being David Greenwood's selection to the All-Rookie team. He led the team in rebounding at 9.4 per game.

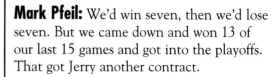

Up High, 1980-81

FOR SLOAN'S second year, the Bulls brought in free agent forward Larry Kenon, who had averaged about 20 points and 10 rebounds for San Antonio. The team's first round draft pick, guard Ronnie Lester out of Iowa, missed 74 games with a knee injury, but the team brought in Bobby Wilkerson from Denver just before the schedule opened. The Bulls got off to a slow start, with Sloan and Kenon feuding.

Tim Hallam: Jerry was such a straight-forward, stand-up guy. This in the days before coaches began using the phoniness and coddling and bull that it took to keep players happy. Jerry wasn't coddled as a person, didn't expect it, and wasn't going to give it. I think he got along with his kind of players. He didn't get along with Larry Kenon. When I met Larry Kenon, I said, "Hello, Larry." He said, "Larry is my slave name. People call me K. or Dr. K."

Sloan threw a chair and had to get his attention. I think he pissed Jerry off quite a bit and was really frustrating for Jerry. But Kenon wasn't about to change. And that was our first big free agent. The Bulls hadn't ever signed a big free agent. Sloan coveted Bernard King, but Jonathan Kovler, our managing partner, wanted Kenon. It probably couldn't have been a bigger disaster. The Bulls were notorious for not making a big trade or signing somebody. So finally we went out on a limb and paid big money to Larry Kenon.

Jerry Sloan: Kenon and I didn't hit it off very well. And I let him know how I stood with him, and he let me know how he felt.

Mark Pfeil: We'd win seven, then we'd lose seven. But we came down and won 13 of our last 15 games and got into the playoffs. That got Jerry another contract.

Rod Thorn: Ricky Sobers won a bunch of games for us with his last-minute heroics. Dwight Jones played strong up front. Reggie played well, and Bobby Wilkerson did a great job as a big defensive guard. Wilkerson, Sobers and Reggie gave us three big, tough people that other teams had trouble with.

Jerry Sloan: I made a big decision with this team in midseason. Larry Kenon had not performed how I thought he should perform for the team, for the kind of player that he was. We made the decision to not start him and not play him, and then we used Dwight Jones instead.

With Gilmore and Theus earning All-Star distinction, the Bulls pulled together for a 45-37 finish and a second-place finish in the Central Division. The reward was a spot in the Eastern Conference playoffs against the New York Knicks, who had finished 50-32. In the best-of-three first round, Chicago swept New York, 2-0.

Tim Hallam: We opened on the road against the Knicks. Jerry flew the team to New York the day of the game. Management was upset that he didn't fly in the night before. But he had a little wrinkle of his own that we were gonna fly in and beat them, which is what he did. He took a lot of heat for that, but we won by 10 and finished them off at the Stadium.

Jerry Sloan: It probably saved my job, the fact that we beat New York, because of the decisions I'd made about Kenon, the decisions I'd made about how we'd play. I had gotten support from the players all of a sudden.

Next came Larry Bird and the Boston Celtics, on their way to the 1981 NBA title. They swept the Bulls in four.

Rod Thorn: Even though we lost 4-0, three of the four games were decided in the last minute. The noise in Chicago Stadium had been incredible. You could see what would happen if the Bulls ever got good.

Larry Kenon (35) and Sloan feuded all season.

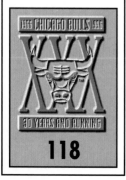

Chicago vanquished NY.

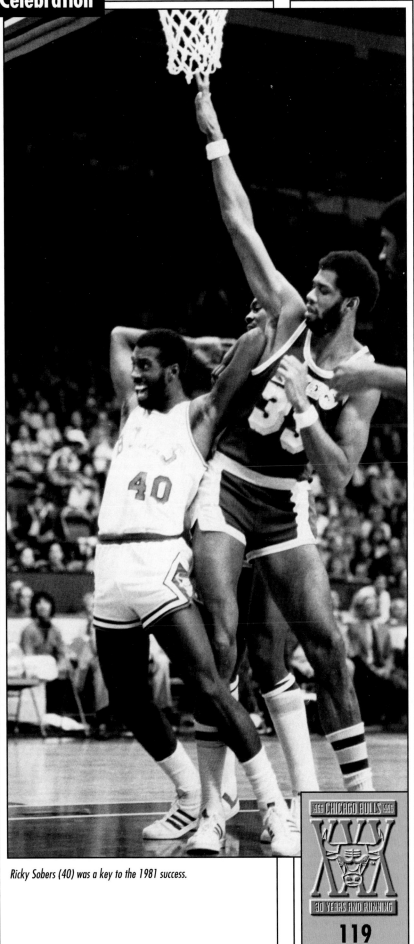

Ricky Sobers (40) was a key to the 1981 success.

119

The Bulls vs. the Celtics in the 1981 playoffs.

CHICAGO BULLS 1981-1982 YEARBOOK

Firing Mr. Bull, 1981-82

*D*ESPITE THE HIGH *of the 1981 play-offs, the Bulls'* *great expectations fal-tered that fall of 1981. The conflicts and missed opportunities quickly added up to trouble. The NBA had not adopted its drug policy. When it did in 1983-84, several former Bulls would be among those identified as being in need of treatment.*

Jerry Sloan: I come in to start the '81-82 season, and Kenon is still here, doesn't want to be here, doesn't want to play for me because I was an old-fashioned coach. I thought you should play defense, try to pass the ball to the open man and try to play with the four other people, which was a lit-tle bit old-fashioned. We had a very good training camp and were 4-0 in exhibition season, if I'm not mistaken, until Kenon came back. We lost the rest of the exhibi-tion games. In the back of my mind, I said, "If he stays here, it'll be the end of my coaching career."

Ronnie Lester: Larry was at the end of his career when we got him from San Antonio. I don't think he fit in well with what we were trying to do here. He was more of a free-lance type of player. Jerry didn't want him and didn't play him.

Rod Thorn: We had drafted Orlando Woolridge. He came into camp late and was of no value to us at all. Ronnie Lester did not prove to be what we thought he'd be. He never really recovered from his knee injuries in college. And Ricky Sobers didn't play as well that year.

Reggie Theus: Not re-signing Bobby Wilkerson, that was their big mistake. He and I played well together. But they let him go to Cleveland. Our management was a nightmare.

Mark Pfeil: Things fell apart. Part of the reason was that we let Bobby Wilkerson go. He was a free agent, and they just didn't sign him. Orlando Woolridge had come in as a rookie and missed training camp. But he made big money, and management wanted him into the lineup right away. Woolridge probably had his drug problem then, but we were unaware of it. He was a disappointment in that he was an unbeliev-able athlete who just didn't work hard. You can imagine how Sloan felt about some-body like that.

Ronnie Lester: It was a tough time in the league. We had some young guys, guys that were immature, guys that when you go on a road trip, the first thing they'd do was go out for the night. They'd come in at two or three in the morning. You gotta play a game the next day. That's not conducive to winning, to being ready to play. And we had too much of that on our team.

On February 16, 1982, after a home loss to Phoenix that left the Bulls' record at 19-32, Rod Thorn fired Jerry Sloan and took over the coaching duties himself.

Rod Thorn: Firing Jerry was really my doing. I felt he wasn't getting as much out of what he had on the roster as he should have. I wanted him to play Woolridge. I thought Woolridge had a big upside. Jerry wasn't one to play a lot of rookies. There's a built-in conflict between a coach and a general manager. As a GM, the people you draft you fall in love with. You want them to do well. Coaches want to play the guys who will help them win games. Coaches aren't opposed to developing young players, but only in practice or over the summer, not in the middle of a season.

Woolridge came in late and out of shape that year. He had just the opposite attitude of what Jerry represented. In retrospect, I don't blame Jerry for not playing Woolridge. He didn't deserve to play.

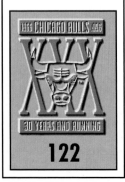

Firing Jerry was one of the toughest things I've ever done because I have a lot of respect for him. He works very hard, is a stand-up guy. He doesn't make excuses. He does everything he can do and is always there. He never bails out.

Ronnie Lester: Some guys did not like Jerry. Not that he was a tough guy to play for. But he demanded things of his players. He would get in players' faces and challenge them personally, and a lot of players did not like that and did not take well to it.

Reggie Theus: I was very upset about Jerry's being fired. After his first year, I saw a massive difference in his approach to the game. The thing I always appreciated about Jerry, if you worked hard for him, he would never screw over you. He was totally loyal. Players loved that in him. They needed it.

Jerry Sloan: I felt I was very loyal to this franchise, and I believed very strongly in it as long as I was here, when I played and when I coached. I thought there was a way that would work. As soon as I had the job, with the lack of experience that I had, I felt like they were looking to replace me. I think that's where there was a lack of support, when you have that feeling. Maybe I didn't handle it the right way.

But they'd always paid me on the first and the fifteenth. That's one of the things I'd always appreciated. That's life. Because we're in sports we think we deserve a little bit more than that, but really we don't.

Ronnie Lester: Rod coached us for the last 30 games of the year. We won half our games. Under Rod,

Sloan's intensity worked against him.

Coby Dietrick chases down a loose ball.

The early Luv-A-Bulls.

the atmoshere was a little bit more relaxed. I think players played a little better under Rod because of that. You weren't so uptight when you made a mistake.

The Bulls finished the season at 34-48. The following November, they waived Larry Kenon.

Quintin Dailey

Move/ Drafting Dailey

THE CHICAGO Bulls made Quintin Dailey their first pick in the 1982 draft, despite the fact that he had recently agreed to plead guilty to a count of felonious assault against a female schoolmate at the University of San Francisco.

Rod Thorn: The draft came down to Dailey or Clark Kellogg. We needed a guy who could really score. When you're in the heat of the battle at draft time, a lot of different things go into your decision-making. Two months later you wonder why you made the choices you made.

Tim Hallam: For some reason his attorney didn't show up for the press conference in Chicago where Quintin was going to explain his actions…. Instead of crying or showing remorse, Quintin kind of stated the facts and pointed out what he had to do to go on with the rest of his life. You could kind of take that either way, but the press chose to take it

and run with it. It was brutal. We had eight lights on the phones back then, and they were lit for two solid days. We've been through a lot of things here in Chicago. Firings. Hirings. But that was the worst week ever for the Bulls in terms of public relations.

Rod Thorn: Of all the decisions I made, drafting Quintin Dailey was the worst. It got our fans down on us and got the press up in arms about us. We lost a lot of fans over that.

Quintin had plea-bargained a felony assault charge against his girlfriend. Then he comes into Chicago, and he's got drug problems and assorted other problems. Then John Schulian of the *Sun Times* wrote the toughest article about an athlete that I've ever read. He compared Dailey to an animal. Women's groups got all up in arms.

While playing in Chicago, Dailey went through a series of very public revelations about his drug use and addiction.

Don Casey: Quintin missed one game for us, and that was the first sign. But he really played well and played hard and had a good jumper. He was a competitor. But he became a sweets eater, and his weight kept fluctuating.

Rod Thorn: The ownership of the Bulls had always had a lot of confidence in me and my decision-making. The Dailey fiasco really undermined a lot of my credibility there with the ownership.

Mark Pfeil: "Q" was a good friend. I felt bad for him. We would try to threaten him, but how do you threaten somebody who came from nothing? He said, "I'm gonna end up on the street? I've been on the street. I survive on the street. You can't threaten me with that." I think the best thing that happened for him, he went ahead and got caught. Today he works as a youth counselor in Las Vegas. The last I heard, it seemed like his life had turned out all right.

Ronnie Lester could never overcome the knee injuries.

Enter Shakespeare, 1982-83

PAUL WESTHEAD, WHO HAD BEEN FIRED by the Lakers in 1981 after coaching the team to the 1980 NBA championship, was named coach of the Bulls in 1982. A scholarly sort, Westhead was given to quoting Shakespeare and reading poetry. From the start, it seemed a bad fit for Chicago.

Other big changes that year included the trading of Artis Gilmore to San Antonio for forward Mark Olberding and the loss of free agent Ricky Sobers to Washington.

Jonathan Kovler: It came down to Westhead or Mike Fratello, and we made the wrong call.

Tim Hallam: Westhead and his people were coming from the Lakers. They wanted to do everything like L.A. did. Well, they were coming to the Chicago Bulls, who really hadn't grown with the league. Our facilities weren't nice. They were archaic. There were mice everywhere at Angel Guardian, that bad little gym. The coaches wanted everything first class. They wanted video equipment, which was their style in LA. God bless 'em, they should have had it. But

we were years behind anything they had done in L.A.

When Westhead first got to town, I went to the airport to pick him up. I'm carrying five bags, his wife is carrying a bag, and he's got his little notebook. I went home and told my wife, "This is Chicago. . ." Westhead was just very difficult. He would never cooperate with our PR staff, but one time, when he ran a race, he phoned me at home and said, "I just ran a marathon. Here's my time. Is there any way you can get that on the news?" Then we played a preseason game in Rockford. We got there, and the gym doors weren't open for practice. He just went nuts on Mark Pfeil, our trainer. He acted like it was Mark's fault.

Don Casey: Chicago people are very provincial and parochial, and Paul's a little loose, a little aloof, quoting Shakespeare and that stuff. It didn't fly there. It just wasn't a good marriage.

Tim Hallam: Westhead had everything in practice organized down to the second. We were gonna run on offense, but you gotta play defense if you're gonna run. Reggie Theus would get 30 a night, but we'd get slaughtered.

The Bulls lost their first 10 road games. In a December 22 road loss to Boston, Reggie Theus scored a career-high 46 points. Orlando Woolridge missed the last 25 games with torn knee ligaments.

Don Casey: On the court, Paul was very sincere, very dramatic and very intense. He was really trying to accomplish something with the up-tempo game, the push game. Maybe we didn't sell it well enough. Maybe

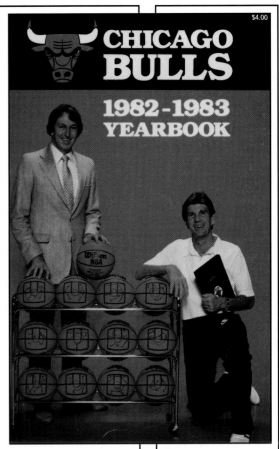

$4.00

CHICAGO BULLS

1982-1983 YEARBOOK

Thorn and Westhead graced the cover of the media guide.

125

For seven seasons, center Dave Corzine, a DePaul product, was a fixture with the Bulls. He usually played better than 2,000 minutes a season and could be depended on for his solid jump shot, rebounding and defense. Regardless, he was far from appreciated by the fans. Each night in the Stadium when he rose from his seat to take off his warmup to enter the game, the booing would begin. Some nights it would persist, ringing out every time he touched the ball. "That has to bother him," coach Kevin Loughery once said. "You're not human if it doesn't. That's bad, especially at home."

One night the 6-foot-11, 255-pound Corzine went into the Stadium stands after a heckler, but usually he brushed the insults off. "The fans pay their money, so they can do whatever they want to do," he said. "I'm not blaming them for my problems. It's not like everyone is against me anyway."

the push game was too dramatic for Chicago after all those years of walking it up. I know Rod Thorn thought the guys had heavy legs and couldn't run. The agents were calling up and saying, "He's beating the hell out of my player." But

that's the price you have to pay to play the push game. The mind-set was not there. The Dwight Joneses and Oberldings didn't want to run.

Ronnie Lester: Westhead stressed running the break and scoring, but we were a terrible defensive team. We never worked on any defensive concepts, anything related to defense. Any time you lose it's frustrating. And it was frustrating here in Chicago.

The Bulls finished 28-54, fourth in their division, and failed to qualify for the playoffs. Westhead was fired after the season.

Don Casey: You can't put the onus on Paul. It was a transition period for the Bulls. I think they pulled the trigger quickly. They should have given Paul another year. In one sense, the numbers speak for themselves. Paul was the eighth coach in seven years. The owners never really promoted the team. They were always minimizing the losses and never maximizing the plusses.

Rod Thorn: Hiring Paul was a mistake. I don't think he was meant to coach the Bulls. He came from L.A. where everything was first class and whatever you wanted you got. That just wasn't the way with the Bulls.

Ronnie Lester: The thing with us is that there were too many changes going on in a short period of time. Coaching changes, big turnover in players. We had some good young talent, some of the best young talent. I think Rod drafted really well. But anytime you get young players and a lot of young players, there's a lot of immaturity that goes along with that. And our young guys were immature.

Dailey works against the Nets

Sidney Green (21) came to Chicago with high expectations.

Greenwood works against Larry Bird.

The Old School, 1983-84

WITH PAUL WESTHEAD'S FIRING, THE Bulls named 43-year-old Kevin Loughery coach in June 1983. Loughery, who had coached the New York Nets to two ABA titles, had just finished coaching the Atlanta Hawks to a 43-39 record and a second-place finish in the Central Division.

From the draft, the Bulls added forward Sidney Green out of Nevada-Las Vegas and guards Ennis Whatley and Mitch Wiggins.

Rod Thorn: I had been an assistant coach with Kevin for the New York/ New Jersey Nets in the ABA and NBA. I had great respect for his ability to deal with players.

Mark Pfeil: Kevin was from the old school. At that time, guys were still having fun in pro basketball. You come in, do your work, then get together afterwards and hit the bars and have some fun.

Seeking a better contract, Reggie Theus held out that fall, which put him at immediate odds with Loughery. The opening night lineup featured David Greenwood and Orlando Woolridge at forwards, Dave Corzine at center and Quintin Dailey and Ennis Whatley at guards. Loughery's decision to keep Theus on the bench resulted in a feud between player and coach. The small Stadium crowds would chant for the coach to play Theus, and Reggie would encourage them by waving a towel on the bench.

Reggie Theus: I admit I was immature in the way I handled it. I'd order pizza from the bench. I knew I wasn't going to play, so I figured I could watch the game and eat. I was a kid.

127

Steve Johnson hooks over Philadelphia's Moses Malone.

Rod Thorn: Kevin had made the decision not to play Reggie, and he knew it was going to be unpopular. In those days we didn't do terribly well at the box office anyway. There were several of our owners looking to sell whatever part of the team they had. Mr. Wirtz had died, and his son Billy was involved. But Billy was more of a hockey guy. I don't think he was nearly as interested in it as his father was.

In February, the Bulls traded Reggie Theus to Kansas City for Steve Johnson and a draft pick. With Quintin Dailey leading the scoring at 18.2 points per game and Greenwood getting an average of 10.1 rebounds, they finished the season at 27-55 and missed the playoffs for the third straight season, bringing yet more speculation that the team would be sold and moved out of Chicago.

Reggie Theus: I cried. My heart was heavy for a very long time after I got traded out of Chicago. I thought I would end my career there. Today, I still think about the respect I got from my fans there. If the Bulls hadn't gotten Michael Jordan the next year, I don't know if the fans would ever have stopped chanting my name. They chanted "Reggie! Reggie!" well into the next year, when I was with Kansas City.

Orlando Woolridge gave Chicago athleticism in the frontcourt.

The Bulls shipped Reggie Theus to the Kings.

MICHAEL JORDAN
CHICAGO BULLS
1984 — 1993

best there ever was. The best there ever will be.

DEDICATED
NOVEMBER 1, 1994

Part Three
Air Show

> That's the beauty of basketball. It's a mystery... It's the unpredictable... It's unwritten stories.
>
> —Phil Jackson

The Chicago Bulls, 1984-96

MICHAEL JORDAN LEFT THE UNIVERSITY of North Carolina after his junior season in 1984 and entered the NBA draft. The Houston Rockets selected Hakeem Olajuwon first. With the second pick, the Portland Trail Blazers took Kentucky center Sam Bowie, a move that they would rue for eternity. Waiting with the third pick were the Bulls, who grabbed Jordan.

He led the U.S. to the Olympic gold medal in Los Angeles that summer, then exploded into an instant phenomenon that fall when he joined the NBA. In one of his early appearances at a Bulls' exhibition game in East Chicago, Indiana, he was greeted by a pack of screaming teen-age girls.

"Michael Jackson eat your heart out," quipped teammate Orlando Woolridge.

Before long Jordan was regularly turning in 40-point performances, but it wasn't point totals that thrilled the crowds. His appeal began with his energy level. He played all-out, every minute. On defense, he was a roaming thief. On offense, he was simply a cornucopia. Jumpers. Elegant dunks. Reverses. Finger rolls. Short bank shots. All executed with a style that bordered on miraculous. When he couldn't get to the hoop by land, he traveled by air. Literally. (The definition of flying, according to the Random House Dictionary of the English Language, is "to be carried through the air by the wind or any other force or agency.")

For the first time in their history, the "force" was with the Bulls, and it meant a profound transformation for both the team and its young superstar. Forging change in the franchise's management were new owner Jerry Reinsdorf and general manager Jerry Krause. Out went the executive committee and the old stodgy manner of doing business. In came a new way of running the team.

After two decades of upheaval and misfires in the team's front office, Bulls fans were openly leery of Krause's seemingly unorthodox approach. There were early unpopular moves greeted by loud hisses from the media and fans.

In retrospect, it seems obvious that a pattern of success was emerging. But at the time, the entire enterprise was a burgeoning gamble with careers on the line. The primary casualties were coaches. A line of them—Kevin Loughery, Stan Albeck and Doug Collins—fell by the wayside.

Meanwhile, Jordan himself was undergoing an unprecedented transformation. Seeing that the Bulls' young star was going places, Nike soon built a multimillion-dollar shoe and clothing deal around his superhuman image. Jordan, the player, quickly became Air Jordan, the incredibly successful corporate entity. Before long, he was making far more money off the court than on it. Rather than dull his unique drive, this off-court success seemed to shove it into a higher gear.

He led the lowly Bulls to the playoffs that first year, where they quickly lost to Milwaukee. The next season, 1986, he overcame a serious foot injury to carry them into the playoffs once more, where they were vanquished 3-0 by Boston, but not before Jordan scared the Celtics blue by scoring 63 points in one game, a playoff record.

He went on from there, shoving the Bulls a notch higher each year. And in the process, he claimed nearly every major individual achievement imaginable. By the 1991 playoffs, he had captured the league scoring title five times. He had been named the league's Most Valuable Player twice. He had been named to the All-NBA first team five times in seven years.

But, alas, the Bulls had won nothing.

With each Chicago loss in the playoffs, observers grew more convinced that the Bulls were flawed because Jordan made them virtually a one-man team. Some pointed out that it had taken Wilt Chamberlain, Jerry West and Oscar Robertson many years to lead teams to the NBA title. Some critics said Jordan fit into the category with those players. Others wondered if he weren't headed for the same anguish as Elgin Baylor, Nate Thurmond, Pete Maravich and Dave Bing, all great players who never played on a championship team.

Jordan was understandably angered by such speculation and by the criticism that he was a one-man team. He was also pained by the loss-

es each year to Detroit. He and Pistons point guard Isiah Thomas weren't fond of each other, which made the losses all the more difficult.

Finally in 1991 that all changed. Jackson had employed the team-oriented triple-post offense devised by veteran assistant Tex Winter. For months the Bulls had struggled with the transition to this new approach until quite suddenly everything clicked. They vanquished the Pistons 4-0 in the east, then thoroughly outplayed a veteran Los Angeles Lakers team led by Magic Johnson to claim the franchise's first NBA title. The tears flowed freely for Jordan afterward. "I've never been this emotional publicly," he said.

It had been a long haul.

"When I came here, we started from scratch," he said. "I vowed we'd make the playoffs every year, and each year we got closer. I always had faith I'd get this ring one day."

Jordan, of course, hadn't hoped alone. The Bulls had begun with a faithful coterie of about 6,000 in 1984. Along the way, they added millions of fans, all captivated by his Air Show. One hundred years earlier, James Naismith had set the height of the goal at 10 feet. A century later, it remained the same challenge. Yet there was little doubt in anyone's mind that Michael Jordan and the Chicago Bulls had elevated the possibilities.

Jordan thrilled his Olympic teammates in 1984.

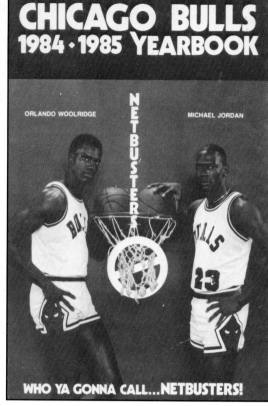

CHICAGO BULLS 1984·1985 YEARBOOK

ORLANDO WOOLRIDGE   MICHAEL JORDAN

NETBUSTERS

WHO YA GONNA CALL...NETBUSTERS!

Here's Mike, 1984-85

WITH THE 1983-84 SEASON COMING *to a disappointing close, Rod Thorn and the Bulls again turned their efforts to improving the roster with another high draft pick. The best of those hopes was that the pick would turn out to be Michael Jordan.*

Bill Blair: We didn't win a lot of games that year before. But Rod reminded us that there was a guy down at North Carolina who was a great, great player. He just kept on and on about Michael Jordan. Rod was always positive and sure that this guy was gonna be one of the great all-time players. But a lot of people said, "Well, he can't play guard. He can't play small forward." Even Bobby Knight [*who would later call Jordan the greatest to ever play the game*] had made a statement like that. But Rod said, "This kid has got something special."

Rod Thorn: Nobody, including me, knew Jordan was going to turn out to be what he is. We didn't work him out before the draft, but we interviewed him. He was confident. He felt he was gonna be good. It was obvious that Michael believed in himself, but even he had no idea just how good he was going to be.

The Bulls held the third pick in the draft, while Houston won the top pick in a coin flip with Portland. Five years earlier, the Bulls had lost Magic Johnson on a flip of a coin. This time luck had been with them.

Irwin Mandel: We could tell that we were going to get Jordan when Houston won the coin flip over Portland. If Portland had won the flip, they would have taken Olajuwon, and Houston probably would have taken Jordan. I remember how excited Rod was. He was thrilled, because in his mind there was a major difference between Jordan and Bowie.

Rod Thorn: Houston had made it clear from the start that they were going to take Olajuwon. About a month before the draft, I had a conversation with Stu Inman, Portland's general manager at the time. Stu told me they wanted Sam Bowie. Their doctors had said Bowie's health would be fine, and they needed a big man and weren't really considering anyone else.

Sure enough, Jordan was there for the Bulls with the third pick. He admitted that he'd like to play for the Lakers, where James Worthy, his college teammate at North Carolina, was becoming a star. But Chicago would be fine,

Jordan said, because the Lakers "are so stacked I probably couldn't have helped them anyway."

Having finished his college career, Michael moved to the U.S. Olympic team, coached by Indiana's Bobby Knight. Although Knight's systematic offense gave him limited playing time and scoring opportunities, Jordan's athletic performances during practices and games thrilled crowds and teammates alike as he led the United States to the gold medal in the games in Los Angeles. "When Michael gets the ball on the break only one thing's going to happen," said Olympic teammate Steve Alford. *"Some kind of dunk."*

"The excitement just sort of builds," agreed teammate Chris Mullin.

"Sometimes the players get into the habit of just watching Michael," Alford said, *"because he's usually going to do something you don't want to miss."*

Rod Thorn: Playing in the Olympics really gave Michael an impetus. He became a household name, because the Olympics were in Los Angeles, because the games became a highlight film every night of his dunks and flashy moves, even though he didn't get to play that much.

On September 12, 1984, the Bulls announced Jordan's signing. Press reports revealed that the seven-year, $6-million deal was the third highest in league history, behind those given to Houston big men Hakeem Olajuwon and Ralph Sampson. "It took some give and take," Kovler quipped. *"We gave, and they took."*

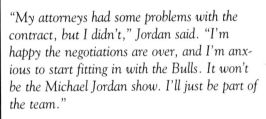

Loughery had the joy of being Mike's first pro coach.

"My attorneys had some problems with the contract, but I didn't," Jordan said. "I'm happy the negotiations are over, and I'm anxious to start fitting in with the Bulls. It won't be the Michael Jordan show. I'll just be part of the team."

A few weeks later, when camp opened, Bob Logan of the Tribune wrote: "For the first time in their frustrating NBA history, the Bulls have a potential superstar in camp."

Bill Blair: His second day of practice, Kevin said, "Let's have a scrimmage and find out if Michael's as good as we think he is." Michael took the ball off the rim at one end and went to other end. From the top of the key, he soared in and dunked it, and Kevin says, "We don't have to scrimmage anymore."

Kevin Loughery: I think the second practice when we started doing one-on-one drills we immediately saw that we had a star. I can't say that we knew we had the best player ever in basketball. But we always felt that Michael could shoot the ball. A lot of people had questioned that. But Michael had played in a passing game

The Youthful Air

John Ligmanowski: This was my expectation of Michael coming in: We always needed a big guard, and I was hoping he'd be like Phil Smith for the Golden State Warriors. I don't think anybody dreamed Michael would become as good as he did.

I know Mark Pfeil—when he first saw Michael at practice, as a rookie just going out there and kicking everybody's ass—Mark told me, "You gotta see this guy play."

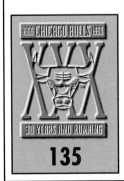

135

Rod Higgins was a stalwart of those early '80s Bulls.

Orlando Woolridge.

system in college under Dean Smith and in the Olympics under Bobby Knight. So people never got the opportunity to see him handle the ball individually the way he could handle it.

Then when we found out how supremely competitive he was, then we knew we had a player who had it all.

Sidney Green: I will never forget the first day he walked into camp right after the Olympics. Everybody said that he would be tired, drained. I remember his first practice. He was jumping from the free-throw line, dunking on drills. And everybody said, "Aw, he's gonna cut that out by midseason." At midseason, it seemed like he was jumping from the top of the key. We said, "By the three-quarter mark of the season his legs are going to die out." At the three-quarter mark, he was still going strong, plus more. That's when I made my quote to the press, "Michael Jordan is the truth, the whole truth and nothing but the truth, so help us God."

And that's what he is: He's the truth.

Mark Pfeil: Michael would pick on somebody every day. You saw this early on. Every day. Somebody was gonna be his goat. It

would be anybody on the team, guys like Ennis Whatley and Ronnie Lester and Quintin Dailey. Michael would shoot, stick it in their faces time and time again. He used to get their goats to make them play harder, mainly because he was so competitive. There were times during his rookie year when practice was unworkable. Loughery would just toss up his hands and let Michael do his thing.

Rod Thorn: In practice, Loughery used to put Michael with different teams, just to see what he could do. Whatever team Kevin put him on would win. Kevin told me, "I don't know if our other guys are that bad, or he's that good."

Mark Pfeil: Kevin always had a thing in practice where he'd divide the roster into two teams, and the first team to 10 won. The team that lost ran 10 laps. Kevin called it 10 points or 10 laps. Michael never ran a lap the whole year. One time Michael's team was up 8-0, and Kevin switched him to the other team. Michael was furious. He scored the first nine points by himself, and his team won.

Kevin Loughery: Once I saw him in camp I changed my thinking about what we were going to do offensively. He dictated what type of offense we were going to need. We weren't a very strong roster outside of Michael, so he was gonna have to do a lot of shooting. I immediately started thinking of ways to isolate him, of having him going one on one. It made sense to post him up because he was stronger than most guards. You had to gear your offense around him.

We saw his skills, but you've got to be around him every day to see the competitiveness of the guy. He was gonna try to take over every situation that was difficult. He was gonna put himself on the line. He enjoyed it.

Jordan played his first game on Friday, October 26, 1984, against the Washington Bullets in Chicago Stadium before a crowd of 13,913. He made five of 16 shots from the floor, scored 16 points and had seven assists and six rebounds. At one point, Jordan was soaring to the hole for a slam when Bulls center Jeff Ruland knocked him to the floor. The Stadium grew quiet as Jordan lay motionless. Finally he got up and later complained of a sore neck and head. Both he and Ruland agreed the collision was inadvertent. "This was a good start for my career," he said afterward.

In his third game, he scored 37 points, including 22 in the fourth quarter, as 9,356 fans in the Stadium saw the Bulls claim a come-from-behind win over Milwaukee.

"He's as much an image as he is a symbol," said Jordan's agent, David Falk, late that October after revealing that Jordan had already signed promotional deals with Nike, Wilson Sporting Goods and the Chicagoland Chevrolet Dealerships Association. The Nike deal alone paid him $500,000 per year. "I know everybody's eyes are on me," Jordan said, "and some of the things I do even surprise myself. They aren't always planned. They just happen."

Bill Blair: Early in the year we went to Milwaukee, and Michael played against Sidney Moncrief. When he started abusing Moncrief, who we considered one of the top five defensive guards in the league, we knew that we had a special person.

Michael was always there at practice 45 minutes early. He wanted to work on his shooting. And after practice he'd make you help him. He'd keep working on his shooting. He didn't care how long he was out there. The thing that I always loved about him, when you'd take him out in practice to give him a rest during a scrimmage, he was constantly back on you to get him back in. Michael loved to play the game.

Kevin Loughery: As much as you talk about Michael's offensive ability, he's probably one of the best defensive players to play the game. His anticipation was so great, he could see the floor, his quickness, and then his strength. That's another thing that's overlooked, how strong Michael is. He really had the whole package.

Rod Thorn: Once Michael started playing and playing well, the fans got interested. At the start of the season, we were selling in the 6,000 range. Then, all of a sudden, we were up over 10,000. He was a show. In his early games, this guy was going to the basket

Wes Matthews.

Sid Green.

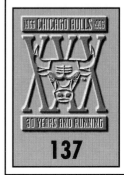

137

Gene Banks

every time he had the ball. He was putting up dunks and whirligig shots. Players on other teams were knocking him down out of the air. We pretty soon realized he was gonna get killed.

In his first game against the Pistons, Jordan was floating for a dunk when Detroit center Bill Laimbeer slammed him to the floor, creating an uproar in the Stadium.

Jordan scored 27 in an early loss to the Celtics in the Stadium. "I've never seen one player turn a team around like that," Larry Bird, the league's reigning Most Valuable Player, said afterward. "All the Bulls have become better because of him... Pretty soon this place will be packed every night... They'll pay just to watch Jordan. He's the best. Even at this stage in his career, he's doing more than I ever did. I couldn't do what he does as a rookie. Heck, there was one drive tonight. He had the ball up in his right hand, then he took it down. Then he brought it back up. I got a hand on it, fouled him, and he still scored. All the while, he's in the air.

"You have to play this game to know how difficult that is. You see that and say, 'Well, what the heck can you do?'

"I'd seen a little of him before and wasn't that impressed. I mean, I thought he'd be good, but not this good. Ain't nothing he can't do. That's good for this franchise, good for the league."

In just his ninth pro game, Jordan scored 45 points against San Antonio. Six weeks later he

burned Cleveland for another 45. Then came a 42-point performance against New York. Another 45 against Atlanta, and his first triple-double (35 points, 15 assists and 14 rebounds) against Denver. Then, just before the All-Star break, he zipped in 41 against defending champion Boston.

Even as he moved through this incredible rookie performance, the men who had owned the Bulls for more than a decade revealed their plans to sell the controlling interest in the team to White Sox owner Jerry Reinsdorf. The deal itself was announced at All-Star Weekend in Indianapolis. Reinsdorf told the press that the transaction would be consummated about March 1, 1985, after the Bulls owners and the Arthur Wirtz estate paid off the $13.3-million settlement to Marv Fishman for the breach-of-contract suit stemming from the 1973 sale of the team.

"The owners are delighted to have Jerry Reinsdorf in the league," said Commissioner David Stern. "There was a feeling before that there were too many owners in Chicago, and now this concentrates ownership."

However, the biggest story of All-Star Weekend 1985 was the "freeze out" of Jordan during the game by other established stars. Dr. Charles Tucker, an advisor to Magic Johnson, Isiah Thomas and George Gervin, revealed to reporters that "the guys weren't happy with his attitude up here. They decided to teach him a lesson. On defense, Magic and George gave him a hard time, and offensively, they just didn't give him the ball.

"That's what they're laughing about," Tucker explained as he stood near the stars as they waited to fly out of the Indianapolis airport. "George asked Isiah, 'You think we did a good enough job on him?'"

Supposedly, the veterans were upset that the rookie wore a black and red Air Jordan jumpsuit at the slam dunk competition. They also complained that he seemed arrogant and standoffish. Jordan had taken just nine of the team's 120 shots during the game, although he had played 22 minutes.

Agent David Falk explained that Jordan had been asked by Nike to wear the prototype of the Air Jordan clothing. "That makes me feel

very small," Jordan said of the snub. "I want to crawl in a hole and not come out."

"How could someone do anything like that?" Isiah Thomas said in denying the snubbing. "It's very childish."

Reportedly, the Detroit guard had become upset because Jordan had little to say during an elevator ride to a player meeting the first night of the All-Star event. "I was very quiet when I went there," Jordan explained. "I didn't want to go there like I was a big-shot rookie and you must respect me."

Said Jordan's Bulls teammate Wes Matthews. "He's got gifts from God. He's God's kid; let him be God's kid."

The Pistons were scheduled to play in the Stadium the first game after the break, and by the time they arrived, Thomas was weary of being asked about his involvement. "That never happened," Thomas said of the alleged snub. "I was very upset when I read that. That could affect a potential friendship between Michael and me."

That night, Jordan addressed the issue by scoring 49 points with 15 rebounds to help the Bulls to a 139-126 overtime win. Afterward, Thomas grew angry with reporters. "It's over. It's over," he told them.

The Chicago/Detroit rivalry, however, was just getting started.

Bill Blair: As the year went on and we made the playoffs, Michael just got bigger and bigger with the fans. I remember the trip in Washington where we won to secure a playoff position. Two days later we played Philly, but Michael stayed in Washington and went with Senator Bill Bradley and made an appearance in Congress. Then he got on the plane and flew up to Philadelphia that night. He had the shootaround the next day and got 35 against Philly. So you knew Michael could handle all the other stuff outside of basketball and still get it done.

Two weeks after finalizing his purchase of the team, Jerry Reinsdorf dismissed Rod Thorn and named Jerry Krause vice president of basketball operations. The Bulls suffered through a 12-game road losing streak before closing out

the season with 35 wins, an improvement of eight over the previous year and good enough to make the playoffs for the first time since 1981. With their frontcourt thinned by injuries, the Bulls lost to Milwaukee, 3-1. Afterward, Krause released Kevin Loughery.

Kevin Loughery: When they fired Rod and hired Krause, I knew what was going to happen. They were gonna bring their people in. We made the playoffs that year, which they hadn't done in three or four years.

I knew Krause for years with the Bullets. So I knew that was [the end of] my job when he came in. I told that to my assistants. I had never had as much respect for him as he wanted me to have.

But I have great memories of coaching the best player who ever played. It didn't take us long to find out we had a great player. We knew his competitive spirit. The team hadn't made the playoffs in a few years. We knew we had a player to elevate us to that level. There was a lot of anticipation.

The crowds didn't develop right away, but it was just a matter of time. He was going to be the premier star in the NBA. You had the man to build around. You knew you were going to get better every year by adding parts. You have to have a star in the NBA to have a good team. When you have a star, you have the opportunity to put the other pieces in.

Not only was he a star, he could do so many things. He could handle three spots, the point, the off guard, the small forward. I guess if you had to put him down low, he could do that. He could rebound, he could pass. A star who could do so many things. He wasn't just one dimensional like a lot of stars are. He made it easier to put a team together.

We're still friends; we still play golf together. I enjoyed Michael, not just his talent, but his zest for the game, his desire to play every minute. He'd take over practice. He loved to play. All great players love to compete. Because of that, he was a little bit beyond his teammates, because he demanded so much of them.

CHICAGO SUN-TIMES   SATURDAY, FEBRUARY 9, 1985   PAGE 88

Sports

BLACK HAWKS:
Get ready for
revved-up
Boston Bruins.
Page 86

ILLINI:
Report details
charges against
Illinois.
Page 87

Reinsdorf gets Bulls

By Mark Vancil

Approval expected from NBA, AL

Jerry Reinsdorf
Awaits routine vote.

INDIANAPOLIS—White Sox chairman Jerry Reinsdorf will become majority owner of the Chicago Bulls, pending a routine vote today by the NBA Board of Governors and approval by the American League.

As first reported in the Sun-Times, Reinsdorf will gain control of 56.8 percent

of the Bulls in a cash deal worth $9.2 million. Including liabilities tied to the ongoing Marvin Fishman antitrust suit, the franchise figures to be worth $18.7 million.

"As far as I can tell, [it] has the potential to go on for several years," Reinsdorf

said of the suit. "And I fully expect Mr. Fishman will enjoin me as a defendant. But we have received very strong indemnities from the people who are already in the lawsuit, so I'm not concerned about any potential liability."

Reinsdorf, part-owner of the White Sox, said he expected no problem securing approval from the American League. He ended weeks of speculation and negotiations that began last August by obtaining Bulls shares previously owned by George

Steinbrenner, William Wirtz, Philip Klutznick and Walter Shorenstein.

Although nearly 75 percent of the league's teams lost money two years ago, Reinsdorf said the steps taken by NBA opened his mind and wallet.

"I'm very impressed with the salary cap," Reinsdorf said. "Without it I wouldn't
Turn to Page 81

Sting's

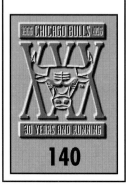

Move/Rein-Ovation

DESPITE THE PROMISE OF MICHAEL *Jordan as a draft pick, a majority of the Bulls' owners had grown weary after a decade of turmoil and frustrations. In 1984, they began looking for a buyer.*

Irwin Mandel: Cumulatively the Bulls had lost millions of dollars over the years. The losses were consistent from '73 until Michael Jordan arrived. The owners kept putting in money. I felt sorry for them, even though they could afford it, because it was frustrating. They didn't like it. It's one thing if you're winning and being praised by the press. You can accept that. But when you're losing money and the team is doing badly and the press and the public are down on you, that's tough. They had a slight profit one year in the seventies. Slight. They had profits for two years in the mid seventies. Other than that, they were not profitable until two years after Jordan joined them. I think the owners felt it was going to be a losing proposition. But I think they felt they were performing a civic duty, having the team in Chicago. That was a source of pride for them. Owning a sports team could be fun. It was something for them to talk about. Something for their families to talk about.

The losses were reasonably big. Fortunately, these were extremely wealthy men. Extremely wealthy. They were able to absorb more losses than another group of owners might have.

I think they always thought there was light at the end of the tunnel, that if we could just get our team good, maybe we could, at a minimum, at least break even.

Steve Schanwald: When I first came to Chicago in 1981, the Stadium was a dead building for basketball. I used to enjoy coming out because I could get a seat and stretch out. But it was really kind of an embarrassment to see. I couldn't believe this was NBA basketball. It seemed more like the CBA, or worse. The Stadium itself was always great when it was filled with people. When it was devoid of people, it was kind of a depressing setting, like a tomb. There was no glitzy scoreboard. I am told that in the early days Bulls fans used to watch basketball games through the hockey plexiglass! That's how little respect the Bulls had. And the Chicago Sting, the indoor soccer team which no longer exists, used to outdraw the Bulls. Benny the Bull was the mascot, but he looked more like a human body with a Bulls head on top. He had human fingers instead of hooves. It was

kind of a bush-league costume. In the early eighties, the experience of attending a Bulls basketball game was nothing like the energy which runs through the building today. It was almost laughable. It had to be depressing to work there because it was sure depressing to watch.

Irwin Mandel: The whole league was down in the late 1970s, so it was crucial that Magic Johnson and Larry Bird came along. And it was crucial that they went to Los Angeles and Boston, the two most popular franchises. Their rivalry in the NBA finals was an exciting east versus west showdown. But more than anything, it was the way those two guys, Larry and Magic, played basketball. Team basketball. Assists. That greatly, greatly changed the public's image of the league. More important, they changed how other players in the NBA viewed the game. The others saw the two best players in the game, how much they gave up the ball, how competitive Magic and Bird were, how much they wanted to win, how hard they played every night. That changed the game, by changing the perception of the public and other players. And it helped set the stage for Michael's coming into the league.

I worried about the owners losing patience with the team in the early eighties. But the Bulls had high number one draft choices then. There was always light ahead because of those draft picks. They figured maybe one of those would pan out.

Luckily, we had that third pick in 1984.

It was through his baseball connections that White Sox co-owner Jerry Reinsdorf learned that he might have a chance to purchase the Bulls. He had grown up in Brooklyn, where his industrious father worked alternately as a mechanic and a cabbie and ice cream truck driver before settling into a business buying and *reselling used sewing machines. In Brooklyn, "being a Dodgers fan was almost a religion," Reinsdorf explained, and he worshipped just as hard as every other kid on Flatbush Avenue. He was also a Knicks fan (Carl Braun was his favorite player), and later in life, even after he had finished law school and was well on his way to amassing a fortune in real estate investment in Chicago, he would hold in awe the Knicks teams of the early 1970s coached by Red Holtzman. As Reinsdorf built the market value of Balcor, his real estate investment company, he realized that he might be able to live the ultimate businessman's fantasy: owning a major league sports team.*

In 1981, Reinsdorf and partner Eddie Einhorn purchased controlling interest in the White Sox from Bill Veeck. They soon began an aggressive revamping of the team, structured around Carlton Fisk, which led to a divisional championship in 1983. A year later, Reinsdorf was in New York having dinner with New York Yankees owner George Steinbrenner, who was also a minority owner of the Bulls. Reinsdorf told Steinbrenner he would love to own and operate the Bulls.

Jerry Reinsdorf: In September 1984, Lester Crown phoned me and said Steinbrenner had told him of our conversation. He asked me if I was serious because some of the other owners in the Bulls really wanted to

Jerry Krause confers with new coach Stan Albeck.

141

Jerry Reinsdorf

Steinbrenner and the Wirtz family, a total of 56.8 percent of the team, for $9.2 million. (The Wirtz family would later reacquire a share of the team.) After learning that he would no longer be the team's managing partner, Kovler sold his seven percent, which increased the Reinsdorf group's share to 63.7 percent. "I will be visible, I will be seen," Reinsdorf said in announcing the sale. "I will be actively involved with this franchise…. I have a theory about how to run a basketball team, and I've always wanted an opportunity to run one."

"I'm still sick," Kovler told reporters. "After 13 years, I still love basketball…. Look at it this way: We lost a $25 million coin flip for Magic Johnson when he came out of college. If we'd won that coin flip, everybody here would've been smart. We'd still be geniuses."

Jerry Reinsdorf: I was stunned, absolutely stunned at what I found when I took over the team. I asked Kovler to meet with me, and when we did, my first question was, "How many season ticket salesmen do you have?" He said, "None." I said, "What?" He said, "We don't really sell season tickets. People who want them just call us."

Jerry Krause: When he heard about the season tickets, Jerry said, "Oh boy, look what I've found!"

Jerry Reinsdorf: The state of the franchise was terrible. The practice facilities were terrible. The offices were terrible. They were dingy. The team charged employees for Cokes if they wanted them. Morale was terrible. The franchise was understaffed. It wasn't that the people running the Bulls were bad, but they all had other things to do. Kovler was the nominal, day-to-day manager, but he didn't have any authority. The committee involved three other people, and they all had their other interests and investments.

Rod Thorn: At the All-Star game in Indianapolis, it became clear that Mr. Reinsdorf was going to take over. I had gone to dinner with Kovler and Reinsdorf, and Reinsdorf asked me to write a detailed analysis of the team, who I would trade if I could and other things. Later we met in the

get out and that we should talk about it. I met with Lester, and he said that he and Lamar Hunt didn't want to sell, but that 55 to 58 percent of the team was available to purchase. I worked out a deal with Lester in October of 1984 before Michael Jordan had played a game. But we couldn't complete the deal until after February. At first, Jonathan Kovler, who had seven percent, was going to stay involved. But then Kovler decided to get out, which left Hunt and Crown as the only holdovers among the owners.

In the settling of Arthur Wirtz's estate in 1984, the Bulls had been valued at $14.8 million. Pulling together a group of 24 investors, Reinsdorf bought out the shares of Phillip Klutznick, Walter Shorenstein, George

office and talked for a long time. We discussed many things, including my relationship with the present ownership, what I thought the team should do.

Then a few weeks later I got a call from Mr. Reinsdorf. He came in my office and informed me he was going to make a change. There is no nice way to do that. I was kind of in shock at the time.

Jerry Reinsdorf: Rod's a wonderful person, a great guy. But I never got into it too deeply with Rod. I just didn't like the whole culture of the organization, and I didn't like the way it was being coached. I felt we had to break from the past, and I wanted someone as a general manager who believed what I believed in. I believed very strongly in two things: 1) A championship team is built around defense. You must remember this was at a time when the NBA was at a peak for points being scored, but very few teams really played any defense; 2) I wanted the offense not to be isolations and one-on-ones. I wanted all five guys participating and sharing the ball. I wanted the Bulls to duplicate what Red Holtzman had done with the Knicks.

Everybody told me the day of defense was gone. But I had visited with Bill Bradley in his office on Capitol Hill and asked him, "Am I wrong?" He said, "No, I think you're right. It's true that today's players are creative offensively and exciting. But by playing good defense you make them shoot further out and at difficult angles."

Reinsdorf announced in late March 1985 that he was replacing Thorn with Jerry Krause, who would become the vice president for basketball operations. In effect, Reinsdorf said the team would no longer have a general manager, per se. Instead there would be three vice presidents: one for basketball, one for marketing and promotions, and one for financial and legal affairs. "I want a team that will play Red Holtzman basketball," Reinsdorf said in announcing the changes. "An unselfish team, one that plays team defense, that knows its roles, that moves without the ball. Jerry Krause's job will be to find the DeBusschere of 1985 and the Bradley of 1985."

Krause had broken into scouting in pro baseball in the 1960s, then had begun his pro basketball career with the Baltimore Bullets before joining the Bulls as a scout in the early 1970s. He

Krause, top pick Charles Oakley and assistant coach Tex Winter after the 1985 draft. Mike Smrek, the second-round pick, is far left.

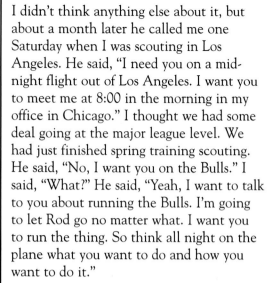

Albeck cheers on a scrambling Gene Banks.

scouted for Phoenix, Philadelphia, and even returned to Bulls briefly in 1976 as player personnel director. From there he had gone on to the Lakers as a scout before returning to baseball. It was while scouting for the White Sox that he got to know Reinsdorf.

Jerry Krause: I wouldn't have taken the Bulls job had it not been for Jerry. Michael or no Michael. I had worked with Jerry with the White Sox for several years. I had turned down chances to come back in the NBA during that time. I'd had a couple of strikes against me, and I didn't want to come back unless I knew I could work for an owner I felt comfortable with and that I knew would back me and do the things that needed to be done.

When Jerry bought the ball club in February, it totally shocked me. I was getting ready to leave for spring training. I said to him, "Take a look at the thing for a year, and if you don't like what you see, I'd be interested in going over there and running the thing for you. You're the one guy I'd go back in that league for. It's a potential gold mine now because you got it."

I didn't think anything else about it, but about a month later he called me one Saturday when I was scouting in Los Angeles. He said, "I need you on a midnight flight out of Los Angeles. I want you to meet me at 8:00 in the morning in my office in Chicago." I thought we had some deal going at the major league level. We had just finished spring training scouting. He said, "No, I want you on the Bulls." I said, "What?" He said, "Yeah, I want to talk to you about running the Bulls. I'm going to let Rod go no matter what. I want you to run the thing. So think all night on the plane what you want to do and how you want to do it."

So the next day I got off the plane at 6:00. I met him at 8:00, and we talked all day. Just about philosophy. How we would do the thing. What the parameters would be. What the responsibilities would be. We met again the next morning about 7:30 or 8:00. About 11:00, he says, "I got to call Rod." He calls Rod downtown. I get in the car with him and drive downtown. He goes up to Rod's office while I wait downstairs in the car. He goes upstairs and he lets Rod go. He walked in and said, "Rod, we're going to end your services." Jerry came back downstairs and he was ashen-faced. The man was white. I looked at him and said, "What's the matter with you?" He said, "You know, in all my years at Balcor I only fired one person. That's only the second person I've fired in my life. I don't like firing people." And I thought, "Gee, that's a great sign. Here's an owner who doesn't want to fire anybody."

Jerry Reinsdorf: Krause was atop the scouting heirarchy at the White Sox, and I had gotten to know him. There had to be a cultural change in the Bulls' organization, and Krause believed the same things I did. I hated to fire Rod. He is one of the two or three nicest gentlemen in the NBA. But the change worked great for us, and it worked great for Rod, who, as you know, is now the league's vice president for operations.

Sidney Green: You gotta look at Rod's big move, though. He drafted Michael Jordan.

144

Rod Thorn: No one likes to get fired. But it has turned out to be a blessing in disguise. It enabled me to go in a different career direction. As the results show, Jerry Krause has done an excellent job putting the people together to complement Michael Jordan.

The success, however, was far from automatic. Putting Reinsdorf's grand vision of Red Holtzman/ Knicks basketball into effect would take years and numerous personnel moves. Krause's first was to fire Kevin Loughery as coach. Then he turned his attention to the roster.

Jerry Krause: I had a brutal start. I had nine players I didn't want and three I did. I wanted Dave Corzine, I wanted Rod Higgins, and I wanted Michael. The rest of them I couldn't have cared less about. And they were talented. All of them were very talented. But it wasn't a question of talent.

Phil Jackson: Jerry took away a lot of things that this franchise didn't need. It didn't need certain types of people on the club. He had a certain idea of what type of person he wanted. He brought in character, or what he liked to think of as character. Good solid people. People who wanted to work hard.

Jerry Krause: I released Wes Mathews without getting any compensation. I just wanted him out of town. Greenwood had a bad foot problem, so we traded him to San Antonio for George Gervin. We traded Ennis Whatley to Cleveland in the Charles Oakley deal.

Reinsdorf made other changes beyond Krause's personnel moves. He hired a phalanx of season ticket salespeople and produced a new source of revenue. He upgraded the team's broadcasting contracts and moved the team's practice facility from Angel Guardian to the Deerfield Multiplex. (In 1992, the Bulls built their own practice gymnasium, the Berto Center.) By 1988, the team had given up flying commercially and begun using a charter service, mainly to avoid the hassle of taking Jordan through public airports. Combined with Jordan's brilliance and the new atmosphere in the league and the changes brought by Reinsdorf, the Bulls' fortunes began to change, if not dramati-cally, at least perceptibly.

Irwin Mandel: Michael's first year started slowly. The first year we sort of stopped the financial skid. It took a little while to become profitable.

Then the numbers started to look real good his second year. I was very excited that finally, the light at the end of the tunnel had arrived. Each week he was becoming more and more popular. There was the feeling that next year he's going to be even more popular. This is a guy who's bringing excitement here, bringing the fans back. He's going to make us successful and popular and profitable. It looked like through him we had turned the corner.

Jerry Reinsdorf: It was a no brainer to make the organization better. It probably was one of the worst in sports. That part was easy.

Over the coming seasons, the men who had sold their interest in the team watched in amazement as the value of the Bulls rocketed from $16 million to well over $100 million.

Irwin Mandel: I don't know if they're bitter, but I feel sorry for them, because they were with the Bulls during the lean years. It's unfortunate that they sold the team in Michael's first year, and they didn't have the benefit of enjoying Michael and the fan adulation and the popularity and the fun and the financial success. I genuinely do feel badly for them in that regard. This is one of the few investments that those people made that lost money and was a negative experience. It was frustrating for them.

For many of them, it must be an unpleasant, disappointing experience. I think they had great expectations.

Jonathan Kovler: I'd be lying if I said I didn't think about it. I was disappointed that we sold the team to Reinsdorf. But I didn't have to sell my stock. It was an error. Unfortunately, I missed the party.

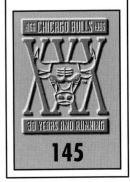

145

Oakley gave the Bulls a frontcourt presence.

A whole new breed.

Feets Don't Fail Me Now, 1985-86

For the 1985 draft, Jerry Krause did some frantic last-minute maneuvering to select Virginia Union's Charles Oakley, a bulky, little-known forward. As with many Krause moves, the pick was not a popular one in Chicago. But Oakley brought the Bulls just the toughness they needed.

Jerry Krause: I took the job on March 26. Three days later I went to Lexington, Kentucky, for the NCAA finals and saw Oakley in the coaches' All-Star game. Boy, did I get excited. I said, "That's the kind of player we need here. Physical, nasty." So I called Bighouse Gaines at Winston-Salem State and 'House tells me all about him, that he's great. Then Oakley goes to the predraft camp in Portsmouth, and he plays great there in front of all the other scouts.

Damn if he doesn't get invited to the predraft camp in Hawaii.

We were expecting to get Oakley with the eleventh pick, but a few days before the draft an agent friend of mine calls and tells me that Jerry Colangelo in Phoenix had brought Oakley in for a physical. Phoenix had the tenth pick.

I thought, "That damn Colangelo's up to his old tricks." I worked for him a long time. I know him. I figure I better go to work on Cleveland, who has the ninth pick. I called Cleveland and said, "Let's talk about a deal." Before long, there must have been four lawyers on the phone. Jerry Reinsdorf was in the room listening. Anyway, we made a trade at three in the morning. We traded our number eleven and Ennis Whatley for Cleveland's number nine and a second-round pick.

About 4:00 to 4:30 the phone rings and it's Colangelo, yelling, "You sonofabitch! You no good sonofabitch!" He's screaming at me. "What the hell did I do?" I asked him. "You screwed me on this draft!" he said. He'd found out through the Cleveland people that we had made a trade. He thought I was going to sneak in and take Eddie

Just days into the season, Jordan was sidelined with a broken foot.

Having fired Kevin Loughery, the Bulls hustled to find a new coach over the summer of 1985. Jerry Krause settled on New Jersey Nets coach Stan Albeck, a veteran. The new assistant coaches were Krause's old mentor, Tex Winter, and veteran college coach Murray Arnold.

With Jordan out, the offense focused on George Gervin, who could stil finger roll.

Pinckney, who Colangelo really wanted. I said, "Jerry, if you've been telling me the truth, then we don't have a problem in the world. If you've lied to me, I don't know if you've got a problem or not."

So the draft comes, and I tell Cleveland, "Take Charles Oakley." They say, "What!?!". I said, "Take Charles Oakley for us." After Phoenix takes Pinckney with the tenth pick, Cleveland tells me to take Keith Lee for them. I took Keith Lee, and our fans went nuts. "How the hell could they take Keith Lee?" they said. Then we announced there was a trade being made. The trade couldn't be announced until the first round was completed. We announced that Oakley was ours, and they went nuts again. "Who the hell is Charles Oakley?" I got ripped for that one, too.

Johnny Bach: Charles was a tough kid, and he didn't take anything from anyone. You could tell he was strong-willed as a person and he wanted to play. He went through the rookie ups and downs where he'd play some games and he wouldn't play a lot in others. You could just tell he had a desire to play. He wanted to prove to people coming from a small school that he was worthy of his selection in the draft and he was committed to playing hard.

Oakley soon developed into just the power forward the Bulls needed. Tough, mean, and best of all, a protector of Michael Jordan from the Bill Laimbeers of the world.

Jerry Reinsdorf: Krause knew Stan Albeck, and we had gotten permission from New Jersey to talk to him, but only for a limited time. We wanted to interview Jimmy Rodgers, but Boston refused to let us talk to him. After we talked to Albeck, Krause said, "He doesn't seem like the old Stan Albeck. There's a fire lacking. There's something lacking. I really have reservations." But we didn't have a coach. We had to do something. The draft was coming up.

147

When Jordan wanted to return, Krause hesitated.

Stan Albeck.

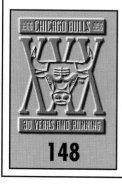

So we hired Albeck. In retrospect, I talked too much in the interview and didn't listen enough. I told him what I wanted, and he said what you wanted to hear.

Jerry Krause: I hired Stan. I knew I made a mistake halfway through the year.

Over the summer, the Bulls traded Steve Johnson to San Antonio for forward Gene Banks. Then, as the season opened, they traded David Greenwood to the Spurs for guard George Gervin and a draft pick. They also signed free agent guards Kyle Macy and John Paxson. They opened the season with three straight wins, but in the third game at Golden State Michael Jordan suffered a broken navicular tarsal bone in his left foot, an injury that had altered or ended the careers of several NBA players. He would miss the next 64 games.

Jerry Reinsdorf: After that, the year was a complete disaster.

Michael Jordan: I was a little bit scared. I didn't want to be bothered by anyone. I didn't want the phone to ring. I didn't want to watch TV. I didn't want to hear music. I just wanted plain darkness because this was something for me to deal with, and it was very painful. For the first time, I had to consider doing something else besides playing basketball, and it was very different.

Mark Pfeil: Michael wanted to go back to North Carolina and rehab there. We were able to get that across to Jerry Reinsdorf and Jerry Krause and set up a program for Michael in Carolina. He rehabbed, finished his degree and had peace of mind. That probably made Michael ready to compete when he returned.

Some observers, including several teammates, criticized Jordan for leaving the team while he was injured. Even though he had played in only three games, Jordan led the Eastern Conference in the fans' All-Star voting that winter.

Michael Jordan: I was very frustrated, and at first I didn't know how to deal with the situation. I walked away from it, went to North Carolina, worked on my degree and watched the team on TV. That's the best way I could deal with it.

Cheryl Raye: Stan tried the best he could under the circumstances. Without Michael that team had a lot of guys who didn't care. During the time-outs you had players who wouldn't even go in the huddles. There was an "I-don't-care" attitude around that team.

Sidney Green: It was hard for Stan. Unfortunately, he had high expectations for the team and for Michael. Once Michael went down, Stan had to change his whole game plan. He tried to build the whole team around George Gervin, but unfortunately George was on his last legs. But he still had the finger roll.

Beyond George, we were all young. But the talent that we had, even excluding Michael, we did pretty darn well. We played hard night in and night out. You must also remember that that was the year Quintin Dailey had his problems, too.

Quintin Dailey's pattern of missed games and late appearances came to a head in February, when he missed a game and Krause placed him on the suspended list. For the second time in eight weeks, Dailey entered a drug treatment facility.

Jerry Krause: Quintin was late to another shootaround, and by then I knew he was messed up on drugs. We were waiting around for him to show up for the game, and Stan said, "I'm gonna play him if he shows up." I said, "Why?" Stan said, "I need him to win." I asked the assistants what they would do. Tex said, "He wouldn't play for me." And Murray said, "Not for me either." I talked to Stan alone and he said if Quintin showed up he was gonna play him. I told him, "The guy's done in a Bulls uniform." I made the decision then to begin looking for another coach.

In March, with the Bulls record at 22-43, Michael Jordan informed the team that his injury had healed and he wanted to resume playing.

Michael Jordan: I didn't want to watch my team go down the pits. I thought I was healthy enough to contribute something.

Jerry Krause: I was scared to death. I didn't want to go down in history as the guy who put Michael Jordan back in too soon.

Jerry Reinsdorf: It was like a soap opera. We were too honest with Michael. We let him hear the report from the three doctors we consulted with over when he could come back. All three said the break had not healed enough. They said if he did play, there was about a 10 to 15 percent chance of ending his career. Michael was such a competitor. He just wanted to play. I thought he was entitled to hear what the doctors had to say. I never thought he'd risk his entire career. It just didn't make any sense to me. But Michael figured that the 10- to 15-percent risk meant the odds were 85 to 90 percent that he wouldn't get hurt. To me, it didn't fit any risk/reward ratio. Here the reward was to come back and play on a team that had already had a bad year. Why risk your whole career for that reward?

Michael insisted that he knew his own body better than I did. So we reached a compromise, that he would play gradually, just seven minutes a half at first.

Jerry Krause: The thing that got Michael and me off on the wrong foot was that he thought I said to him, "You're our property, and you'll do what we want you to do." I don't remember ever saying it that way. He just misinterpreted me. I was trying to keep him from playing because he had a bad foot and the doctors were saying, "No, no, no." And Reinsdorf was telling him about risk. We were all sitting in that room, and Stan wouldn't do a damn thing to help. Stan could have helped us explain the situation to Michael, but he was being selfish. He could have stood with us and the doctors who said Michael wasn't ready to play.

Mark Pfeil: That's the way Mike was. If he didn't think something was gonna hurt him, he'd focus past it and play. Sprains, groin pulls, muscle spasms, flu, Michael's first question always was, "Is it gonna hurt me to play?" If I told him no, it was gone. He'd focus past it.

Oakley proved to be a mature rookie.

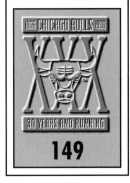

The 1985-86 season brought Paxson to the Bulls.

Cheryl Raye: They put a limitation on how many minutes Michael could play. They literally ran a clock on how many minutes he could play. Stan would sit there and have to calculate the time. He was under duress the whole time with Michael's return.

Jerry Krause: I was scared every time he stepped on the floor until I knew his foot was gonna be sound.

Jerry Reinsdorf: One game Albeck played Michael longer than seven minutes a half. I told Krause to tell him not to do that again. Stan told us what he thought of that. The next game was at Indiana, and with 25 or 30 seconds to go, the Bulls were down by a point. Just then Michael reached the seven minute mark, and Stan pulled him from the game. He pulled him just to show us how ridiculous he thought the seven minutes were, how arbitrary it was. We still won the game on a jump shot by a little guy named Johnny Paxson. But I was really angry because Stan had made us look bad. I thought he could have managed Michael's minutes better.

Mark Pfeil: The one thing I could never understand, how could Michael practice for two hours, yet he couldn't play but 14 minutes?

John Paxson: It was very hard for Michael to understand where the franchise was coming from. They wanted to be careful bringing their young superstar along. But, from a head coach's perspective, Stan wanted to win games, too. That could mean your job, and Stan was in the position where he had to win and that made it a very uncomfortable situation.

Jerry Krause: When Michael got hurt, Stan reacted in a way that I wasn't happy with at all. Stan basically got very selfish. He didn't back Jerry and me at all. Michael really liked him, and Stan could have stood up with us and agreed with the doctors who said Michael was not ready to play.

The night in Indiana was the turning point in getting Stan fired. That one single night had as much to do with it as anything. Jerry looked at me and said, "That's your coach." I said, "No, that's our ex-coach."

With Jordan back in the lineup, the Bulls went 6-7 over their last 13 games and despite a 30-52 finish somehow made the playoffs with a late-season win over Washington.

Jerry Reinsdorf: Michael's minutes increased after it became obvious we could make the playoffs. Finally, Krause went down at halftime of a game late in the season and told the trainer to tell Stan to play Michael as many minutes as he wanted. I shouldn't have let him play at all that year. It was wrong.

In the first round of the playoffs, the Bulls encountered the Boston Celtics, who were on their way to their sixteenth world championship. Boston swept Chicago, but not before Michael set the NBA abuzz with a 63-point performance in a double-overtime loss on April 20 in Boston Garden. "That's God disguised as Michael Jordan," Larry Bird said afterward.

Sidney Green: We made the playoffs, and we made room for Michael, who came back and scored his fabulous 63 points against Boston.

That was something I'll never forget. It was marvelous. I know Michael. He's the type of guy who loves for people to think that he can't do something. And that just added more fuel to his fire, to prove not only to himself but to prove to everybody else that he could play injured and that he was ready to play.

It was total silence in the locker room before the game. Michael was extremely focused, and we knew he was intent on doing something big.

Jerry Reinsdorf: That game was when we began to realize just how great Michael could be.

In May, the Bulls fired Stan Albeck and hired Doug Collins.

Jerry Krause: We were fooling around, trying to work things out with the Spurs. San Antonio owed us a hundred thousand dollars from the Artis Gilmore/ George Gervin deal. One day I phoned the Spurs and said, "You know the hundred thousand that you owe us? Keep it, and give me John Paxson." They said, "Done."

For years after that, we kept bringing in guards trying to replace him, and every year he just kept beating them out.

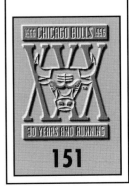

Jordan was maginficent in the 1986 playoffs against the Celtics. He scored 63 points, the NBA playoff single-game record, although the Bulls fell 3-0 in the series. The performance, says Bulls owner Jerry Reinsdorf, was the first big indication that Jordan's talent was overpowering.

153

Starting The Fire, 1986-87

J ERRY KRAUSE MADE A FLURRY OF decisions during his 1986 makeover of the team. First was the hiring of 35-year-old Doug Collins and assistants Johnny Bach and Gene Littles. Then Krause got back to reworking the roster. Out went David Greenwood, Orlando Woolridge, Jawann Oldham, and Sidney Green. In their place, Krause began stockpiling draft picks and cash. For 1987 alone, he squirreled away three first-round picks. But the Bulls suddenly had only one player on the roster who averaged better than 10 points a game, and that player was coming off a major foot injury. Collins, the media, the public, the players—all called for Krause to bring in scorers. Sacramento's Eddie Johnson and Golden State's Joe Barry Carroll were mentioned. But Krause elected not to move, which led to a round of preseason predictions that the Bulls would struggle to win 30 games.

Who was going to score? observers asked.

Michael Jordan gave the first big clue to that in the opening contest against the Knicks in Madison Square Garden. The Bulls' starting

lineup included Earl Cureton and Charles Oakley at forward, Granville Waiters at center and Steve Colter in the backcourt with Jordan. The Knicks, with Twin Towers Patrick Ewing and Bill Cartwright, were in control with a five-point lead midway through the fourth quarter when Jordan looked at Collins and said, "Coach, I'm not gonna let you lose your first game."

He then scored the Bulls' last 18 points to finish with 50 and give Collins the win, 108-103. It was the most points ever scored by an opponent in the Garden, erasing the 44-point mark shared by Rick Barry and former Bull Quintin Dailey.

"I've never seen anything like Michael Jordan. Ever. Ever. Never," Collins said after hugging each of his players. Yet, as the coming months would reveal, the Air Show was just getting started.

Jerry Reinsdorf: I remember the first game that Doug coached, we beat the Knicks in the Garden. The excitement that came to the club from winning the opening game of the season, that was a turning point. That was the year things started to build, and Michael was unbelievable.

Michael Jordan: When I first came here, I had to be the igniter, to get the fire going. So a lot of my individual skills had to come out.

Twenty-eight times that season, Michael scored better than 40 points. Six times, he ran up better than 50. Over late November and early December, he scored more than 40 in nine straight games, six of them coming on a western road trip.

January and February brought another flurry of big nights, prompting fans to cast a record-setting 1.41 million All-Star votes for a player sportswriters had begun calling "His Royal Airness." "I think it's great the fans admire my style so much," Jordan said. "I'm not going to do anything to disappoint them."

At the 1987 All-Star festivities in Seattle, he claimed the $12,000 prize in the Slam Dunk contest, and upon his return to Chicago promptly split it into twelve $1,000 shares for his teammates. Then he resumed his assault on

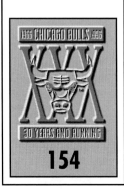

Brad Sellars.

155

With Jordan in town, the Luv-A-Bulls weren't the only attraction at the Stadium.

the league's rims and records. In late February, he scored 58 against the Nets, breaking Chet Walker's old Bulls regular-season, single-game scoring record of 57. A few days later, despite a painful corn on his left foot, he blasted the Pistons for 61 in an overtime win before 30,281 screaming fans at the Pontiac Silverdome. Down the stretch, Jordan and Isiah Thomas and Adrian Dantley of the Pistons swapped baskets furiously.

Michael Jordan: Isiah's play at that time pumped me up to another level. He was making great shots and then I'd come down and make a great shot. It was great entertainment for the fans and great basketball.

John Paxson: I don't know how he did it. Every night someone else was standing in his face, and he never took a step back.

March brought another scoring outburst, including a streak of five 40-plus games. In April, he had an opportunity to become the first and only player since Wilt Chamberlain in 1962-63 to score better than 3,000 points in a season. (Chamberlain had done it twice.) Jordan scored 53 against Indiana, 50 against

Corzine was workmanlike in the post.

Oakley was a jump shooter.

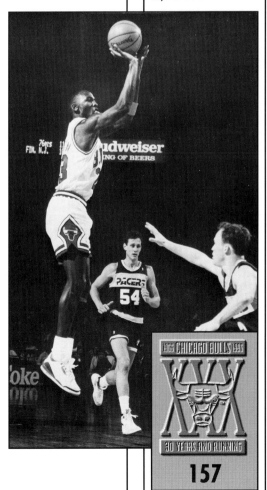

Jordan's performances were beyond All-Star.

Milwaukee and 61 against Atlanta in the Stadium to finish with 3,041 and a league-best 37.1 scoring average. He also set Bulls records in six different single-season categories, all enough to drive Doug Collins first team to a 40-42 record and another first-round playoff meeting with the Celtics. Bird and Boston, however, swept the series in three and taught the Bulls a primary lesson—that team strength could easily outshine a one-man show.

"I think he is by far the most exciting player I've ever seen," said Boston guard Danny Ainge. "He's a guy whose highlight films you most want to watch. But I don't know how much fun he'd be to play with."

Players around the league seemed to concur. Jordan was a great show, but that didn't seem to be driving the Bulls any closer to a championship. "When Michael's average drops to 25, 28 points," said Lakers coach Pat Riley, "the Bulls will have a better team."

The performances, however, earned Jordan the first of seven straight All-NBA first team distinctions. Yet for some reason he was left off the league's All-Defensive team, despite the fact that he became the first player in league history to record 200 steals and 100 blocks in a season.

In the frontcourt, Charles Oakley averaged 13.1 rebounds and pulled down more boards than any other player in the league.

This newfound success brought an unprecedented cash flow for the Bulls, as the franchise broke all attendance records with an average of 15,871 a night.

Jordan, meanwhile, was laboring under a contract that paid him only $710,000 a year, far below what other stars in the league earned. Business, though, was booming for his Air Jordan line, with 2.5 million pairs sold for a gross of nearly $150 million.

Doug Collins.

Cheryl Raye: It was very uncomfortable because Collins was a broadcaster. Stan Albeck would look over his shoulder, and there was Doug Collins. He served as a consultant briefly, and there was speculation that Collins was taking Stan's job.

Jerry Krause: When I hired Doug, everybody laughed at me. A lot of people said, "What the f—- are you doing hiring a TV guy?"

Doug Collins: At the time, I was 35, and there had been nine coaches in 10 years in Chicago. I was the kind of guy to roll up my sleeves and make something happen.

Michael Jordan: When I first met Doug, I didn't think he knew what he was talking about. I wondered when he first got the job. I mean, he was so young. But once I got to know him, I liked him a lot. He was bright, he was in control, and most of all, he was positive.

Johnny Bach: I had coached him at the Olympics in 1972 and we had a good friend-ship and respect for each other. Doug called me and said, "I'd like you to come here and join the staff."

It was a pleasure to go with Paul Douglas Collins. He was emotional and exciting, fired-up. He really started this franchise, the Bulls, to winning again.

John Paxson: Doug was a perfect coach for our team when he got the job because we needed some young, aggressive guy that you could feed off of. He was energetic, and a lot of games we fed off of his energy. Michael was in the early stages of his career and athletically could do some amazing things, but Doug got us going. He was very active, very vocal up and down the side-

Profile/Doug Collins

DOUG COLLINS WAS A CBS *broadcaster when the Bulls hired him as their coach in 1986. He had no coaching experience whatsoever. But he had been a player. A star at Illinois State, he was the top pick of the 1973 draft and had played a pivotal role on the ill-fated 1972 U.S. Olympic team that lost a controversial last-second decision to the Russians. Selected by the Philadelphia 76ers, Collins helped that club climb out of the wreckage of its disas-trous 1973 season into championship contention by 1977. A 20-points-per-game scorer in his best seasons, Collins ultimately fell victim to the injuries that prematurely ended his career.*

lines, and at that time that was what we needed.

Cheryl Raye: He was good with the television media. They loved him. He was very accessible to them.

Doug was screaming and yelling and jumping and throwing… . He definitely was demonstrative in his actions, and the guys who were key to this team were extremely young. Horace and Scottie, they hated him.

He was growing up with them. He was new to the job. Here's a guy who came from the television booth. He was learning the process, too.

John Ligmanowski: Doug was such an intense guy. It was almost like he wanted to be in the game. He'd come downstairs soaked in sweat, totally drained after a game. It was fun because we were just really

starting to get good. The team had come around.

Mark Pfeil: Doug was a great guy. He was interested in everything about people. He cared about them.

Jerry Reinsdorf: Doug Collins played a great role in the development of this franchise. He was a great part in our ultimately winning the championship. He came here and took a team that had been losing and instilled in them a desire to win. He taught them how to win. So Doug Collins was the right guy at that particular time. I'm not sure that Phil Jackson would have been as good, or would have won as fast if he had come instead of Doug at that time.

In 1987-88, Collins led the Bulls to their first 50-win season in 13 years.

Collins gave the Bulls just the enthusiasm they needed.

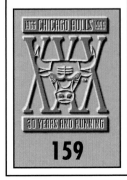

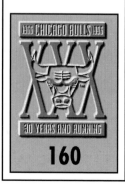

Krause worked the phones all night before the '87 draft to get Pippen and Grant. Assistant Billy McKinney is in the background.

Move/Drafting Scottie and Horace

*J*ERRY KRAUSE SCRAMBLED TO GET INTO *position to select Scottie Pippen and Horace Grant in the 1987 NBA draft. Once the two rookies were secured for Chicago, people across the organization began to sense that the Bulls were about to undergo dramatic change.*

Jerry Krause: Late in the season I got a call from Marty Blake [*the NBA's director of scouting*], and he said, "There's a kid named Pippen in a little small school in Arkansas that's gonna play on a Monday night, and there's gonna be a bunch of scouts down there. You ought to go take a look at him." So I sent Billy McKinney, my assistant at that time, down there. Billy comes back the next day and says he couldn't tell anything about him because the competition was so poor. So I said, "Tell me about him." He said, "Well, he's got long arms, he's a good athlete, but it's really hard to tell." I called the coach down there and had him send me some tapes, but we didn't get a chance to look at them before we went to the pre-draft camp at Portsmouth.

On the second night at Portsmouth, the players come out to warm up and I look out and say, "Billy, that's Pippen right there." He said, "How'd you know?" I said, "You

told me he had long arms. That guy's arms are longer than any I've ever seen." We watched him, and I just got excited. I just got really shook up bad, so shook up that I left Portsmouth a day early just so other people wouldn't know that I was interested.

Then Pippen got invited to the pre-draft deal in Hawaii. He plays very well there and very well at the pre-draft camp in Chicago. I knew through my sources that Sacramento was seriously considering taking him with the sixth pick. We were picking eighth, and I knew we wouldn't be able to get Pippen there. So we began trying to move up past Sacramento.

At 4:00 to 4:30 in the morning before the draft, I had a long conversation with Seattle's Bob Whitsitt. We agreed to switch our eighth pick for their fifth, if the player they wanted wasn't available when their fifth pick came around. Whitsitt wouldn't tell me who that player was, and I wouldn't tell him the player I wanted at five. In return for trading picks with us, he would have the right to switch again during the next two years, plus we gave him a second-round pick.

I still wasn't sure, so I got on the phone with the Clippers, who were picking fourth. The Clippers finally told us right before their pick that they were taking Reggie Williams. I then told Whitsitt that they were taking Reggie Williams. He said, "OK, our deal is on. Who do you want me to take for you?" The Sonics had wanted Reggie Williams. I said, "Take Pippen for me." They do, and then we take Olden Polynice for them. The minute both picks were made we called the league to announce the trade.

The Grant pick has been widely reported wrong. We saw Horace during the season that year. We weren't really enthused about him one way or another. He was a good player, but we weren't nuts about him. Doug Collins asked me to bring him in for a workout. Doug had watched a tape of him and wanted to bring him in. We thought he was going to go fairly high. I saw him at the All-Star game in New Orleans, and he played better there than he had during the year.

We brought him in for a workout, and that changed my mind to a certain extent. I liked North Carolina's Joe Wolf, and I didn't think that Horace would be there available for us when we picked tenth. But he fell to tenth and I had to make up my mind between him and Wolf. We had five minutes. The coaches were very interested in me taking Horace. I walked outside the draft room, and Reinsdorf walked out of the room with me. He put his arm around me and said, "Go with your guts. Your guts have gotten us where we are, and we trust your guts. Go with them." I walked around about a minute or two longer and went back in and said, "We're going to take Horace." I based it on Horace being the better athlete.

The next day, Dean Smith called me from Carolina and said, "How could you do this?" Dean just ripped me. And Michael, who always loves Carolina players, says, "How could you be that damn dumb? To take Horace Grant over Joe Wolf?"

When they got here as rookies, I used to call Scottie and Horace "Frick and Frack," like the old Siamese twins, because they were never separated. The two of them went everywhere together.

Jerry Reinsdorf: That night, when the draft was over, we were in the conference room in the old Bulls office with the coaching staff. There were a lot of high fives going around that night because we really felt that we had pulled a coup. And I think that draft won Jerry the NBA Executive of the Year Award.

Cheryl Raye: We went with the other general managers to watch Scottie work out at the University of Illinois-Chicago during the Chicago pre-draft camp. It was unbelievable. This guy was just explosive. Scottie jumped higher than everybody. He was big, much bigger than we thought he'd be. You knew he was something special.

They were making so many moves to turn this team around. And then to get Horace.... The two of them came to Chicago the next day and went to a White Sox game. They were sitting in the dugout

with their Bulls caps on. They forged a friendship immediately. I mean it was instantaneous that they became friends. From that point on, you could see that those two had bonded. And it translated onto the court because they felt really good about each other. They both had a lot of maturing to do. Scottie had it the most difficult coming from an NAIA school. Not being used to ever having media around, it was quite a shock for him. Also coming from Central Arkansas into Chicago, it was overwhelming. But when the Bulls got those two, you knew this team was going in a wonderful direction.

Grant and Pippen were a major draft coup.

Few had heard of the lanky Pippen.

Given time, Pippen and Grant would develop into what assistant coach Johnny Bach called the "Dobermans," the athletic attack players in the Bulls' pressure, trapping defense.

Johnny Bach: Doug brought them to a level of competing hard every night. He drove them. He emotionally got involved with them and got them to understand how important each game and practice was, and he drove them. Some people lead young players; he drove them.

Sellars, Grant and Jordan.

Grant hits a jumper

Getting There, 1987-88

IN THE THREE SEASONS SINCE JORDAN'S arrival, the value of the Bulls' franchise had more than tripled and was growing with each tipoff. Reinsdorf was so pleased with these developments that he extended Doug Collins' year-old contract and began plans to give Michael Jordan a new, extended deal.

With the increased popularity and cash flow came a new atmosphere of confidence around the team. "We've reached a respect factor in this city," Collins told reporters. "We're no longer considered the Bad News Bulls."

Yet there was little argument that the team still faced major challenges. To plug their perenniel hole in the middle, the Bulls brought back 38-year-old Artis Gilmore to share center duties with Dave Corzine. Oakley was well-established at power forward, but he continued to call for more opportunities to get the ball in Collins' play-oriented offense. The coach seemed to agree with him. "We have to get to the point where Michael Jordan is not the sole source of energy on this team," Collins said.

There were hopes that the two rookies—Scottie Pippen and Horace Grant—could contribute, and that the veterans had gained from another year's experience playing with Michael. "We have not proven anything yet," Collins told reporters. "Last year we were overachievers that played on emotion. Oakley's rebounding, Jordan's scoring, Paxson's steadiness, Corzine's toughness—all fell into place and allowed us to be average."

Just as they finally seemed to concentrate on getting better, yet another storm appeared on the horizon. In late October, the hypercompetitive Jordan angrily stalked out of practice after accusing Collins of doctoring the score of a scrimmage. The incident made headlines in Chicago and left in its wake a stony silence between the young coach and his star.

"He has his pride; I have mine," Jordan told reporters. "We're two adults. In due time, words will be said. I'm not going to rush the situation." The team issued Jordan a light fine, but the task of re-establishing relations with the superstar was left to Collins.

John Paxson: Doug knew he had to kiss and make up, and that's what he did. He had to calm his superstar. That was a little test he had. Had another player done that, you don't know what would have happened because guys just don't walk out of practice. Just don't take off.

Some observers questioned if Collins hadn't lost some respect and undermined his authority by seeking the soothe Jordan's anger.

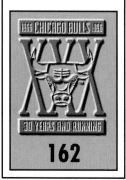

SCOTTIE PIPPEN

John Paxson: It's got to be very difficult as a head coach to have a relationship with Michael and try to have that same type of relationship with other players. You just can't do it. You have to give Michael leeway. On the floor you can't be as critical of him as you can with other players because of what he can do and what he means. As a head coach you're walking a fine line with Michael Jordan. Not that he would ever do anything like that, but we all knew about the situation with Magic Johnson and Paul Westhead at the Lakers, when Westhead got fired after disagreeing with Magic. That's the power Michael could have wielded if he chose to. So Doug was walking a fine line. Early in Doug's career he handled it the best way he knew how.

Even though he had been rewarded with a contract extension, some observers saw signs that the pressure of trying to mold the Bulls into a winner was taking its toll on Collins.

Another key addition during the 1987 offseason was the hiring of assistant coach Phil Jackson, another Krause protege. Jackson had spent 11 of his 13 seasons as an NBA player with the New York Knicks. His hiring meant that Jerry Reinsdorf now had a Red Holtzman disciple on the payroll.

The opening night lineup in 1987 featured Brad Sellers, the Bulls' first-round pick in 1986, at small forward, with Gilmore at center and Oakley at power forward. Jordan and Paxson were the guards. Management had planned for Jordan to play fewer minutes and to share the responsibility with his teammates, but just the opposite happened. Collins continued to run a large number of isolation plays for Jordan and to rely on him heavily. The reasoning was simple: They needed him.

Chicago ran off to a 10-3 start, which earned Collins coach-of-the-month honors for November. A five-game losing streak in late December dipped them back toward .500, and the hopes for Gilmore soon vanished. The team released him before Christmas. But the Bulls zoomed off again from there on their way to a 50-32 record.

Pippen got his baptism in the '88 playoffs.

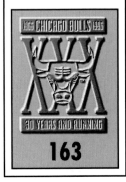

163

Phil Jackson: Red Holtzman had a saying, that the difference between superstars and great players is that a superstar makes everybody on his team a better player.

I told Michael about it, and Michael thanked me for it. That was one of the most amazing things, that he took it. And that's one of the best things about Michael Jordan. He's a very coachable player.

The Bulls paused long enough in their progress to host the All-Star game in February, where Jordan claimed his second Slam Dunk title in a narrow win over Atlanta's Dominique Wilkins, which was accomplished with a perfect 50 score on Jordan's final dunk. Some observers smelled a little Chicago home cooking, but Air Jordan fans were pleased with the outcome. Michael again planned to share the $12,500 prize with his teammates.

Michael Jordan: I did it because my teammates had been so understanding. There was a lack of animosity over all of the attention I got, and they had all been very caring. They had worked so hard, and I had gotten all of the publicity and credit.

The next night Jordan scored 40 points to earn the MVP honors in the All-Star Game, and the media took note that Detroit's Isiah Thomas fell all over himself getting Jordan assists. In fact, the last points came on an alley-oop slam dunk from Isiah to Michael, after which they paused and pointed at each other. It would be perhaps the last sign of peace before the coming storm.

The Bulls' haul of honors continued right into the postseason. Jordan again led the league in scoring, this time with a 35.0 average, and for the first time he was named the NBA's MVP. "It's a thrill," he said. His 3.2 steals per game also led the league, and he was named Defensive Player of the Year and a member of the All-Defensive team.

Krause, meanwhile, was named Executive of the Year, and Oakley again pulled down more rebounds than any player in the league with 1,066.

The biggest prize, though, was the Bulls' first playoff series win since 1981, a 3-2 defeat of the Cleveland Cavaliers. In the decisive fifth game, Collins decided to give Pippen his first-ever career start. Pippen replaced the ineffective Sellers and scored 24 points. Krause was overcome afterward. "This is a baby from Conway, Arkansas, upon whom we've put tremendous pressure," he told reporters.

"When I played against Scottie last summer, I could see he had the skills," Jordan said. "It was just a matter of, how do you get them out of him in a season? It took 82 games for him to do it, but he's done it. And I think it's going to help him for the rest of his career."

To celebrate, the Bulls donned T-shirts that said, "How do you like us now?"

"We're ready for the next round!" Jordan had announced after the victory. At first, it seemed they were. They claimed the second game at the Pontiace Silverdome in their seven-game series with the Detroit Pistons, and suddenly the Bulls had the homecourt advantage. But from there the Pistons zeroed their double- and triple-teaming defense on Jordan and forced him to pass. They also resorted to their Bad Boy tactics. In Game 3, a 101-79 Piston blowout in the Stadium, Jordan and Detroit center Bill Laimbeer scuffled. "I set a pick," Laimbeer said. "I guess he wasn't looking."

Detroit then took Game 4 and was in control in Game 5 when Jordan hit Isiah Thomas in the face with an elbow and sent him to the locker room. The blow knocked Thomas unconscious, but he returned later in the game to make sure the Pistons advanced, 4-1.

Michael Jordan: During those playoffs the other teams dedicated themselves more to stopping me. And doing that exposed certain weaknesses on our team.

Most of all, the Bulls needed a center, somebody to play tough in the middle. Shortly after the season ended, Jerry Krause went shopping for one.

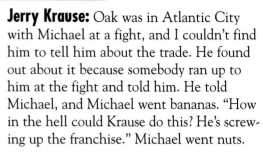

Giving up Oakley was a tough choice for Krause.

Move/Trading Oak for Teach

*J*UST BEFORE THE 1988 DRAFT, THE BULLS *traded forward Charles Oakley to New York for center Bill Cartwright. The move created yet another stir among Bulls players and fans, because Oakley had established a reputation as a strong rebounder, and Cartwright, a 7-foot-1 post-up center, had been plagued by foot injuries and was thought to be near the end of his career. Several days later, the Bulls drafted Vanderbilt center Will Purdue in the first round as a backup.*

Johnny Bach: Charles was strong and tough and mean. He was the hardest trade that we had to do because Jerry Krause not only loved him as a player, but I think he had a great affection for him as a person. And, to give him up and get Cartwright was almost against the grain. But the coaches really believed we couldn't win without Bill Cartwright, so we made the trade.

Jerry Krause: Oak was in Atlantic City with Michael at a fight, and I couldn't find him to tell him about the trade. He found out about it because somebody ran up to him at the fight and told him. He told Michael, and Michael went bananas. "How in the hell could Krause do this? He's screwing up the franchise." Michael went nuts.

Michael Jordan: I didn't find out about it until Oakley told me during the fight between Mike Tyson and Michael Spinks. We were in Atlantic City watching the fight. I was pretty upset about the deal and also to have to find out about it that way.

Johnny Bach: It was traumatic for the team, but I think it just took us the next step up. Our defense was anchored by a real professional. Bill was good in the locker room. He was good in practice, and he earned the respect of the team because he could play Patrick Ewing straight up. We didn't have to double Patrick Ewing. And that gave us a great deal of confidence.

What made the trade so tough was that Michael looked at Oakley as a protector. Charles was ready to fly into any tangle. You hit Michael, you had to face Charles. But Bill, in his own way, toughened up the big guys we had, and, in his own quiet way, Bill became very much of a terminator. Things stopped at the basket.

Jerry Reinsdorf: We knew we couldn't win without a dominant defensive center. I didn't care about offense. We needed a defender. We needed a guy who could clog the middle, and we weren't going to win without one. We also knew that Horace Grant was coming on and thought that he'd be a better player than Oakley anyway.

With Grant at forward, our team was built around a quick defense. Johnny Bach called them the Dobermans. With Grant, we could keep on pressing and pressuring the ball, which we couldn't do with Oakley.

Tex Winter: It was a big gamble for this franchise. A huge gamble. We were giving up a young guy for an old guy, but we felt like we needed to start with a good post-up center, particularly someone that could anchor our defense.

$5.00

1988/89 YEARBOOK

The First Run, 1988-89

SPURRED BY THE JORDAN PHENOMENON, the Bulls experienced unprecedented financial growth with each season in the late 1980s.

Steve Schanwald: In the 1986-87 season, which was Michael's third year, we had 4,800 season ticket holders. By the start of the 1987-88 season, that number had jumped to 11,200 season ticket holders, due largely to Jordan, the Pippen/Grant draft and the fact that we held the 1987 All-Star game in Chicago. By the 1988-89 season we capped our season ticket sales at 13,000. The summer of 1988 was really the last opportunity anyone had in Chicago to get Bulls season tickets. Since November of 1987 we've sold out the last 387 consecutive games with and without Michael. Roughly from 1989 to the present, the Bulls have been ranked number one in sales of NBA licensed merchandise. To put that in proper perspective, about 40 percent of all NBA licensed merchandise sold was Bulls-related.

The team rewarded Jordan with a contract extension in September 1988 worth a reported $25 million over eight years. A short time later, Reinsdorf also extended Jerry Krause's contract.

This financial success did little, however, to alleviate Jordan's frustration over the team's seeming inability to compete for a championship. Writers and reporters often compared Jordan to Larry Bird and Magic Johnson by pointing out that Bird and Johnson were the type of players to make their teammates better while Jordan often seemed to be playing for himself. This criticism infuriated Jordan, and the trade for Cartwright only deepened his anger because he thought the team had been weakened.

Michael Jordan: At the beginning of the year it was frustrating and hard to accept. Things were not going well, and it was getting to me. I had very high expectations, just like everyone, but there was a transition period we had to go through.

The season opened with Cartwright at center, Sellers and Grant at forwards and Jordan in the backcourt with Sam Vincent, who had come to Chicago from Seattle in a trade for Sedale

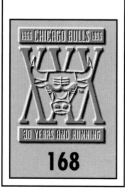

John Ligmanowski: When Michael hit that shot against Cleveland, that was where we kind of made it over the hump, because they had beaten us like six straight times that season during the regular season. Then we beat 'em in the playoffs. I don't think Cleveland ever got over that.

Threatt. On opening night, the Bulls got shoved around in the Stadium by the Pistons. The tension built from there. Jordan again scored at a league-leading clip, but by January the club still struggled to stay above .500.

Discord on the coaching staff mounted until Collins blocked Tex Winter from coming to practice.

Phil Jackson: Tex was basically out of the picture at that time. He did some scouting for Jerry Krause and took some road trips. He didn't go on all of our game trips. When he was with us, he sat in a corner and kept notes on practice and didn't participate in the coaching. He was out of it.

Jerry Krause: I was upset because Doug basically wasn't listening to Tex, and he wasn't listening to Phil Jackson. Doug did a great job for us for a couple or years. He took the heat off me from a public relations standpoint. Doug was great with the media. But he learned to coach on the fly, and he didn't listen to his assistants as much as he should have. Doug had a thing with Phil, too. As time went on, he was like Stan in that he got away from what we wanted to do.

By January, the team had begun a turnaround with a series of winning streaks. A big factor in the change was the improvement of Pippen and Grant.

Will Perdue: I think Michael saw what kind of players Scottie and Horace could be, and he was very difficult on them at that time. Yet at the same time he was supportive. I mean he wasn't negative to the point that it drove them out of the game, or drove them to become not as good as they are. He did it in a positive way, but at the same time he was challenging them to see if they would answer the challenge.

By March, Vincent had become the latest point guard to displease Collins. He was benched, and Jordan made an unprecedented move to the point while newly acquired Craig Hodges stepped in at shooting guard. "It'll be interesting to see how Michael likes it," Collins said. Jordan responded by turning in seven straight triple-doubles, and the Bulls went on a six-game winning streak. But that was followed by

The Pistons' game was intimidation.

a six-game losing streak, and the team's management worried that Collins, who had placed more of a burden on Jordan, might just wear the superstar out. They finished the schedule at 47-35 for fifth place in the conference.

Once again, Cleveland was the first-round opponent, but this time the Cavaliers had the home-court advantage. The Bulls took a 2-1 series lead and had a chance to close it out in the Stadium in Game 4. But, despite scoring 50 points, Jordan missed a key late free throw and the Cavaliers evened the series in overtime.

Game 5 in Cleveland produced an incredibly tight fourth quarter. There were six lead changes in the final three minutes. Craig Ehlo scored for Cleveland and seemed to give them a 100-99 victory with just seconds left. But Jordan got one final shot, for which the videotape has been replayed thousands of times. With Ehlo draped on him, Jordan put up a spinning, double-clutch jumper as time expired to break the Cavaliers' hearts, 101-100.

"I saw him go up," said Cleveland center Brad Daugherty, "and I turned to box out, to look for the flight of the ball. I didn't see it, because Michael pumped, then brought it down. Then he went back up and hit the bottom of the net. I still don't know how he fit all of that into three seconds."

The dominant image from the videoclip was Jordan's fist-pumping celebration as he was mobbed by teammates.

The energy of that win carried over into the second round, where the Bulls dispatched the Knicks in six games as Jordan averaged 35 points despite playing with an aggravated groin injury. For the first time since their ill-fated 1975 loss, the Bulls returned to the conference finals. Once again, they faced the Pistons, known around the league as the "Bad Boys," and once again, the rivalry hit new lows. In an April game, Isiah Thomas had slugged Bill Cartwright and been suspended for two games. Hanging over the series was the air of that tussle and the 1988 fight in which Detroit's Rick Mahorn had thrown Collins over the scorer's table.

Jordan broke loose against Detroit in the '89 Eastern Finals, giving the Pistons their only two losses of the playoffs on their way to the league title.

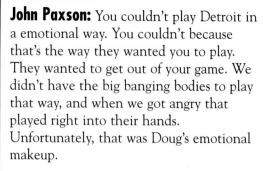

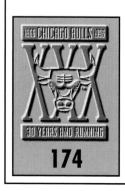

Stacey King, a first round pick in '89, faces down the Palace crowd.

John Paxson: You couldn't play Detroit in a emotional way. You couldn't because that's the way they wanted you to play. They wanted to get out of your game. We didn't have the big banging bodies to play that way, and when we got angry that played right into their hands. Unfortunately, that was Doug's emotional makeup.

Our crowd would play into that whole thing, too. And it never worked to our advantage. The Pistons were so antagonistic that it was just hard to maintain that control. It turned out to be a terrific rivalry for us, once we learned how to beat them. But for a while it looked like we were never going to get past them.

With Jordan at point guard, the Bulls surprised the Pistons in Game 1 at the Palace of Auburn Hills. The loss ended Detroit's 25-game home-court winning streak and nine-game playoff winning streak. It also marked the first time in nine games that the Bulls had beaten the Pistons.

The Pistons won Game 2 at home, but Chicago fought back for a 2-1 lead when the series returned to the Stadium. But the Pistons stepped up their intimidation in Game 4 and covered Jordan so closely that he took only eight shots. Detroit won in Chicago, then went on to finish the series, 4-2. Piston center Bill Laimbeer infuriated the Stadium crowds with his rough treatment of Pippen, leading Bulls fans to chant over and over, "Laim-beer sucks!"

John Paxson: I never played with Bill at Notre Dame. He graduated in May of '79, and I entered in September. I tried early in my career to talk to Bill Laimbeer. But he never wanted to talk, never wanted to acknowledge the Notre Dame connection. I tried one or two times early on in my career and I never tried again after that. I guess there are some nice qualities about him, but I don't know what they are.

Jerry Krause: I would have killed to have Laimbeer on my team.

Mark Pfeil: The Bulls always seemed a little intimidated by the Pistons, except for Michael. And he was always trying to get it across to the guys that this is the team we have to bridge ourselves over to get to the next level. Sometimes it took some yelling to get his point across. But against the Pistons, I think that's when Michael started stepping up as a leader.

But in the backs of their minds, our guys were always thinking that something dirty would happen against the Pistons. Detroit would intimidate you every time they came in your building. We had a big fight with them one time. There was a tussle in front of our bench, and Doug Collins tried to grab Ricky Mahorn. Hell, Ricky threw Doug down twice. Threw him down on the floor. Doug jumped back up, and Ricky threw him over the scorer's table. Those were the things that always stood out in our minds. The Pistons were constantly doing those kinds of things. They just constantly beat and battered you.

Move/Releasing Doug Collins

ON JULY 6, 1989, JERRY REINSDORF AND Jerry Krause abruptly released Doug Collins, citing the management's "philosphical differences" with the coach. The move surprised and outraged many of the team's fans and led to a round of gossip and media speculation about why Collins had been let go.

Cheryl Raye: Most of the local media weren't too surprised that Doug was fired. There was a lot of anger by the fans. They didn't understand it. The Bulls had gone to Cleveland and won that series, and everybody thought, "Gosh, Cleveland should have won."

The fans reacted bad, but there was so much tension, there was tension amongst the players; there was tension between Doug and management, it didn't seem like it was gonna be long-term.

Jerry Krause: Doug was extremely popular with the media. Everybody loved him except me. We were in the Eastern Finals against Detroit when I said to Jerry, "I want to let Doug go." Most owners would have said, "Wait a minute. You brought him in here. He's your creation. He's just won 50 games and got us to the Eastern Finals." Jerry didn't say that. He said, "Why?" And I told him I didn't think we could win the world championship this way, and I thought this was a club that could win the world championship. That's the only reason we let Doug Collins go.

Everybody with a typewriter castrated me. "That dumb little sonofabitch," they said. "He went and did it again."

Jerry said, "I'll back you totally. We'll co-fire him. I don't want all the heat on you." And in the end, the owner has to go along with you. No general manager, no matter how strong he is, can fire the head coach without the owner's approval.

When I first told Jerry, he said, "Who do you want to coach the team?" I said, "I don't want to make that decision until we decide that we're going to let Doug go. Let's decide Doug's merits first." So we did that. After that, I said, "I want to hire Phil Jackson." I'd brought Phil on two years earlier as assistant coach. Jerry said, "Fine."

We brought Doug into the office, and I think Doug thought he was going to talk about a contract extension. He had his agent with him. Jerry said, "Doug, we're going to have to let you go." The look on his face was shocking. We had our conversation with him, and I called Phil, who was fishing out in Montana. I told him, "I just let Doug go." He said, "What!?!?" And I said, "Doug's gone, and I want you to be the head coach. You need to get your ass in here on a flight today. Soon as you can. I got to talk to you."

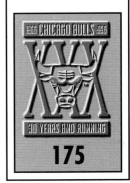

175

To replace Collins, Krause turned to assistant Phil Jackson.

I brought Phil in and we talked philosophy. The first thing he said was, "I've always been a defensive oriented guy, as a player with Red Holtzman, and as a coach. That's what you want me for?" I said, "Yeah." He said, "I'm going to turn the offense over to Tex, and I'm going to run the triple-post."

I think a some people who know me thought that I had set that all up, that I'd brought Phil in because he'd run Tex's stuff. I wish I'd been that smart, but I wasn't. It was all his idea. But I said, "Great. That's super." Because I knew the damn stuff would work. But I couldn't impose that on

Doug. I would never impose what a coach runs on them anyway.

Jerry Reinsdorf: I made the decision to fire Doug Collins in large part because I thought it was the best thing for Doug Collins. And I thought it was the right decision for the Chicago Bulls. I knew it was the right decision for Doug Collins. I have a very strong attachment, personally, to Doug Collins. I really like him as a person, I think he's brilliant, but he's driven, maybe to the detriment of his own benefit, overly driven, and I wanted to remove him from a situation where I thought he was

going to grind himself up.

Mark Pfeil: Doug didn't get along with Jerry Krause, and on a day-to-day basis, that began to grind on us.

Jerry Krause: Basically "philosophical differences" meant that I felt we lacked a system. It got to be a play-of-the-day thing with Doug. There wasn't a fundamental way we were playing. Collins would see a play that Boston or somebody ran, and he'd add that to our playbook all the time.

Phil Jackson: Doug had a lot of plays. There were 40 or 50 plays we ran. We had a lot of options off of plays. We had five or six different offensive sets. You see that with a lot of teams. But that's not where I came from as a basketball coach, and that's not where Tex was philosophically. We believed in Tex's organized system.

Doug's a very emotional guy. He throws his heart into it, and from that standpoint he was very good for this basketball club. He was good at getting them directed to play with intensity and emotion. Then there came a level where they had to learn poise and control.

In a prepared statement, Collins responded to his release: "When hired three years ago, I willingly accepted the challenge of leading the Bulls back to the type of team this city richly deserves. I'm proud of the fact that each year the team has taken another step towards an NBA championship, and played with intense pride and determination. Words will not describe the void I feel not being a part of Chicago Stadium and this great team."

John Paxson: Everybody liked Doug. The thing about it was, we had just come off of getting the conference finals, of taking Detroit to six games. Our future was out there. The coach who had spent three years helping us do that was gone. That's where you give Jerry Reinsdorf and Jerry Krause credit. They truly believed that Doug had been good for that team to a certain point, but that there had to be a different type coach to get us to the next level.

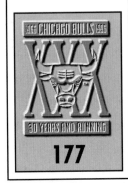

Jackson was somehow less frenetic than Collins.

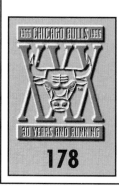

Profile/The Maverick

T he son of a Pentecostal preacher, Phil Jackson was raised in Montana. By the end of high school, he longed for relief from his strict upbringing. He found escape in an athletic scholarship at the University of North Dakota, where he played basketball for an engaging young coach named Bill Fitch. The 6-foot-8 Jackson developed into a two-time NCAA Division II All-American, a legitimate pro prospect, the only problem being that few pro scouts found their way out to North Dakota. One who did was a chubby young Baltimore Bullets representative named Jerry

Krause, who was entertained by Fitch's trick of having Jackson sit in the back seat of a Chevrolet and use his long arms to grab the steering wheel or unlock the front doors on either side. "I had quite a wingspan," Jackson recalled with a chuckle.

After his 13-year playing career, Jackson worked as an assistant coach and broadcaster for the New Jersey Nets before moving on to become head coach of the Albany Patroons in the Continental Basketball Association for five seasons. In 1984, Jackson's Patroons won the CBA title, and the next season he was named CBA Coach of the Year. He was doing a brief stint coaching in Puerto Rico when Jerry Krause contacted him about an assistant coaching job with the Bulls in 1985.

Jerry Krause: I had wanted to draft Phil for Baltimore in the second round in 1967. We took a gamble on another player, and New York got Phil. I kept up with Phil as a player through the years. We'd talk from time to time, and I followed his coaching career in the CBA. When I got the job in Chicago in 1985, I talked to him again. I told him I needed scouting reports on the CBA. Within a week, I had typewritten reports on the whole league, detail on every player. What I saw in Phil was an innate brightness. I thought that eventually he'd become the governor of North Dakota. I saw a lot of Tony LaRussa in him. A feel for people. A brightness. A probing mind.

Phil Jackson: I went to the CBA and had some success, but still nothing came in my direction. I had no mentor in the NBA. My coach, Red Holtzman, had retired and was out of the game. Although Dave DeBusschere, my former Knicks teammate, was a general manager, he had no control over my destiny as a coach. Jerry Krause was like the only person that really stayed in touch with me from the NBA world. And he had just gotten back in it. But that was my connection. Jerry had seen me play in college, and we had a relationship that spanned 20 years.

Jerry's a remarkable guy. He's an enigma to the athletic world. He's not what you would consider an athlete. And even as a scout back there 30 years ago, he was a very unusual type of fellow to be out there scouting a basketball player.

Jackson himself was known as an unusual fellow during his playing days with the New York Knicks. In Maverick, his 1975 autobiography written with Charlie Rosen for Playboy Press, Jackson recalled his exploration of sixties counterculture.

Phil Jackson: The only thing in that book that's an embarrassment for me today is that people have picked out one or two phrases and said, "This is who Phil Jackson is." Sportswriters in the past have seized on one experience with psychedelic drugs or some comments I've made about the type of lifestyle I had as a kid growing up in the 'sixties and seventies. I've tried to make sure people don't just grab a sentence or phrase to build a context for someone's personality.

Jerry Krause: I've never read the book. I didn't need to. I knew about Phil's character.

Shortly after coming to the Bulls in 1985, Krause called Jackson to interview with Stan Albeck for the job of assistant coach.

Phil Jackson: I was coaching in Puerto Rico, and I flew up directly from San Juan. It was a quick trip. I had to drive into San Juan and catch a morning flight. When you live in the subtropics, you get a lifestyle. I was wearing flip-flops most of the time. I wore chino slacks, because of their social standards down there, and a polo shirt. I had an Ecuadorian straw hat. Those hats are really expensive. They're not like a Panama, which costs 25 bucks. It's a $100 hat. You could crush proof it. As a little flair item, I had a parrott feather that I'd picked up at a restaurant. I had messed around with a macaw in the restaurant and pulled a tail feather out and stuck it in my hat.

There was a certain image I presented. I had a beard, had had it for a number of years. I was a little bit of an individualist, as I still am. I have a certain carriage about myself that's going to be unique. I just came in for the interview. I don't know how it affected Stan Albeck. Stan was a good coach. He'd been around and had some success.

Stan and I had a very short interview. It wasn't very personal, and I knew right away that Stan wasn't looking to hire me, although Jerry Krause had locked us in a room and said, "I want you guys to sit down and talk X's and O's." Stan found a different topic to talk about.

From his days as a role player for the Knicks.

Jerry Krause: Stan came back to me after the interview and said, "I don't want that guy under any circumstances." When we brought Phil in again to interview for the assistant's job two years later, I told him what to wear. And to shave.

Jerry Reinsdorf: One of Jerry Krause's greatest decisions that he gets no credit for was finding Phil Jackson in the CBA.

Phil Jackson: The next time I came in for an interview, with Doug Collins in 1987, it went a little better. Doug was a much more open person to deal with.

John Paxson: I've always been impressed by Phil. He's an intellectual guy, and I think that's the first thing that stood out to me. You don't run into too many intellectual guys in the NBA. The thing that impressed me is that he hasn't allowed this game to consume him. It can be so consuming for a coach. But Phil has other interests. His family has always been important to him. And he has never let the game take a toll on him mentally.

When Krause fired Collins in 1989, he knew that the 43-year-old Jackson was the perfect coach for the Bulls. He had been a member of Reinsdorf's beloved Knicks when they won the

179

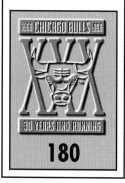

Former Knicks teammate Willis Reed says of Jackson, "I'm surprised Phil became a coach. But he's become a very good one. He's a very smart guy, very opinionated, has strong beliefs and I think those are some of the characteristics that have made him a good coach... He put in his time and dues, and he was lucky enough to have Michael Jordan on his team. I'm very proud of Phil, proud of what he has been able to accomplish, even as a player. He came back from the worst surgery that could happen, back surgery. He came back from that to play on our championship team in '73. And now he's coached three teams that have won it. He made himself a famous coach."

NBA title in 1973. Yet Jackson actually cites the Knicks' 1970 season, when he was on the injured list after undergoing major back surgery, as the breakthrough season in his pro basketball career. That year he sat in the stands at Madison Square Garden watching Knicks' coach Red Holtzman's every move. It was then, Jackson wrote in Maverick, *that he came to understand the game. That season also laid the foundation for the philosophy he sought to instill when he became head coach of the Bulls in 1989.*

Phil Jackson: The Knicks in the late sixties and early seventies were one of the dominant teams in the NBA, yet they were a collection of very good individual players but without a dominant star that could change the context of the game.

The whole of idea of the Knicks playing together was how well the ball moved, how well they played together defensively, the fact that any of the five players could take a key shot down the stretch. It was a difficult team in that regard to defend against. They were unselfish, and Red Holtzman, the mentor, was really the guy who taught us that. Surprisingly enough, he taught us teamwork through defense

That was the concept when I came to the Bulls, that the ball had to move. They all had to touch the ball regardless of who was gonna score. Everybody had to become interdependent upon each other and trusting on the offensive end. Defensively, we

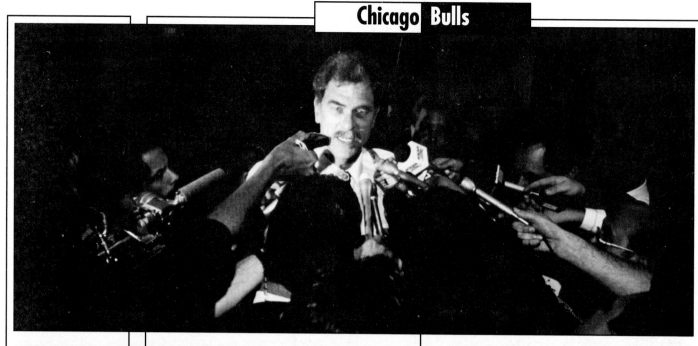

were gonna play full-court pressure. We were gonna make defense where we started our teamwork.

Tex Winter: I think Phil came in with the basis of some very sound philosophy. I mean the philosophy of life. He recognizes that there are a whole lot of things more important than basketball. He doesn't take himself too seriously. We all take basketball pretty seriously at times. Even then, he's inclined to relax. I'm amazed at times in the course of the game how he sits back

and lets things happen. He likes people to be able to solve their own problems, and so he gives his players the reins. On the other hand, when he sees they're out of control, then he starts to pull them in a little bit. I think this is his strength, the way he handles the players and his motivation, his personal relationship with the players. That's borne out by the fact that they'll accept his coaching, they'll accept the criticism, even though sometimes it's pretty severe with certain players. They accept that because it's who he is, because he's Phil.

183

includes **hoop** insert

Profile/ To Air is Divine

THE DETAILS OF HIS LEGEND ARE WORN *now, as smooth as the marble at the base of his statue outside the United Center. The fourth of James and Deloris Jordan's five children, Michael Jeffrey Jordan was born February 17, 1963, in Brooklyn, New York. Not long afterward, his family moved to Wilmington, North Carolina, where his father worked at an electric plant and his mother was employed by a bank.*

Michael's older brothers were Ronnie and Larry, and Delores was his older sister. Behind him was little sister Roslyn.

With both parents working, the setting was idyllic enough, a two-story brick house, from which Michael launched his daily adventures in baseball, football, and basketball. Baseball was

his favorite (he pitched a one-hitter in a Dixie Youth league championship game at age 12), as he has explained many times. He was good at baseball, but roundball was his gift.

Jordan was 14 when his father measured off a court in the family's back yard and placed a hoop at each end. The surface was grass, but Michael and his brothers soon wore it smooth.

He was about 5-10 and playing for Wilmington's D.C. Virgo Junior High School when he stole a ball in a game and dunked for the first time.

Michael Jordan: It was a baby dunk, just basic. I didn't even know I did it until after the fact. I surprised myself. Other kids had done it, but still it was spectacular for a junior high kid to be dunking. I felt proud that I could do it.

The next year, 1978, he failed to make the varsity at Laney High in 1978 as a sophomore. Instead, he dropped back to the junior varsity team. He grew to 6-3 before the next season and played so well as a junior at Laney that he was invited in the summer before his senior year to the Five-Star Camp in Pittsburgh, Pennsylvania, where he wowed the many col-

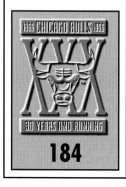

Jackson wanted to lessen the distance between Jordan and his teammates.

lege recruiters in attendance. Jordan, however, was not recruited as heavily as other better-known high school stars, and he decided to play for Dean Smith at the University of North Carolina.

James Worthy: I remember Michael coming into North Carolina as a freshman, a very confident young man, not arrogant, but confident. Since then, a couple of times, I've told him that I taught him everything he knows, but not everything I know.

I beat him one-on-one a couple of times his freshman year. Michael and I were a lot closer in college. We're still close, but in college it was almost like a bond. He was a freshman and I was a junior. I cherish those memories

Back then, I knew he had the potential to be an All-Star, but I never dreamed he was going to take it to this level. I didn't think he would dominate and just "be" the league. A couple of times on the golf course, we've talked about it, about how amazing it all is.

Jordan's legend gained tremendous momentum when as a freshman at North Carolina he hit the jumper that gave the Tar Heels the 1982 NCAA championship. Although Carolina never won another championship during his tenure there, Jordan's play earned him honors as the College Player of the Year the next two seasons, which in turn set up his selection by Chicago in 1984.

By the time Phil Jackson took over as head coach of the Bulls in 1989, Michael Jordan was 26 years old and facing explosive fame and wealth. His annual off-court income was ballooning from $4 million to $30 million. Overnight, he had become a cultural icon. Just as Jordan struggled personally to cope with this newfound status, Bulls management feared the team might well be consumed by it, too.

Phil Jackson: I was nervous when I took over the Bulls, but it wasn't the kind of nervousness where you lose sleep at night. I wanted to do well. I was anxious about having a good relationship with Michael. I was anxious about selling him on the direction in which I was going.

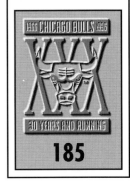

You knew what Michael was going to give you every single night as a player. He was gonna get those 30 points; he was gonna give you a chance to win. The challenge was, how to get the other guys feeling a part of it, like they had a role, a vital part. It was just his team, his way.

He had such hero worship in the United States among basketball fans that living with him had become an impossiblity. Traveling in airports, he needed an entourage to get through. He had brought people along on the road with him. His father would come. His friends would come on the road. He had just a life that sometimes alienated him from his teammates. It became a challenge to make him part of the team again and still not lose his special status because he didn't have the necessary privacy.

I had roomed on the same floor of hotels as he did. Michael always had a suite because of who he was, and the coaches got suites, too, because we needed the space for team meetings and staff meetings. Michael basically had to have someone stay in his room with him. I'd hear murmuring in the hallway, and there'd be six or eight of the hotel

staff, cleaning ladies, busboys, getting autographs and standing in the hallway with flowers. It was incredible, and he was constantly bothered.

So I knew that we had to make exceptions to the basic rules that we had: "Okay, so your father and your brothers and your friends can't ride on the team bus. Let's keep that a team thing. Yeah, they can meet you on the road, but they can't fly on the team plane. There has to be some of the team stuff that is ours, that is the sacred part of what we try to do as a basketball club."

I got a curtain for our practice facility, so that practice became our time together. It was just the 12 of us and the coaches, not the reporters and the television cameras. It wasn't going to be a show for the public anymore. It became who are we as a group, as people. Michael had to break down some of his exterior. You know that when you become that famous person you have to develop a shell around you to hide behind.

Michael had to become one of the guys in that regard. He had to involve his teammates, and he was able to do that. He was

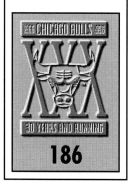

able to bring it out and let his hair down at the same time.

Over his years in pro basketball, Michael had learned to mark out his own territory. He had his own stall at every arena where he might find the most privacy, or he might find a territory in the trainer's room. He had two stalls in the old Chicago Stadium. That was his spot because there were 25 reporters around him every night.

We continued the protocol of all that, but we also made efforts to create space for him within the team. If we hadn't done that, the way he was going to treat us was that the rest of the world was going to overrun us, if we hadn't done things the right way. So we said, "Let's not all suffer because of his fame. Let's give ourselves space and exclude the crowd." I guess I created a safe zone, a safe space for Michael. That's what I tried to do.

John Paxson: If I could ever take a page out of the manual for handling a superstar, it would be the way Phil's handled Michael Jordan.

Phil Jackson: Some nights he could take on a whole team. They'd say, "That son of a gun, he beat us all to the basket." As a coach, you can run that tape back all day.

You say, "Look at this guy go around that guy and that guy. He beat four guys going to the basket that time." That's destructive. That's something that Michael's been known for, and I know it grates at the heart of the other team.

It's an amazing feat this guy has been able to accomplish. But I think his power is very addictive. You know the fans were there looking for him. Everybody's waiting. They loved it. He had this tremendous vision of basketball. He was this tremendous entertainer.

Tex Winter: He lives in his own world a great deal. I don't think he wants people to figure out what Michael Jordan's thinking. It's one of his strengths.

Phil Jackson: After having a game that was mediocre or average, a game where maybe he did too much, a game that we lost, Michael had an ability to walk through the plane and say, "Guys, we're gonna kick butt tomorrow. They're gonna have to beat us. They can't put it together."

That attitude, that tremendous competitiveness, sometimes makes it tough to be a teammate, because you see that tremendous competitiveness is gonna eat you up everywhere. It's gonna eat you up playing golf

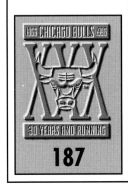

He was about 5-foot-10 and playing for Wilmington's D.C. Virgo Junior High School when he stole the ball in a game and dunked for the first time. "It was a baby dunk, just basic," Jordan recalled. "I didn't even know I did it until after the fact. I surprised myself. Other kids had done it, but still it was spectacular for a junior high kid to be dunking. I felt proud that I could do it."

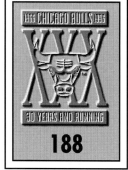

with him next week, playing cards with him next month. That attitude of arrogance is gonna be there. It's not always the best for personal connections and friendship. But it certainly makes for greatness.

By 1989, Jordan's "greatness" had become an issue. Was he the kind of player who could lead a team to a championship? Or was he the kind of superstar whose gifts were good only for the show? The kind of player whose game tended to minimize his teammates? Those questions haunted and angered Michael Jordan. He faced a strait gate. If he complained about the abilities of the players on the Bulls' roster, he was seen as arrogant. If he tried to do too much himself, he was seen as a ball hog. Never had his basketball skills been a question. But now his leadership skills, and his character, were. Unfortunately, there was only one way for Jordan to answer the questions and the criticism.

John Paxson: I think there came a point where he understood his greatness was going to be defined by winning. That's why I saw a change in his real commitment to winning championships and, to that end, dealing with teammates and getting guys he

felt comfortable with, that were able to play with him. It was really that understanding that championships mean a lot, when it comes down to who's the greatest. There are great NBA players who've never won championships, and it's always been a blot on their careers.

Mark Pfeil: When Scottie and Horace came in, Michael sensed the thing could be turned around. But the thing that frustrated him was that they didn't have the same attitude. They were young enough to say, "Hell, we get paid whether we win or lose." And it was good enough for them just to get close. In their second year, we went to the Eastern Finals and lost. Then with Phil we lost again. After that second loss, Michael said, "Hey, now we've gotta go over the top, and I'm gonna take us there. If you don't want to be on the boat, get off." I think those guys really matured. You had your petty jealousies, but Michael, to me, bent over backwards to help all kinds of people, from Oakley to Paxson to Scottie to Horace.

John Paxson: Michael is easily the most demanding athlete I've been around. I don't want any of that to sound like there's something wrong with that because there's not. There came a point in his career that winning championships was going to be one of the defining things in his career. He put more pressure on himself than he did on his teammates. As much pressure as he puts on guys around him he puts more on himself. That says a lot about him.

Michael Jordan: I guess I expected more from a lot of them. But some of them didn't want to take more responsibility… . We were inconsistent and I was frustrated.

John Paxson: If you showed weakness around him, he'd run you off. He was always challenging you in little ways. The thing you had to do with Michael Jordan is you had to gain his confidence as a player. You had to do something that gave him some trust in you as a player. He was hard on teammates as far as demanding you play hard, you execute. So there had to come some point where you did something on the floor to earn his trust. That was the hardest thing for new guys coming in, and some guys couldn't deal with it. Some guys could not play consistently enough or well enough, or they would not do the dirty work or little things. That's one of the reasons why Michael liked Charles Oakley because Charles played hard. He did little things on the floor that Michael appreciated, but a lot of guys didn't understand that.

Michael demanded nothing less than playing hard. If you missed shots when you were open, he didn't want to see that either. If Michael came off the screen and roll a couple of times and threw a quick pass to Bill Cartwright and he couldn't handle it, Michael wasn't going to go there again. That was kind of what happened early. If you do something and one of your teammates doesn't respond to it you're going to think twice about going there. It's a natural thing.

You always sensed with Michael that he was looking for perfection out of himself. There's a part of him that expected that of those around him, too.

Michael Jordan: I feel I'm very observant about the game. If things were going well, I didn't have to score too much. I could stay in the background and get everyone else involved.

John Paxson: Michael challenged guys, and for some, their game didn't live up to that challenge. Brad Sellers, for example. It was tough for him to handle what Michael expected of him. Michael had a tendency to look at certain guys and say, "You're capable of doing this. Why aren't you? I look at your physical skills. Why can't you?" I'm sure he looked at me many times and said, "You're not capable of doing that on the floor." But I had an advantage with Michael in our basketball relationship. We spent a month overseas together when we were in college as part of an international team in 1981. I made a shot to win a game over in Yugoslavia, and I've got to believe that in the back of his mind, Michael remembered that about me as a player. He was able to trust me.

At the same time, I don't remember Michael early on putting any pressure on Scottie Pippen or Horace. He knew that a lot of guys have to grow into the league.

Michael was always more than fair with me. He was always positive with me and never said anything negative about me in the papers. That meant a lot to me. You can get battered down when the great player of the team says something critical of you personally. He didn't do that. I thought early on he was too reserved toward players at times. I'm sure he felt he was walking a fine line. "Should I be critical? Should I just lay back and let these guys do their own thing?"

I felt the more vocal he became as a leader, the better we were. Once he really started challenging guys, it made us better. We had to learn how to play with Michael as well as Michael had to learn to play with us.

Winter, Jackson and Bach.

Profile/
Tex and Johnny

ONE OF PHIL JACKSON'S FIRST REQUESTS as Bulls head coach was to hire Jim Cleamons, an old teammate, as the team's third assistant. Cleamons, in his early forties, fit in nicely with the staff, the core of which was the veteran braintrust of Tex Winter and Johnny Bach.

In 1989, Winter was in his late sixties and possessed more than four decades of first-rate coaching experience. He had been the head coach at five colleges—Marquette, Kansas State, Washington, Northwestern and Long Beach State—and had served as head coach of the San Diego/Houston Rockets. His specialty over the years had been the development of the triple-post offense, which would figure greatly in the Bulls' championship seasons. One of Jerry Krause's first acts upon being named Bulls general manager in 1985 was to phone Winter, his old mentor, and offer him a job as assistant coach.

It was a source of irritation to Krause that the first two head coaches he hired—Stan Albeck and Doug Collins—decided not to follow Winter's offensive advice. If they had, they just might have kept their jobs.

Bach, like Winter, was in his late sixties when Jackson took over the team in '89. And like Winter, Bach had a host of college head coaching experience—at Fordham and Penn State—and a top pro job at Golden State. But where Winter focused on offense, Bach was a defensive specialist and a Collins protégé.

Together with Cleamons, they gave Jackson perhaps the most experienced staff in the NBA in 1989.

Mark Pfeil: Johnny's an old Navy officer. His twin brother was a pilot who was lost at sea and never found. Johnny was a true gentleman, the kind of guy who even sewed a crease in his pants. He was his own man; he loved to play devil's advocate. Sometimes people took him too seriously. I always called him Doctor Doom. I don't

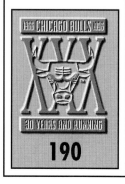

care what we were doing, he always thought the worst was going to happen.

Cheryl Raye: Phil had called Johnny the locker room coach, which meant he was the liaison with the players, especially for Horace Grant. Horace was extremely sensitive, took everything at face value. So Johnny was there to explain everything. While Phil would be screaming at him, Johnny would be there, "Okay, Horace." He'd be stroking him and telling him everything was all right. So Johnny was very close to Horace. The players had so much respect for him, especially defensively.

And they seemed to take their pride from him. It just rubbed off, especially the defense. When he put the Aces up, the military term, that signalled for the pressure, it got everybody going.

Mark Pfeil: Tex is like a grandpa to all of us. But the players would mock him. Michael used to tease him and stuff. Over everything. One time in practice, Michael sneaked up behind him and pulled Tex's shorts all the way down to his knees, and there was Tex's bare butt sticking out.

Tex Winter: Michael's sort of his own man. I think he's talked to Phil occasionally about what we do offensively and how he fits into the scheme of things. I let Phil handle that. My basic job is of teacher. When we step out on that floor at a practice session, I'm going to coach whoever shows up. And I'm going to coach them the way I coach, whether it's Michael Jordan, Scottie Pippen, or Pete Myers, or whoever it is. It doesn't make any difference. They know that. If I see Michael making a mistake, I'll correct him as fast as I will anyone else. On the other hand, he's such a great athlete you have to handle him a little differently than you do the other players. I don't think you can come down on him hard in a very critical way, whereas some younger guy or some other guy you feel you might be able to motivate by coming down on them pretty tough.

Chip Schaefer: Tex is a few years younger than my parents and a product of that Depression era. To say that he is frugal

would be an understatement. Johnny Bach used to call him penurious. I think that's a very apt description of him. But I think Tex in a lot of ways is the way we all should be. He doesn't like to see things get wasted. He takes that attitude at the dinner table, too. If there's a little bit of meat on your bone, he may just pick up your steak bone and finish it off for you.

Tex Winter: The teaching is the reward for me. You get a big thrill watching a guy like Pete Myers grow in the scheme of things. You can take a role player and see how they fit in our system of play. You can see their improvement, especially with a guy like Will Perdue, who's really had a struggle with some of the things we do.

Chip Schaefer: Basketball is his absolute passion in life. He's 73 years old, and that's what keeps him going. There's times when he'll look tired, and I'll wonder if he has the energy for it. Then all of a sudden practice will start, and he's out here barking at these guys like he's coaching the K-State freshman team and it's 1948.

Tex has three or four real passions in life. One of them's basketball. Certainly one of them's food. He really enjoys his finances. He pores over the business section of the paper as intensely as he does the sports section. He's a real joy. I hope he keeps on going.

Working with Winter and Bach made Jackson feel like he'd been to hoops grad school.

Profile/The Triple-post Offense

*T*EX WINTER HAD SPENT YEARS *developing the triangle, or triple-post offense. It was an old college system that involved all five players sharing the ball and moving. But it was totally foreign to pro players of the 1990s, and many of them found it difficult to learn. Where for years the pro game had worked on isolation plays and one-on-one set ups, the triple-post used very little in the way of set plays. Instead the players learned to react to situations and to allow their ball movement to create weaknesses in defenses. It was this system that Phil Jackson decided to use upon taking over as Bulls head coach. The subsequent transition was not easy. Some observers, such as* Chicago Tribune *reporter Sam Smith in his book,* The Jordan Rules, *sensed an atmosphere of mutiny over Jackson's first two seasons. The team had yet to win a title, and Michael Jordan's frustration was building.*

Tex Winter: I've always been very much impressed with Michael as well as everyone else has been. I've never been a hero worshiper. I saw his strong points, but I also saw some weaknesses. I felt like there was a lot of things that we could do as a coaching staff to blend Michael in with the team a little bit better. I thought he was a great player, but I did not feel that we wanted to go with him exclusively. We wanted to try and get him to involve his teammates more. Until he was convinced that that was what he wanted to do, I don't think we had the chance to have the program that we had later down the line.

Phil Jackson: Tex's offense emulated the offense I had played in with New York. The ball dropped into the post a lot. You ran cuts. You did things off the ball. People were cutting and passing and moving the basketball. And it took the focus away from Michael, who had the ball in his hands a lot, who had been a great scorer. That had made the defenses all turn and face him.

Tex's offense required Jordan to share the ball with Cartwright and other teammates.

Suddenly he was on the back side of the defenses, and Michael saw the value in having an offense like that. He'd been in an offense like that at North Carolina. It didn't happen all at once. He started to see that over a period of time, as the concepts built up.

John Paxson: It was different for different types of players. For me it was great. A system offense is made for someone who doesn't have the athletic skills that a lot of guys in the league have. It played to my strengths. But it tightened the reins on guys like Michael and Scottie from the standpoint that we stopped coming down and isolating them on the side. There were subtleties involved, teamwork involved. But that was the job of Phil to sell us on the fact we could win playing that way.

Michael Jordan: Everything was geared toward the middle, toward the post play. We were totally changing our outlook… and I disagreed with that to a certain extent. I felt that was putting too much pressure on the people inside.

Phil Jackson: But what Michael had trouble with, was when the ball went to one of the big guys like Bill Cartwright or Horace Grant or some of the other players who weren't tuned in to handling and passing the ball. They now had the ball. Could they be counted on to make the right passes, the right choices? I brought Michael in my office and told him basically, "The ball is like a spotlight. And when it's in your hands, the spotlight is on you. And you've gotta share that spotlight with some of your teammates by having them do things with the basketball, too."

He said, "I know that. It's just that when it comes down to getting the job done, a lot of times they don't want to take the initiative. Sometimes it's up to me to take it, and sometimes that's a tough balance."

All along the way it was a compromise of efforts. Everybody made such a big issue of the triple-post offense. We just said, "It's a format out of which to play. You can play any way you want out of the triangle." Because if it's a sound offense, you should be able to do that. One of the concepts is to hit the open man.

Paxson was perfectly suited for the triple post.

193

There were times when Michael knew he was going to get 40 points. He was just hot those nights. He was going to go on his own, and he would just take over a ball game. We had to understand that that was just part of his magnitude, that was something he could do that nobody else in this game could do. And it was going to be okay. Those weren't always the easiest nights for us to win as a team. But they were certainly spectacular nights for him as a showman and a scorer

John Paxson: It took some time. Michael was out there playing with these guys, and unless he had a great deal of respect for them as players, I think he figured, "Why should I pass them the ball when I have the ability to score myself or do the job myself? I'd rather rely on myself to succeed or fail than some of these other guys." The thing I like about Michael is that he finally came to understand that if we were going to win championships he had to make some sacrifices individually. He had to go about the task of involving his teammates more.

Phil Jackson: A lot of times, my convincing story to Michael was, "We want you to get your thirty-some points, and we want you to do whatever is necessary. It's great for us if you get 12 or 14 points by halftime, and you have 18 points at the end of the third quarter. Then get your 14 or 18 points in the fourth quarter. That's great. If it works out that way, that's exactly what it'll be." Who could argue with that? We'd tell him, "Just play your cards. Make them play everybody during the course of the game and then finish it out for us." I think that's why sometimes Michael has downplayed the triangle. He says it's a good offense for three quarters, but it's not great for the fourth quarter. That's because he took over in the fourth quarter. He can perform.

This last four or five years has been remarkable for us. It's been a marriage of guys playing an offense together, and Michael Jordan doing the things he's able to do on his own.

Tex Winter: Phil was definitely set on what we were going to do and he wouldn't waiver. Even though the triple-post offense evolved through my many, many years of coaching, Phil was sold on it even more than I was at times. There's times when I would say. "We should get away from this. Let Michael have more one-on-one opportunities." And Phil was persistent in not doing so. It's to his credit that we stayed to his basic philosophy of basketball. It may sound sort of self-serving, but I think it has very definitely been one of the Chicago Bulls' strengths. Because the program has perpetuated itself. Even when Jordan left us, I think people were amazed—and we were too—that we could win 55 games.

John Paxson: I think guys that come in new to this situation are always a little reluctant because it's different. The NBA game is not a system game. The NBA is a play game. You have sets, and you have called plays. You see coaches running up and down the sidelines all the time making a play call, which to me, especially in play-off series, plays into your hand. If you scout well, you know how to defend against those set plays. Phil sold us, then made us believe the more subtle you are on your offense, the more successful you're going to be. You can do some damage if you're reading the other team's defense and reacting rather than worrying about calling some play that the coach wants from the sideline. That's really what happened. That's what this offense is all about. I'm a believer in it. I think it's a wonderful way to play a game.

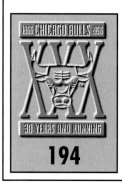

Closing In, 1989-90

HIS HOPES MAY HAVE RESTED WITH TEX *Winter's offense, but Phil Jackson opened his first training camp as head coach of the Bulls by focusing solely on defense. Baseline-to-baseline pressure defense.*

John Paxson: When Phil came in, our first training camp was as difficult a camp as I'd ever had. It was defensive-oriented. Everything we did was start from the defensive end and work to the offensive end. Phil basically made us into a pressure-type team. Defensively, he knew that was how we would win.

Phil Jackson: This was Bill Cartwright's second year with the Bulls. We were kind of getting solid in who we were. We were adding a system and trying to learn to play within a system. Sometimes there were little inconsistencies, and some guys had trouble really understanding the direction of the system. But we got the defense down. We were gonna play full-court pressure defense. We were gonna throw our hearts into it.

Key to the Bulls' growth would be the maturing of Scottie Pippen and Horace Grant, the two young players with enough athleticism to give the defense its bite. "He's on the cusp of greatness," Bach said of Pippen. "He's starting to do the kinds of things only Michael does."

"It's just a matter of working hard," Pippen said. "I've worked to improve my defense and shooting off the dribble. I know I'm a better spot-up shooter, but I'm trying to pull up off the dribble when the lane is blocked."

In the '89 draft, Krause had brought in another three rookies, all first-round draft picks— point guard B. J. Armstrong, center/forward Stacey King and forward Jeff Sanders. That August, Krause signed free agent guard Craig Hodges and picked up an old standby, forward Ed Nealy, in a trade with Phoenix.

Coming out of camp, they knew they were much better, and the energy was tangible as they finished the preseason 8-0. Yet everyone knew that a big adjustment lay ahead. The Bulls had to find a comfort level playing in the strange new offense. And then there was the

BILL CARTWRIGHT

matter of Cartwright. Jordan was openly skeptical of the big center, who seemed to have trouble catching the ball in traffic.

The Bulls went 8-6 over the month of November, and there were few smiling faces. December, however, brought a trend: They would find bursts of momentum and consume the schedule with winning streaks. First came a five-game run right before the holidays, then another five heading into the new year. Their offense continued to struggle, but the secret was their defense. Across the league, other coaches began talking about it—and fearing it.

Then, just as suddenly, their magic faltered, and during a west coast road trip things reached a low point with four straight losses. Even worse, Cartwright was struggling with sore knees and missed several games. Fortunately, the All-Star break provided relief. Pippen joined Jordan on the Eastern squad for

THE ADVENTURES OF

CHICAGO BULLS
1989/90

FIGHTING THE NEVER ENDING BATTLE FOR HOOPS, VICTORIES, AND THE N.B.A. TITLE!

FASTER THAN A SPEEDING BULLET!

UGH!

MORE POWERFUL THAN AN EL' TRAIN!

ABLE TO LEAP SEARS TOWER IN A SINGLE BOUND!

DID YOU SEE THAT?

UN-BE-LIEV-A-BULL!

IN-CRED-I-BULL!

YEAH!

LOOK IN THE STANDS, THE CROWD IS WILD!

ECSTATIC! JUBILANT! FOR THEIR...

SUPERHEROES

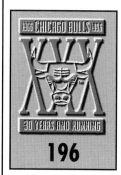

1966 CHICAGO BULLS 1996
XXX
30 YEARS AND RUNNING

196

the first time, and Craig Hodges won the three-point shootout.

Afterward, the Bulls regained whatever confidence they'd lost and won nine straight. They lost a game to Utah in the Stadium, then won six of eight and followed that with another nine-game win streak. Almost every night, Jordan led them in scoring, but it was Pippen who gave opposing coaches nightmares. Few teams had a means of matching up with him, particularly when they also had to worry about Jordan.

The win streaks propelled them to a 55-27 finish, good for second place in the Central behind the 60-win Pistons, the defending World

Champions. Stacey King was named to the All-Rookie second team, and Jordan harvested another batch of honors: All-NBA, All-Defense, and his fourth consecutive scoring title. Plus he led the league in steals.

The Bulls sailed into the playoffs with new confidence and Pippen playing like a veteran. First they dismissed the Milwaukee Bucks and followed that by humbling Charles Barkley and the Philadelphia 76ers. But Pippen's 70-year-old father, Lewis, died during the series, and the young forward rushed home to Arkansas for the funeral. He returned in time to help finish off Philly. Next up were the Pistons and the Eastern Finals. The year before in the playoffs, Bill Laimbeer had knocked Pippen out of Game 6 with an elbow to the head. The Detroit center claimed the shot was inadvertent, but that wasn't the way the Bulls saw it. To win a championship, they knew they had to stand up to the Bad Boys.

Jerry Reinsdorf: I thought the Pistons were thugs, and you know, you have to hold the ownership responsible for that. I mean, Bill Laimbeer was a thug. He would hit people from behind in the head during dead balls. He took cheap shots all the time. Mahorn and Laimbeer, I mean, they tried to hurt people.

They called themselves the Bad Boys, and they marketed themselves under that name. I would never have allowed that. You know I blame the league and David Stern a little bit for that, too. It was terrible.

Scottie Pippen: There were times, a few years before the flagrant foul rules, when guys would have a breakaway and (the Pistons) would cut their legs out from under them. Anything to win a game. That's not the way the game is supposed to be played. I remember once when Michael had a breakaway, and Laimbeer took him out. There was no way he could have blocked the shot. When you were out there playing them, that was always in the back of your mind, to kind of watch yourself.

The series developed as a classic, with each team winning tight battles at home to tie it at 3-3 heading into Game 7 at the Palace of Auburn Hills. The Pistons had homecourt advantage, but the Bulls had worked for years to get to this point. In 1975, they had come to a seventh game of the Eastern Finals, only to lose a close contest. Now, 15 years later, they were back again, and just like before, things went dreadfully wrong, beginning with Paxson's badly sprained ankle and Pippen's migraine headache just before tipoff.

Mark Pfeil: Scottie had had migraines before. He actually came to me before the game and said he couldn't see. I said, "Can you play?" He started to tell me no, and Michael jumped in and said, "Hell, yes, he can play. Start him. Let him play blind."

Horace kind of backed up a little bit that game, too. It was more a matter of maturity

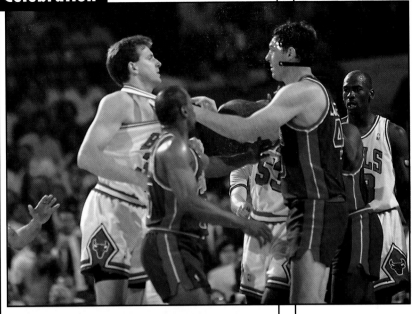

In 1990, the Pistons intimidated the Bulls one last time.

197

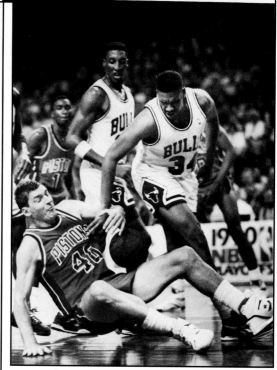

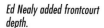

Ed Nealy added frontcourt depth.

than wimping out. It took a certain period of time before they would stand up and say, "Damn it, I've been pushed to the wall enough." Scottie played with the headache, and as the game went on he got better.

Scottie Pippen: It grabbed me and wouldn't let go. It's something the fans will never let die. Then again, it's something I look over. I really don't think much about it.

Pippen played, but the entire roster seemed lost. They fell into a deep hole in the second quarter and never climbed out. With their skull 'n' crossbones banners flying, the Pistons advanced easily, 93-74.

Phil Jackson: My worst moment as a Bull was trying to finish out the seventh game that we lost to the Pistons in the Palace. There was Scottie Pippen with a migraine on the bench, and John Paxson had sprained his ankle in the game before. I just had to sit there and grit my teeth and go through a half in which we were struggling to get in the ball game. We had just gone through a second period that was an embarrassment to the organization. It was my most difficult moment as a coach. But I learned a lot from that moment. I learned a lot of things about being a sportsman.

The burden of the loss fell on Pippen. Everyone, from the media to his own teammates, had interpreted the headache as a sign of faint-heartedness. Lost in the perspective was the fact that the third-year forward had recently buried his father.

Jerry Reinsdorf: When we lost to Detroit seven games and I went down to the locker room. It's something I rarely do, but I just knew we would win the next year. We had gotten close, and you could sense we were going to beat them.

Profile/ The Anti- Piston

*T*HE BULLS ALMOST selected Bill Cartwright out of the University of San Francisco when they had the second pick in the 1979 draft. Instead, Chicago took David Greenwood, and the 7-foot-1 Cartwright went on to the New York Knicks, where he had an outstanding rookie season, averaging better than 21 points and 10 rebounds per game. After that, however, his career became one frustrating battle after another with injuries, all played out before the merciless New York media. He went through foot surgery after foot surgery, until the newspapers dubbed him "Medical Bill." The Knicks' problem was that they didn't know how to play Cartwright with Patrick Ewing. They tried putting them in a Twin Towers alignment with modest success. Finally, they traded him to the Bulls, where Cartwright's reputation preceeded him. He had come into the league as a big-time, low-post offensive threat. But what the Bulls saw in him was the defensive intimidator they needed. Either way, Jordan still couldn't believe they had traded Oakley for Cartwright. Phil Jackson, however, had seen his value, not only as a defender but as a leader. The coach began calling Cartwright "Teach," and the name stuck.

More than that, his teammates and opponents around the league knew Cartwright for his

Jerry Krause: When Phil Jackson was an assistant on the staff, he wanted Bill Cartwright badly. We talked about it. I knew we had to get a center. I phone Robert Parish, who was playing with the Celtics then, and old friend of mine. He told me how tough it was to play against Cartwright.

elbows. He held them high when he rebounded or boxed out. Cartwright's elbows weren't as notorious as the Pistons' style of play, but they were close.

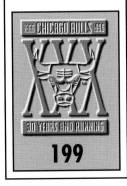

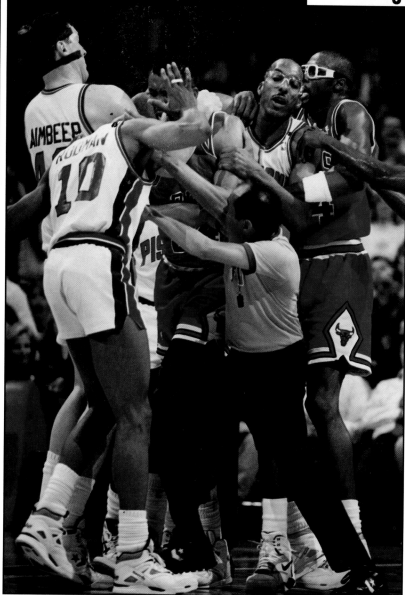

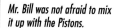
Mr. Bill was not afraid to mix it up with the Pistons.

He was a traditional low-post player.

200

Jerry Krause: Michael really didn't know Bill Cartwright as a person. Michael made Bill prove himself. Michael did that with everybody. That was Michael's way. I knew what Bill was. Bill was gonna be fine with Michael. I told Bill, "It's coming. He's gonna needle you. Michael's gonna drive you crazy." Bill said, "He ain't gonna do nothing to me."

Bill Cartwright: Michael and I had a comfort problem, the fact that he wanted to do some things, and I was in the way. It took some getting used to. It took him getting used to me. And I had to get used to Scottie and Horace. It wasn't a Michael problem; it was a team problem.

Johnny Bach: I think once Michael saw what the big guy was doing, he could for-

give someone who dropped the ball occasionally and might be getting older.

Phil Jackson: I'll never forget the battles Willis Reed had to fight against Kareem to get to the championship in 1970, the fight Willis had to wage against Wilt Chamberlain in both '70 and '73. We, the Knicks, had to have this guy who said, "You're gonna have to come through my door, and you're gonna have to get over me to win a championship." At some level, that sacrifice had to be made. That's what Bill Cartwright brought to the Bulls as a player. He was the one who said, "You're gonna have to come through me."

Bill's an extremely stubborn person, and he believes you've got to work real hard to get what you want in life. He gave us that ele-

ment, that "I'm-gonna-work-real-hard-to-get-this-accomplished" attitude. He was dogged, dogged persistence.

One of the things that got to us was that Detroit used to have a way of bringing up the level of animosity in a game. At some level, you were gonna have to contest them physically, if you were gonna stay in the game with them. If you didn't want to stay in the game with them, fine. They'd go ahead and beat you. But if you wanted to compete, you'd have to do something physically to play at their level.

Bill stood up to the Pistons. In one of the great wins we had in Detroit, Bill got thrown out. We had to beat Detroit on their home floor, in the Palace of Auburn Hills. We hadn't been able to accomplish that.

It was a game in the spring of 1991. Bill got thrown out in the first half on an elbow call with Laimbeer. But he had to do it. He had to stand up to Laimbeer, because of what Laimbeer had done to him.

The year before against the Pistons, Bill had gotten thrown out and suspended for a game because Isiah had come back at him and hit him after Bill set a pick on him from behind. Isiah broke his hand in that one.

Bill's statement was, "This isn't the way we want to play. This isn't the way I want to play. But if it is the way we have to play to take care of these guys, I'm not afraid to do it. I'm gonna show these Detroit guys this is not acceptable. We won't accept you doing this to us."

You can't imagine how much that relieved guys like Scottie Pippen and Horace Grant, guys who were being beseiged constantly and challenged constantly by more physical guys like Dennis Rodman and Rick Mahorn.

Bill Cartwright: The Pistons seemingly always tried to attack, and I was able to stop them from getting off. If you did that against Detroit, they didn't go back to that stuff.

Tom Boerwinkle: Bill is one of the most workman-like people you could ever be around. He doesn't say a lot; he keeps to himself. But you can't find a two-minute flim clip where he isn't working hard. He was a tremendous asset to the Bulls.

Eventually Jordan came to appreciate him.

Bill could defend Ewing straight up.

Horace Grant:
Without Bill Cartwright, we don't get three championship rings.

The atmosphere in the Stadium had undergone a dramatic transformation since 1984.

The Ritz, 1990-91

JORDAN AND HIS TEAMMATES MATURED into a determined unit over the 1990-91 season, although their progress was sometimes frutstrating and difficult. Jordan again led the league in scoring at 31.5 points per game (to go with six rebounds and five assists per outing). But the key development came with the 6-foot-7 Pippen. He had been stung by criticism, most of it stemming from his migraine headache in Game 7 of the 1990 Eastern Conference finals. A gifted swing player, Pippen performed with determination over the 1990-91 campaign, playing 3,014 minutes, averaging nearly 18 points, seven rebounds and six assists.

"I thought about it all summer," he said of the migraine. "I failed to produce last season."

Other key factors were power forward Horace Grant (12.8 points, 8.4 rebounds); point

guard John Paxson (8.7 points while jump-shooting .548 from the floor); and center Bill Cartwright (9.6 points and interior toughness on defense). Coach Phil Jackson also made great use of his bench with B. J. Armstrong, Craig Hodges, Will Perdue, Stacey King, Cliff Levingston, Scott Williams (a free agent rookie out of North Carolina), and Dennis Hopson (who had come over in a trade with New Jersey) all contributing.

Phil Jackson: John Paxson was one of the people who made all of the difference in the world, because of his attitude. He was going to play full court pressure and be a facilitator in this offense.

Horace Grant learned and matured while having to pick up a system of offense that was not natural to him. Yet he made every effort to be good at it.

For Pippen, it was ultimately taking him from being a wing into a point guard role. He

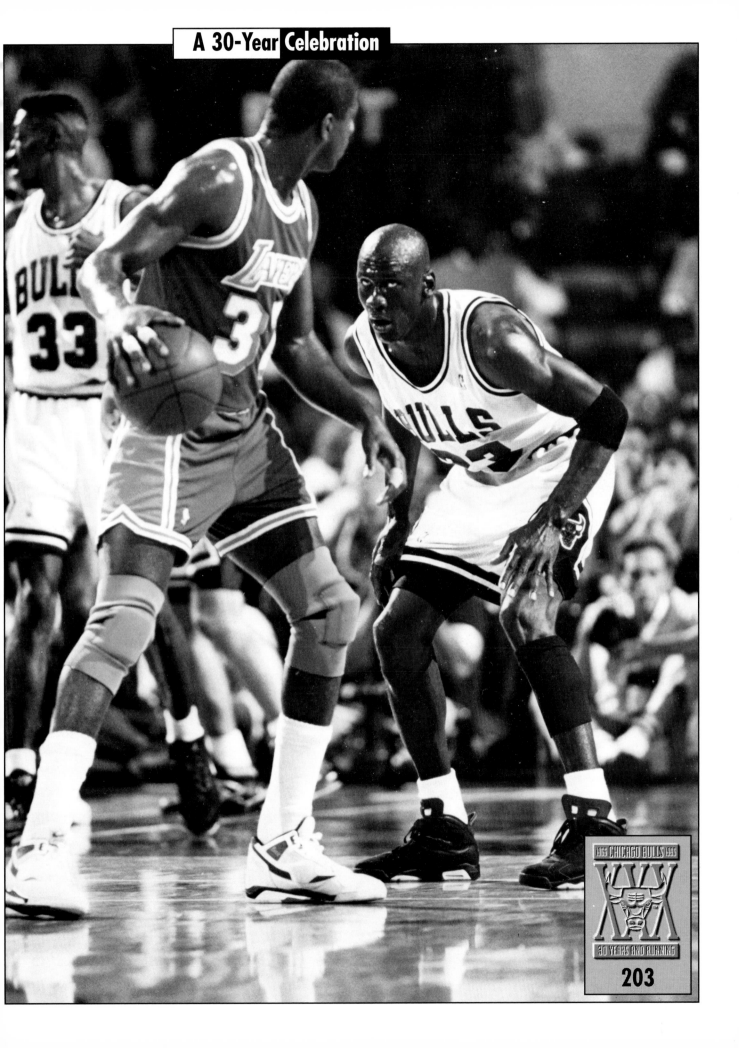

Chicago Tribune

Thursday, June 13, 1991   35¢

NBA Championship Final

146th Year — No. 164 © Chicago Tribune   8 Sections   N   S   D   NW   NW/L   D/F   D/W   N/L   ★

High five! Bulls are champs!

Bulls
108
Lakers
101

Jordan soars: For the first time in 17 playoff games, Michael Jordan didn't lead Bulls' scorers. But his team's night was still tops. **In Sports.**

Big shot: The Bulls "other" guard, John Paxson, was 32 of 49 from the field, shooting 65 percent against the Lakers. **In Sports.**

Saying thanks: Reserve Craig Hodges led his teammates in a post-game prayer while national television cameras rolled. **In Sports.**

"[The championship] means so much. Not just for me but for this team and this city. It was a seven-year struggle. It's the most proud day I've ever had."

**Michael Jordan, in tears,
after the Bulls' victory**

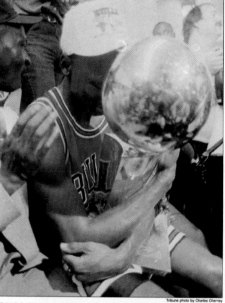

Tribune photo by Charles Cherney

Michael Jordan, alone with his thoughts in a jubilant Bulls locker room, clutches the championship trophy that eluded him for six seasons—and Chicago for 25.

1st title sweeps away 25 years of frustration

By Sam Smith
Chicago Tribune

INGLEWOOD, Calif.—All this started with New York almost two months ago and, fittingly, ends with Los Angeles.

The Bulls have swept across the National Basketball Association landscape in a remarkable cross-country run to the title that has left no doubt about the location of the basketball capital of the world.

Chicago is second to none.

"[The championship] means so much," said Michael Jordan, in tears after the game talking to a national television audience. "Not just for me but for this team and this city. It was a seven-year struggle. It's the most proud day I've ever had."

Jordan was named Most Valuable Player of the NBA Finals, which the Bulls won 4 games to one—including three straight on the road in Los Angeles.

Yes, the Bulls have taken the gold in their silver anniversary season, a tempest of effort finally sending the proud Lakers sinking into the Pacific Wednesday night in a hard-fought 108-101 game and letting loose a tidal wave of exhilaration and emotion.

The Bulls are champions!

Roll it around in your mouth and savor the sweet taste of victory. Close your eyes and see them raising the banners in honor of the Bulls, in honor of all Bulls teams and, really, in honor of all Chicagoans. Get ready for Friday's noon rally at the Petrillo Band Shell in Grant Park.

Because the Bulls have been Chicago's team, winning with a bit of Gold Coast glamor and a lot of stockyards effort.

This not only has been an inexorable march to glory, it has been a 100-yard dash to success. The Bulls sped through the playoffs with a 15-2 record, equaling the best since the NBA went to the current postseason format and posting the second-best all-time playoff winning percentage.

The Bulls did it with some of the best marksmanship an NBA Finals has seen and a suffocating defense that broke records for fewest points scored by their opponents, yet they refused to allow the beauty and grace of the game to be diminished.

Jordan, with 30 points and 10 assists Wednesday night, danced on air. Scottie Pippen, who tallied a

See **Champions**, pg. 16

This time the waiting isn't until next year

For 1 special night, everyone's a fan

By Charles Leroux
and Charles M. Madigan

■ Fans throw impromptu parties; some get out of hand. Page 16.

Before Chicago erupted into a late-night shout, a thumbs-up, triumphant, "YES," before the Bulls' 108-101 victory over the Los Angeles Lakers, before fans spilled cheering into the streets and fireworks crackled and car horns honked in glee, there was the wait.

You found Chicago fans in the strangest places during the game Wednesday night, waiting for the Bulls to take the National Basketball Association championship. And for some of them, it seemed nothing could get in the way of watching the battle with the Los Angeles Lakers.

At Hinsdale Hospital, in one class on natural childbirth, seven pregnant women and their husbands ate cookies colored and shaped like basketballs. Some of them had snapshots taken beside a full-sized cutout of Michael Jordan.

In another classroom, a TV displayed the game without sound while teacher Nadine Thornton instructed men on how to coach their wives during labor. Learning how to breath properly helps with having babies, and with watching the Bulls too.

"I take a cleansing breath every time Michael Jordan throws the ball," said Renee Sipek, 32, of Westmont, who is in the 8th month of her pregnancy. She inhaled deeply and exhaled to demonstrate.

"It didn't even hurt," she said.

In one of the hospital's operating rooms, an anesthesiologist placed a small television set into the far corner of an operating room where a woman was undergoing a bowel resection.

The doctor "assured the patient that 'We'll take real good care of you despite the fact that we have the Bulls game on,'" according to one of the night nurses.

In the birthing room at the hospital, Donald Porter, 40, was with his wife, Shirley, 32, as she was working through labor. Their first child, they had already learned, would be a daughter.

"I bought her a Bulls T-shirt already. I hope the Bulls take this tonight, so I can always remember her birthday."

● ● ●

There was no parking problem at Chicago Stadium Wednesday night.

Michael Scott, 26, of Cicero, and a dozen friends and family members gathered around his Bulls-red Chevy Blazer to watch the game on a TV perched on the hood. They were the sole occupants of the vast parking lot.

"We wanted to celebrate at the stadium," Scott said. "So we took

See **The wait**, pg. 18

Bulls win respect for themselves and their town

By Bernie Lincicome
Chicago Tribune

INGLEWOOD, Calif.—Respect.

This has been about respect from the beginning, from the time Michael Jordan first arrived in Chicago, an Olympic hero and an infant conglomerate, to the dawn of this day, the day the Bulls are champions of basketball.

Respect for Jordan, who has to imagine more critics than he has in order to reach ever higher.

"Ten years ago," Jordan said, "I was just a kid scared to death, leaving high school, wondering if I could play at the next level.

Commentary

"Now, 10 years later, I'm at the highest level."

The nagging accusations of ego and selfishness against Jordan no longer have a voice, for this is a trophy with the fingerprints of an entire team on it.

Genius is, by its nature, selfish, but invaluable to anyone wise enough to use it properly. Genius can carry heavy loads to where it must go.

"Ten years down the road, no one would ever remember Michael Jordan, the challenger," said Jordan, the champion.

This is about respect for the Bulls, a team so obscured by Jordan it must fight its own invisibility.

"Thank you for asking me a question," said John Paxson, seated next to Jordan in one of the media sessions.

This is about respect for a bumbling franchise, a quarter of a century into alibis, a franchise that can consider the luckiest day in its history the day that Houston selected Hakeem

See **Respect**, pg. 16

How the Bulls won the title

1 **Michael Jordan.** Enough said.

Tribune photos by Jim Prisching, Charles Cherney

2 **Development of Scottie Pippen and Horace Grant.** Pippen now has NBA star status; Grant was a key man in playoffs.

3 **Defense.** Team committed to executing a high-intensity defensive pressure system.

4 **Phil Jackson.** The second-year coach exuded a calming influence on an excitable team.

5 **No major injuries to starters.** Jordan, Pippen, John Paxson played every game. Grant missed 4; Bill Cartwright sat out 3.

Anti-Semitic outbreak stains Leningrad election

By Thom Shanker
Chicago Tribune

LENINGRAD—As residents in this most European of Russian cities voted Wednesday whether to restore its historic name, St. Petersburg, an outbreak of virulent anti-Semitism proved that Leningrad also remains the most xenophobically Russian of Soviet cities.

Just hours before the polls opened, a wall along an entire block of Nevsky Prospect, Leningrad's main thoroughfare, was covered with posters crudely depicting hook-nosed Jews.

They alleged a Zionist conspiracy—behind the centrist reforms of Soviet President Mikhail Gorbachev, behind the radical platform of Boris Yeltsin, who is seeking the presidency of the Russian Republic and even behind the idea of dropping the communist-era name of Leningrad.

One, for example, was a particu-

■ Yeltsin the likely new leader of the Russian Republic. Page 20.

larly nasty caricature of a member of the Rothschild financial dynasty. The individual was pulling puppet strings to control Gorbachev and Yeltsin.

Another, put up by Vladimir Fursov, a leader of Leningrad's "Fatherland" society, depicted a Nazi mapmaker trying to erase Leningrad in 1941.

Beneath it was a drawing of a ballot used in Wednesday's voting, leaving the clear impression that voters opting for a return of the name St. Petersburg were as intent on destroying the city as Hitler's Wehrmacht.

Although the site has become Leningrad's Speakers Corner, open to appeals for all causes, a cell of right-wing fanatics forcefully ejected a Yeltsin supporter seeking to

See **Name**, pg. 20

Thursday

Road trips: Memories of summers past include dream-like visions of beaches, faraway cities and pretty towns. But, when families traveled by car, getting there could be a nightmare. **In Tempo.**

Kitchen crusaders: The most obvious and easiest place to start a recycling revolution of your own is in the kitchen. Some tips, **in Food Guide.**

Weather

Chicago and vicinity: Thursday: Mostly sunny; high 82 degrees. Thursday night: Partly cloudy, chance for late storms; low 64. Friday: Cloudy, humid, chance for storms; high 89. The national weather report is in **Sec. 2, pg. 7.**

Schwarzkopf: Expand combat role for women

By Elaine S. Povich
Chicago Tribune

WASHINGTON—Moving out in front of many military leaders, Gen. H. Norman Schwarzkopf said Wednesday that the role of women in combat should be expanded, but not to the point of fighting in infantry units.

Setting the stage for upcoming Senate votes on permitting the armed services to assign women to combat roles, Schwarzkopf said the current line separating women from all combat participation has to be moved. But he refused to say if he favored allowing women to fly Navy and Air Force combat missions, a step already taken by the House.

The Senate Armed Services Committee, where America's best-known combat general was testifying Wednesday, will take up the

Tribune photo by Ernie Cox Jr.

Gen. Norman Schwarzkopf testifies before a Senate panel.

issue of women in air combat shortly. Under current law, women can fly transport and tanker planes and serve on crews of repair and supply ships.

But women are not assigned to combat aircraft or ships. The Army also has a policy barring women from direct combat roles.

The invasion force that Schwarzkopf led into the desert

See **Women**, pg. 20

1966 CHICAGO BULLS 1996
XXX
30 YEARS AND RUNNING

204

became a guy who now had the ball as much as Michael. He became a dominant force.

These efforts resulted in impressive displays of execution. In December, the Bulls' defense held the Cleveland Cavaliers to just five points in one quarter at the Stadium. Crowds there presented an atmosphere that no opponent wanted to face. The Bulls lost to Boston there the third game of the season. They wouldn't lost at home again until Houston stopped them March 25, a run of 30 straight home wins.

Their best month was February, which they finished at 11-1. During the All-Star break Craig Hodges won his second straight three-point title by hitting 19 straight shots. The Bulls were hot. Most important, they got a road win in Detroit. Isiah Thomas was out with an injury, but the victory still boosted the Bulls' belief that their time had come.

John Paxson: That February, we finally won a game in Detroit. Just winning a game in their building gave us confidence because we'd had such a tough time beating them.

Phil had sold us on playing our game, not being retaliatory against the Pistons. That's what really helped us along.

Michael Jordan: When we went in there and beat them right before the All-Star break, that's when I knew we could beat them in the playoffs. We had been on the road for something like two weeks, and it just came together. I could feel it then.

The Bulls won the Eastern Conference with a 61-21 record, and Jordan claimed his fifth straight scoring title with a 31.5 average. During the playoffs, he was named the league's MVP for the second time. The Bulls, however, had seen all that window dressing before. The only awards they wanted came in the playoffs. They opened against the Knicks and won the first game by a record 41 points, then went on to sweep them, 3-0. Next Charles Barkley and the 'Sixers fell, 4-1, setting up the only rematch the Bulls wanted: the Pistons in the Eastern Conference Finals.

Jerry Reinsdorf: I have nothing but contempt and disgust for the Pistons organization. I don't think I've ever had any unpleasantries with the owners, but I wasn't

Cliff Levingston and Jordan scramble for a loose ball.

Bulls fans were in the pink.

the only one that felt that way about it. I mean, ultimately, David Stern felt the pressure and made rules changes to outlaw their style of play. It wasn't basketball. It was thuggerism, hoodlumism.

Phil Jackson: Chuck Daly and I never had a difficult moment. But I always said, "Don't be deceived. Chuck is the coach of that team. It comes down from the top."

The Bulls hammered the Pistons, who were reeling from injuries, in three straight games, and on the eve of Game 4 Jordan announced they were going to sweep. "That's not going to happen," responded an infuriated Isiah Thomas. But it did.

At the end of the Game 4 the next day in Detroit, Thomas and the Pistons stalked off the

205

The Knicks wanted to rumble but wound up going quietly, 3-0 in the first round of the '91 playoffs.

Will Perdue and B.J. Armstrong watch Pippen elevate over old teammate Charles Oakley.

floor without congratulating the Bulls, a snub that angered Jordan and thousands of Chicago fans.

Jerry Reinsdorf:

That's one of the things that made us so popular. We were the white knights; we were the good guys. We beat the Bad Boys, 4-0, and they sulked off the court the way they did. I remember saying at the time that this was a triumph of good over evil.

The Portland Trail Blazers had ruled the regular season in the Western with a 63-19 finish, but once again Magic Johnson and the Lakers survived in the playoffs, ousting Portland in the conference finals, 4-2.

For many observers, the Finals seemed a dream matchup: Jordan and the Bulls against Magic and the Lakers. Many, including former Laker coach Pat Riley, figured the Lakers' experience made them a sure bet. Los Angeles was making its ninth Finals appearance since 1980, and had five titles to show for it.

"The Lakers have experience on us," Pippen said as the series opened in Chicago Stadium, "but we have enough to win."

Just as important, the Lakers' James Worthy had a badly sprained ankle, limiting his mobility. Some insiders figured Worthy's injury would cost the Lakers the series. But Los Angeles

won Game 1, 93-91, on a late three-pointer by Sam Perkins. The Bulls got the ball to Jordan, but his 18-foot jumper with four seconds left went in the basket and spun out. It seemed the Lakers' experience might just deliver them, after all.

The Bulls, though, blew out the Lakers in Game 2, 107-86. The Chicago starters shot better than 73 percent from the floor, with Paxson going eight for eight to score 16 points. "Does Paxson ever miss?" the Lakers' Perkins asked.

Paxson shrugged at reporters' questions and said his job was to hit open jumpers. "When I'm in my rhythm, I feel like I'm going to make them all."

Jordan himself had hit 15 of 18 to finish with 33.

Even with the loss, the Lakers were pleased. They had gotten a split in Chicago Stadium and were headed home for three straight games in the Forum. The pressure was on Chicago.

But the Bulls met the challenge in Game 3. Jordan hit a jumper with 3.4 seconds left to send the game into overtime. There, the Bulls ran off eight straight points for a 104-96 win and a 2-1 lead in the series. Jordan was elated, but he refused to dwell on the victory. The Lakers had plenty of experience in coming back, he said.

Yet experience proved no match for the Bulls' young legs and determination. Chicago's Game 4 weapon was defense. The Bulls harried the Lakers into shooting 37 percent from the floor. Chicago won, 97-82. The Lakers' point total was their lowest since before the shot clock was adopted in 1954. They managed a total of 30 points over the second and third quarters.

Perkins had made just one of his 15 shots.

"I didn't even dream this would happen," Magic said.

But the Bulls did. Suddenly, they were on the verge of the improbable.

"It's no surprise the way they've been defending," Laker coach Mike Dunleavy said of the Bulls. "They are very athletic and very smart."

And very hot.

On the eve of Game 5, Jordan publicly acknowledged the team's debt to Cartwright. "He has given us an edge in the middle," he said. "He has been solid for us…. . This guy has turned out to be one of the most important factors for this ball club, and he has surprised many who are standing here and who play with him."

Told of Jordan's comments, Carwright said, "That stuff really isn't important to me. I've always figured what goes around comes around. What's really important to me is winning a championship."

They turned to their offense to claim the title in Game 5, 108-101. Pippen led the scoring parade with 32 points, and Paxson did the damage down the stretch, hitting five buckets in the final four minutes to score 20 points and seal the win. Time and again, Jordan had penetrated, drawing the defense, then tossing the ball out to Paxson, who hit the open shots. In the bedlam on the Forum floor following the Bulls 108-101 victory, Laker superfan Jack Nicholson hugged Phil Jackson, and Magic Johnson tracked down Jordan to offer his congratulations. "I saw tears in his eyes," Johnson said. "I told him, 'You proved everyone wrong. You're a winner as well as a great individual basketball player.'"

By the time Jordan squeezed through the crowd to the locker room he was openly weeping. "I never lost hope," he said, his father and wife nearby. "I'm so happy for my family and this team and this franchise. It's something I've worked seven years for, and I thank God for the talent and the opportunity that I've had."

Jackson and Jordan agreed that the key to the game had been Paxson hitting the open shots. "That's why I've always wanted him on my team and why I wanted him to stay on my team," Jordan said.

Phil Jackson: It was done and over, and it was dramatic, like a blitzkrieg. Afterward, there was a lot of joy. There was Michael holding the trophy and weeping. For me, it was doubly special because the Forum was where I had won the championship as a player nearly 20 years earlier, in 1973.

John Ligmanowski: I remember going up to Michael's room. He told me to order like a dozen bottles of Dom Perignon and enough hor d'ouevres for 40 people. We're at the Ritz Carlton, and I call down to the concierge. I said, "Yeah, send up a dozen bottles of Dom and hor douevres for 40 people." So they were like, "Wait a second." They didn't want to send it up because they knew it wasn't Michael on the phone. So I handed the phone to him. He grabbed the phone and said, "Send it up!"

They had a nice party downstairs. Michael went downstairs about 11:00 at night, and he was still in his game shorts. That was a lot of fun. I think the Ritz Carlton out in L.A. is always gonna be a special place for us when we go out there. We've stayed there ever since, and that's kind of the memory we have, of winning the championship.

The Bulls returned to Chicago and celebrated their championship in Grant Park before a crowd estimated at between 500,000 and a million. "We started from the bottom," Jordan told the screaming masses, "and it was hard working our way to the top. But we did it."

Craig Hodges won the second of his three straight three-point shootouts in 1991.

Vanquishing the Pistons 4-0 made the Eastern Finals complete.

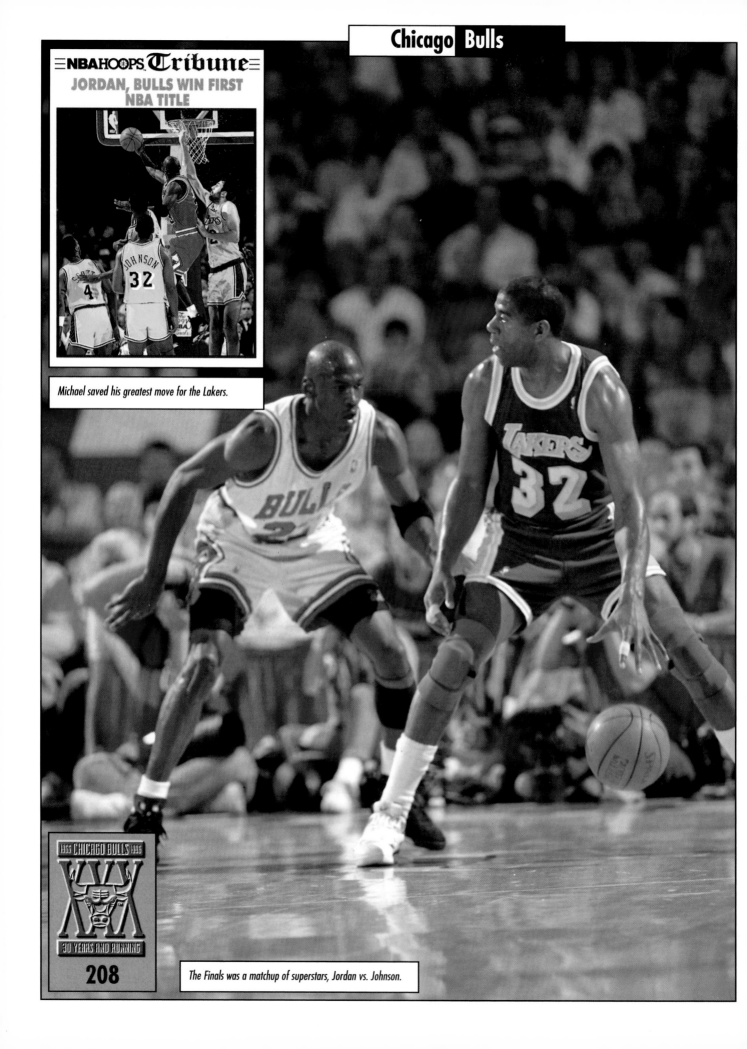

≡NBAHOOPS. Tribune≡

JORDAN, BULLS WIN FIRST NBA TITLE

Michael saved his greatest move for the Lakers.

The Finals was a matchup of superstars, Jordan vs. Johnson.

≡NBAHOOPS. Tribune≡

BULLS ROUT LAKERS TO EVEN SERIES 1-1

After losing Game 1, the Bulls came back strong in Game 2.

B.J. soared.

1966 CHICAGO BULLS 1996

XXX

30 YEARS AND RUNNING

Jordan shared a special moment with his father in the locker room afterward.

Back home in Chicago, the Bulls celebrated with a parade and a rally before hundreds of thousands at Grant Park.

The trip to see President Bush featured stopping for a few hoops at the White House outdoor courts, then a Rose Garden ceremony where the operative word was "Champions!"

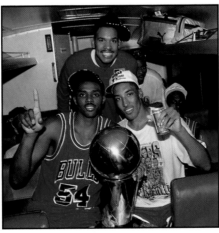

The realization soon settled in on the trip home.

211

Scottie erased all doubters with his '91 performance.

212

Profile/Scottie Pippen

AFTER PLAYING ALL OF HIS YOUNG LIFE *in relative basketball obscurity, Scottie Pippen quite suddenly and dramatically sprang to the NBA's attention in the spring of 1987. He came from the hamlet of Hamburg, Arkansas, (population 3,394) where he had grown up, the baby in Preston and Ethel Pippen's family of a dozen children. "It was fun," Pippen said . "With all those brothers and sisters I always had a friend around."*

He attended Hamburg High, where as a junior he hardly got off the bench for the basketball team. As a 6-1, 150-pound senior, he became the school's starting point guard. That hardly brought him any notice from college recruiters, however. The fall of his junior year, he had agreed to become manager of the football team, and if his prospects for higher education seemed bright, it was there.

Don Dyer, the basketball coach at Central Arkansas, arranged for Pippen to attend school there on a federal grant while serving as manager of the basketball team.

Scottie Pippen: I was responsible for taking care of the equipment, jerseys, stuff like that. I always enjoyed doing that, just being a regular manager.

Don Dyer: He wasn't recruited by anyone. He was a walk-on, a 6-1 1/2, 150-pound walk-on. His high school coach, Donald Wayne, played for me in college, and I took Pippen as a favor to him. I was prepared to help him through college. I was going to make him manager of the team and help him make it financially through college. When Scottie showed up for college, he had grown to 6-3. I had had a couple of players leave school. I could see a little potential; he was like a young colt.

Scottie Pippen: I really wasn't that interested in playing. I had gone through some hard times not playing in high school, but my coach had it in his mind that basketball was the way I would get an education.

Don Dyer: By the end of his first season, he had grown to 6-5, and he was one of our best players… . He had a point guard mentality, and we used him to bring the ball up the floor against the press. But I also played him at forward, center, all over the floor.

Scottie Pippen: I felt myself developing late. I kept seeing myself getting better and better. It was a great feeling, something like I could be as good as I wanted to be. I developed confidence in my abilities.

For Central Arkansas, Pippen became a two-time NAIA All-American. As a senior he averaged 23.6 points, 10 rebounds and 4.3 assists while shooting 59 percent from the floor and 58 percent from three-point range. NBA scouting guru Marty Blake had gotten a tip about Pippen, which he passed on to the Bulls and other teams. Pippen was invited to the NBA's tryout camps, and the rest of the story became the Bulls' sweet fortune. They selected him fifth overall in the 1987 draft.

Don Dyer: His is one of those stories that you read about happening somewhere else. It's rags to riches, a guy coming from nowhere. One of those fantastic stories. Just amazing.

Jerry Krause: When we told Doug Collins about Scottie, he was skeptical. So I put together a video of all the players in the Hawaii tournament and gave it to the coaches. I gave them names and rosters but no real information on the players. We let them see for themselves. After they came out of the video session, I asked if they had any questions, and the first thing out of their mouths was, "Who the hell is Scottie Pippen?"

Michael Jordan: I'd never heard of him. He was from an NAIA school.

Scottie Pippen: Honestly, I didn't expect to be drafted that high. I figured after I went through the camps that I'd have the opportunity to be drafted. I didn't know how high.

As a player from a small town and a small school who was suddenly thrust into the spotlight in Chicago, Pippen was understandably lost. But he quickly developed a friendship with the Bulls' other first round pick that year, Horace Grant. They did everything together. Shopped. Dated girls. Partied. They both drove $74,000 Mercedes 560 SELs. They moved within a mile of each other in suburban

Northbrook. And eventually, they both got married within a week of each other, serving as each other's best man.

In the Bulls' 1988 yearbook, Pippen's profile contained a question: If you were going to the moon who would you take along?

Pippen's answer was, "Horace Grant."

"Scottie is like my twin brother," Grant told reporters.

"We talk about every two hours," Pippen agreed. "Just to see what's going on. Horace is my best friend, the closest anyone's ever been to me."

Mark Pfeil: Scottie called in one day and skipped practice because his cat died. Horace called about 15 minutes later and said he was with Scottie because of the grieving. Johnny Bach was absolutely furious. He got Horace on the phone and said, "You get here. You oughta throw the cat in the garbage can." Horace, when the team got together, wanted to have a moment of silence for Scottie's cat.

Jim Cleamons: My first year here you could read their facial expressions like a book. They were easily frustrated when things did not go right. But over their first three years, they learned how to play, and they learned to keep their composure on the court. They matured and grew more confident.

Cheryl Raye: I think the physical demands on Scottie were what get to him the most. When he got here, he was very fragile mentally. I tie that to his being from a very small school, being from a different background, a different setting.

Scottie never had any of the grooming that guys like Michael who went to big programs had. At the big schools, they groom those guys with the media. Usually they have some sort of maturity about them when they get to the NBA. Scottie did a couple of things on his own. He hired a speech coach from Chicago. She's a radio person and worked on how he handled questions, what to say.

Scottie Pippen: My first year or two, I admit that I messed around a lot. I partied, enjoyed my wealth and didn't take basketball as seriously as I should have. I'm sure a lot of rookies did the same thing I did. You're not used to the limelight or being put in a great situation financially.

Phil Jackson: Starting out, you could see Scottie's possibilities. He could rebound yet still dribble. He could post up, but he also had those slashing moves. You knew he could be very good, but you didn't know how good. He played a few times at guard in his first few sesasons, bringing the ball up against teams with pressing guards, but mostly we used him at small forward.

As more and more teams pressed, however, we decided we had to become more creative. More and more we had to go to Michael to bring the ball up. We didn't want to do that. We came up with the thought of Scottie as a third ball advancer, of an offense that attacked at multiple points. From that position Scottie started to take control, to make decisions. He became a bit of everything.

His first public setback didn't come until Game 7 of the 1990 conference finals against the Pistons, his infamous "migraine game."

Never mind that Kareem Abdul-Jabbar's play-off record was spotted with performances hindered by migraines, Pippen's headache was seen as a classic choke job.

Determined to prove his detractors wrong, Pippen answered with his play over the 1990-91 season. When he was finished, the Bulls had their championship, and observers began to realize that Pippen was one of the league's best players. "I thought that Scottie Pippen would be, at best, a very good journeyman player in this league," Utah executive Frank Layden told Lacy Banks of the Sun Times. "But to tell you the truth now, I'd have to think real hard not to place him as the second best player in this league. I think he's that good. I get the feeling that his development has been enhanced by playing alongside Jordan. He's picked up some good habits from him."

Michael Jordan: It was just a matter of him believing in himself. When he got here, just playing with him, you could see he had all the right tools. It took some time for him to get his confidence on this level because he was competing against some of the best.

214

Gary Glitter Again, 1991-92

PERHAPS THE MOST AMAZING THING *about the Bulls' second championship was the amount of discord and controversy they had to overcome to win it. Long-festering resentment surfaced during the 1991 championship celebration when Michael Jordan decided not to join the team in the traditional Rose Garden ceremony with President George Bush. Much of the discord stemmed from the relationship between Horace Grant and Jordan.*

Phil Jackson: I think it was a situation where Horace felt demeaned, felt that he was made light of, and he wanted to be a person of importance.

There were some things about Horace that bothered Michael. Basically, Horace says whatever comes into his mind in front of the press. One of the situations that was exacerbating to Michael came after our first championship when Horace and his wife and Michael and his wife went to New York. They went to dinner and to see a play. While they were out, Michael basically told Horace that he wasn't going to see President Bush. Michael said, "It's not obligatory. It's on my time, and I have other things to do."

Horace at the time had no problem with it. He knew about this in a private situation and said nothing. Yet when the press came into the picture later, after the story became public, and asked Horace if it bothered him, he made a big issue of it. Basically, the press had put the words in his mouth, and he felt it was a good time to make this kind of statement.

It was immediately team divisive and made Michael look bad and basically got that whole thing started. That bothered Michael about Horace, that he would do something personal like that. Horace had problems in that area, where a lot of times he said things that the press had put in his mind, or in his consciousness.

I would call him in and remind him that he could be fined for making comments that

were detrimental to the team. I'd say, "Horace I have every reason to fine you, but I'm not going to because I know the press put words in your mouth."

He would say, "I'm not ever gonna tell lies."

I told him, "No one's saying you have to tell lies. You have to be conscious of what you're saying. You don't want to be divisive."

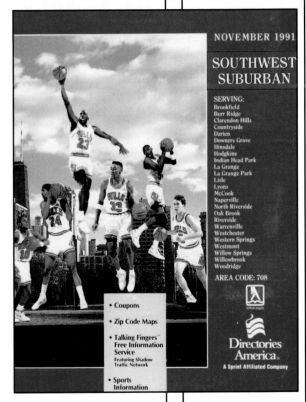

Steve Schanwald: Visiting the White House was a great thrill. The players got to shoot hoops with the President on the White House's outdoor basketball court. The President couldn't have been a more gracious host.

Grant also served as a major source for the book, The Jordan Rules *by Chicago Tribune sportswriter Sam Smith. Marketed as the inside story of the Bulls' championship season, the*

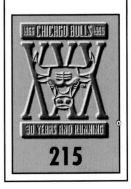

215

Chicago Tribune

Monday, June 15, 1992

NBA Championship Final

35¢ City, suburbs   50¢ Elsewhere

146th Year — No. 167 © Chicago Tribune   6 Sections   N S D NW   ★

Two for two: Bulls still champs!

Bulls repeat

The Chicago Bulls beat the Portland Trail Blazers 4 games to 2 to win their second consecutive NBA title.

GAME 6	Bulls	97
The final game—the final score	Trail Blazers	93

Tribune photo by Charles Cherney

Bobby Hansen receives a high-five from Horace Grant during the Bulls' win.

Mike's momentum: MVP Michael Jordan, who started slowly, finished with 33 points. He had hot 2nd and 4th quarters, including 12 points in the game's final six minutes.

King for a day: The Bulls' Stacey King led a strong Chicago bench effort with five critical points in the fourth quarter.

King

Fourth and won: After three quarters in Game 6, the Bulls were down 64-79, but they roared back and outscored Portland 33-14 in the fourth quarter.

' Last year was a honeymoon. This year has been an odyssey.'

Chicago coach Phil Jackson

Trailing the Blazers... ...but not when it counted. Portland opened Game 6 by missing its first six field goal attempts; however, the team still led 25-19 after the first quarter and 50-44 at the half.

Game 6 line score

	1st	2nd	3rd	4th	Total
Bulls	19	25	20	33	97
Trail Blazers	25	25	29	14	93

Celebration breaks out repeatedly

By Steve Johnson and Susan Kuczka

Those who complained that the Chicago Bulls and their fans were complacent during this year's championship playoffs got their comeuppance Sunday night.

If what led to the Bulls' winning the National Basketball Association title was complacency, then bungee jumping is a stroll to the 7-Eleven. If what followed it was world weariness, then a wedding is merely a church social with an oversized cake.

Chicago sports fans, accustomed to loving losers, cheering also-rans, and suffering with teams that look better on paper

■ Bulls fans stampede parts of city after victory. Page 8.

than in the paper, could be forgiven their exuberance, if not their scattered displays of criminality.

Those fans were handed Sunday a second successive NBA championship by the Bulls, the first time a Chicago sporting franchise has won a title at home since the 1963 Bears. It also was the first time a Chicago team claimed back-to-back championships since the Bears in 1940 and 1941.

As time ran out in Sunday's game and the Bulls clinched their 4-games-to-2 series victory over an underdisciplined Portland Trail Blazers team, John Paxson's toss of the ball toward the rafters served much the same function as the orb that drops in New York's Times Square on New Year's Eve.

It was Paxson's way of saying: Let the partying begin.

Throughout Chicago, the faithful obeyed, raising fists, steins and even cans in celebration. In a few areas, victory brought broken windows and uninvited shopping. And mopes citywide chose to draw and fire their guns in the air, as though only actual menace could match the moment.

But the predominant noise on the streets was more benign. Motorists leaned into their car

See Fans, pg. 14

Tribune photo by Jim Prisching

Atop the scorer's table, and the basketball world, Michael Jordan celebrates the Bulls' victory.

Late rally secures aura of greatness

By Sam Smith

There can be no doubt now about what the Bulls accomplished during the last few weeks in winning their second straight NBA title.

They have made greatness and history their principal opponents. They have taken their place beside the Celtics and the Lakers in NBA folklore and excellence. They have taken over a decade.

They did it Sunday night at the Stadium, overcoming a 17-point deficit and defeating the Portland Trail Blazers 97-93 to win the NBA Finals four games to two.

With Michael Jordan on the bench, an unlikely combination of Bulls reserves helped cut the margin to three in the fourth quarter. Stacey King scored five fourth-quarter points and Bobby Hansen—the only Bull without a 1991 championship ring—contributed a key three-point shot plus a steal. Jordan returned to score 12 of his 33 points in the game's final six minutes, and Scottie Pippen also hit some key shots down the stretch.

"We had to get some energy out there," responded a champagne-soaked Bulls coach Phil Jackson when asked about his unusual lineup to start the final period.

"This is so gratifying," said Jordan, also bathed in the bubbly. "I've had some hard times this season. I stayed strong with the support of my teammates. I'm glad for Bobby Hansen.

The 1990s, no doubt growing into a time of massive change, have taken on the Bulls as a partner, much as the '60s did for the Celtics and the '80s did for the Lakers. By winning twice in a row, even if it hasn't been the artistic and overwhelming triumph of their maiden voyage a year ago, the Bulls have combined talent, genius and hard work into a special treat for their followers. They have entered the cathedral of greatness because they were the architects of their own success.

"Who cares how many games it took?" said Jordan.

It took 17 games in 1991 to earn that elusive title for which a city had yearned for more than a

See Bulls, pg. 8

This championship was a promise kept

By Bernie Lincicome

Commentary

One championship is a souvenir. Two is an inventory.

They look identical, like polished twins, the pair of NBA trophies that now belong to the Bulls and, by extension and devotion, to Chicago itself.

And yet they are as distinctive as a Michael Jordan tomahawk jam from a Michael Jordan postup jumper, one uncontested, one earned, but worth the same.

This second trophy ought to be just a little larger or come

with distinctive dents, something to mark the effort it took to get it, a season of entitlement followed by a playoffs of challenge.

This was the greatest of all seasons for any modern Chicago sports team because it was a promise kept. In a town that always gives its warriors next year, this was the year after next year, and it came without regrets or

alibis.

From the moment the fresh and flushed winners of 1991 joined in the Grant Park chant of "Re-peat! Rep-eat!" failure was not going to be accepted, and neither they, nor we, understood how much easier it is to put a boast on a T-shirt than in an almanac.

These Bulls were not the one-ring Bears of the '80s or the half-title Sox and Cubs, not the recent next-to-first Blackhawks, full of reasons and wishes.

The Bulls have raised the standard for all Chicago sports teams of what is acceptable. One is no longer enough.

These are, now and at last, the good old days.

Phil Jackson, the coach, has won as many NBA titles as his own mentor, Red Holzman, and more than his first teacher, Bill Fitch.

The child has exceeded the father figure, without compromising his soul, cutting much of

See Promise, pg. 8

All ends well: Ecstasy of a repeat was worth the struggle. Melissa Isaacson.

Curtain call: The Bulls take their celebration back upstairs. Bob Verdi.

Bench delivers: Four subs help turn the game around. Skip Myslenski.

In Sports.

Perot camp tries to keep up with unbridled momentum

By Thomas Hardy
Chicago Tribune

[...] piece of the Ross [...] is the story of [...] colt himself, he [...] in horses and [...] nose in the process. [...] himself astride [...] force, a nearly [...] petition drive and [...] movement that [...] undeclared candidate [...] of President Bush [...] Democratic nominee [...] in presidential

[...] and his growing [...] advisers rein in [...] force and direct it [...] campaign [...] whether the Texas [...] into the White [...] remarkable independence [...] thrown on his [...] fashion unfamiliar to

billionaires.

Perot will travel to four states this week to be on hand when volunteers file nominating petitions to place his name on the presidential ballot. A formal campaign declaration is expected in early July. Meanwhile, the Perot operation spent the weekend moving into an expanded headquarters at a north Dallas office complex.

"Ours is not a problem of creating movement, it's keeping up with it," said James Squires, a senior adviser in the Perot camp.

But as Perot and his staff work to keep pace with the nationwide petition drive and plan for the

See Perot, pg. 2

Election 92

Monday

License to sell: The licensing industry offers up Slick the crash dummy, Burp Balls and dinosaurs in search of the successor to the Ninja Turtle bonanza. **In Business.**

Stars shine for Ringo: Ringo Starr gets by with a little help from his famous friends during a Poplar Creek concert. **In Overnight.**

Weather

Chicago and vicinity: Monday: Partly cloudy, less humid; high mid to upper 70s. Monday night: Partly cloudy; low 58 to 63. Tuesday: Chance of thundershowers late; high near 80. The national weather report is in Sec. 2, pg. 5.

American firms wake up to world market demands

By Ronald E. Yates
Chicago Tribune

WASHINGTON—The year was 1975, and Barry Hannon, like most Americans, was not concerned about such things as trade imbalances or America's international competitiveness.

In fact, there was no reason Hannon, a machine-tool engineer from Cleveland, should have cared. Since the end of World War II, America had been the strongest industrial and financial power the world had ever seen. Like most of us, Hannon expected that condition to continue from generation to generation.

"I thought it was an American birthright to always be the strongest, the richest, the best at everything," he says. "Hell, that's what being an American was all about. If somebody had told me back then that things would be the way

Back to business

If U.S. business is to regain its competitive global edge, it must grapple with fundamental change. Second in a series.

they are now, I wouldn't have believed it. This is the country where everybody is supposed to live happily ever after, right?"

Wrong.

For millions of Americans, the 17 years since 1975—the last year the U.S. registered a trade surplus, $8.9 billion—have not been at all like that American fairy tale. Between 1975 and 1990, America's trade deficit with the rest of the world totaled a staggering $1.12 trillion, and the U.S. moved from being the world's largest creditor

See Compete, pg. 16

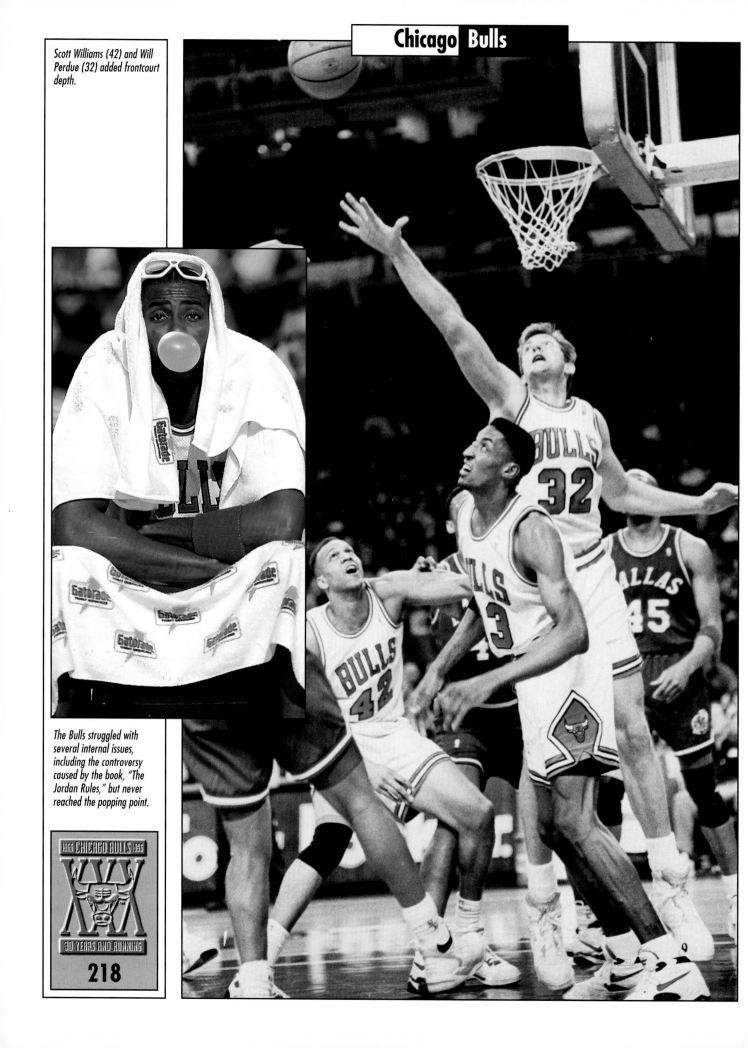

Scott Williams (42) and Will Perdue (32) added frontcourt depth.

The Bulls struggled with several internal issues, including the controversy caused by the book, "The Jordan Rules," but never reached the popping point.

218

book and its unflattering portraits of Jordan and Jerry Krause rocked the franchise just as the 1991-92 season opened.

Phil Jackson: Those kinds of stories there's no reason for. And people believe it's the truth. I read about 70 pages of it, and I realized there's a lot of things represented that I didn't believe to be true, or that I knew didn't happen to the team. I felt, "This is like anything else. It's one guy's perspective on life. Another guy knows it's not real."

The Jordan Rules was very divisive to the team. But the one great thing about this group of guys, they never let the external stuff bother the team's play on the floor.

Indeed it didn't. Krause set the roster with a November trade, sending disgruntled Dennis Hopson to Sacramento for reserve guard Bobby Hansen. The Bulls raced out to a 37-5 record including a 14-game winning streak, the longest in team history. They slipped over late January and February, going only 11-8. Jordan and Pippen were both named as starters for the East in the All-Star game, and Craig Hodges won his third straight long-distance shootout during All-Star Weekend.

By the first of March, the Bulls were back on track and closed out the schedule with a blistering 19-2 run to finish 67-15, the franchise's best record. Jordan claimed his sixth straight scoring crown and won his third league MVP award. He and Pippen were named to the All-Defense first team, and Pippen earned All-NBA second team honors.

Phil Jackson: We really had an outrageous year. We won 67 games, and basically I felt like I had to pull back on the reins, or they would have tried to win 70 or 75.

Chip Schaefer: We had a phenomenal start to the season. We had a 37-5 record. But then we headed west and lost four of six games before the All-Star break. Michael got ejected in Utah when he head-bumped Tommie Wood, the official. We were in a triple-overtime game, and Wood called a foul on Michael in the third overtime. It was an accidental head butt. Michael was vehement in his argument, and they bumped heads. Wood ejected him from the game, and we wound up losing with Jeff

Malone's free throws. Then Michael had to sit out the next game, which was the game in Phoenix. So he just flew on to the All-Star game in Orlando. We just coasted the rest of that season through one winning streak after another. The team was almost bored with success and could turn it on and off whenever they wanted to.

Steve Schanwald: It was a galling loss. The game was a great commercial for the NBA. If not for that call, it likely would have been the NBA's first quadruple-overtime game ever. It was a shame. Our guys played their asses off.

Phil Jackson: The playoffs were an entirely different story from the regular season. We had injuries, and we had New York. And teams were coming at us with a lot of vim and vigor.

In the first round of the playoffs, the Bulls faced the Miami Heat, a 1989 expansion team making its first postseason appearance. Chicago quickly claimed the first two games in the best-of-five series, then headed to Miami for Game 3.

They rose above the Knicks again in the playoffs.

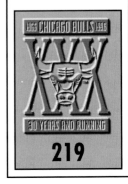

The 1992 Finals featured a showdown of amazing athletes. Jordan and Pippen vs. Clyde Drexler and Cliff Robinson.

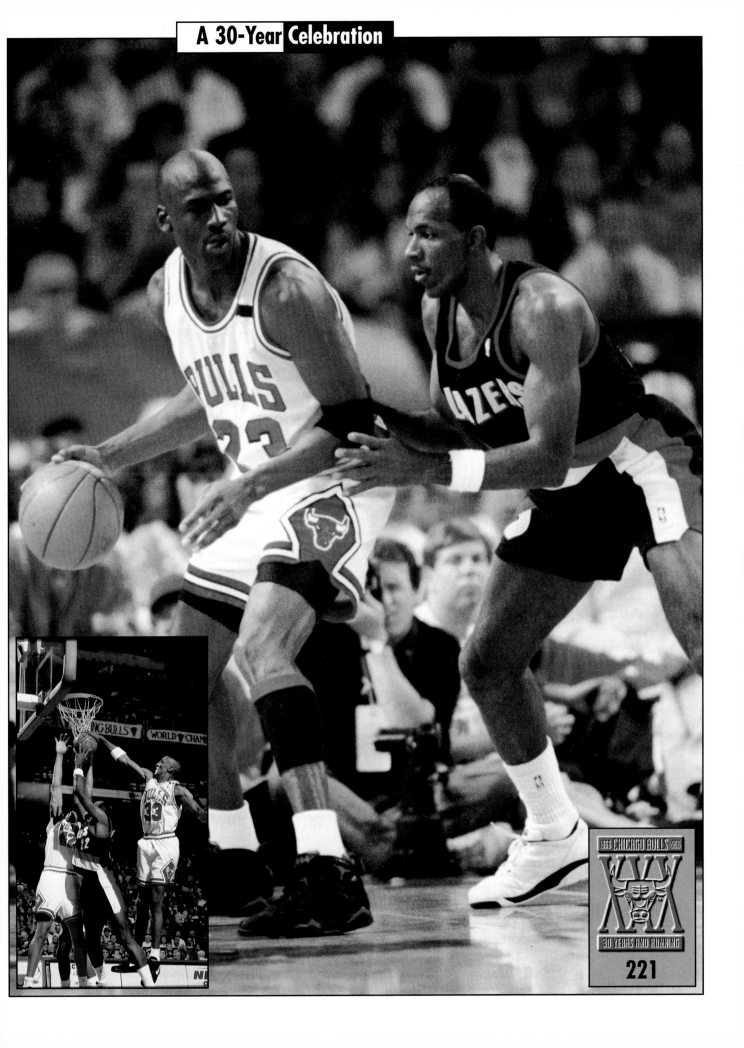

The Bulls' amazing rally in the fourth quarter of Game 6 gave them a championship to celebrate at home.

Tom Dore: In Miami's first playoff game ever, it was clacker night. What they said was, any time Michael gets the ball or shoots a free throw, go nuts with those clackers. Make all kinds of noise. Well, it worked in the first quarter. The Heat had a big lead. And, in fact, we were wondering, can the Bulls come back from this? And Michael stopped by the broadcast table and looked at Johnny Kerr and me and said, "Here we come." That's all he said. Boy, did he ever. He went absolutely beserk, scored 56 points, and the Bulls won, swept the series.

Next up were the New York Knicks, now coached by Pat Riley and employing a physical style strikingly similar to the Pistons. The

Knicks used their muscle to claim Game 1 in Chicago Stadium. B. J. Armstrong helped even the series at 1-1 by hitting big shots in the fourth quarter of Game 2. Then the Bulls regained the home-court advantage in Game 3 in New York when Jordan finally broke free of New York's cloying defense for his first dunks of the series.

The Knicks, powered by Xavier McDaniel, fought back to even it with a win in Game 4.

In critical Game 5, Jordan took control by going to the basket. The Knicks kept fouling him, and he kept making the free throws, 15 in all to finish with 37 points as the Bulls won, 96-88. "Michael is Michael," Riley said afterward. "His game is to take it to the basket and challenge the defense. When you play against a guy like him, he tells you how much he wants to win by how hard he takes the ball to the basket."

The Knicks managed to tie it again with a Game 6 win in New York, but the Bulls were primed for Game 7 in the Stadium and walked to the win, 110-81. "We got back to playing Bulls basketball," Armstrong explained.

They resumed their struggle in the conference finals against the Cavaliers and lost Game 2, 107-81, in Chicago Stadium. "I never sat through an exhibition of basketball like that in my life," Jackson said. "This team deserved to be booed off the floor."

The Cavaliers managed to tie the series at 2-2, but the Bulls had just enough to escape Cleveland, 4-2. "John Paxson turned to me in the locker room and said, 'What a long strange trip it's been,'" Jackson confided to reporters. "Last year was the honeymoon. This year was an odyssey."

The Finals against the Portland Trail Blazers brought more turbulence, which was intermittently calmed by Jordan's memorable performances. In Game 1, he scored 35 points in the first half, including a record six three-pointers, enough to bury the Blazers, 122-89.

Michael Jordan: I was in a zone. My threes felt like free throws. I didn't know what I was doing, but they were going in.

Portland struggled back and somehow won Game 2 on the strength of Danny Ainge's nine points in overtime. The Blazers had their split and the series headed to Portland for three games. But the Bulls' defense and a solid team effort—Pippen and Grant scored 18 each to go with Jordan's 26—ended thoughts of an upset with a win in Game 3.

The Blazers evened it at 2-2 in Game 4, but Game 5 was another Jordan showcase. Going to the hole repeatedly, he drew fouls and made 16 of 19 free throws to finish with 46 points, enough to give the Bulls a 119-106 win and a 3-2 lead.

Game 6 back in the Stadium should have been a Chicago walk, but the Bulls fell into a deep hole, down 17 points late in the third quarter. Then Jackson pulled his regulars and played Bobby Hansen, B. J. Armstrong, Stacey King and Scott Williams with Pippen. Hansen stole the ball and hit a shot, and the rally was on. Strangely, Jordan was on the bench leading the cheering.

With about eight minutes to go, Jackson sent Jordan back in, and the Bulls powered their way to their second title, 97-93, bringing the Stadium to an unprecedented eruption.

Phil Jackson: The final game against Portland was a dramatic night for us and all Chicago fans. We came from 17 down at the end of the third quarter to win the championship. What followed was an incredible celebration.

Steve Schanwald: Jerry Reinsdorf and Jerry Krause and Phil Jackson and Michael and Scottie stood on the stage in the locker room and accepted the trophy. But we didn't have instant replay capability, so the fans were not able to share in that moment. Up in the Stadium, we were playing Gary Glitter on the loudspeaker, and the crowd was just reveling in the championship. It had been a great comeback in the fourth quarter, really initiated by our bench. So the victory was a total team effort.

I went down and asked Jerry Reinsdorf if we could bring the team back up. He said, "It's alright with me, but ask Phil." I said, "Phil, the fans are upstairs. They're not leaving; they're dancing. We've got to bring the team back up and let them enjoy this thing." Phil thought for a moment, and Bobby Hansen was standing nearby. Phil asked Bobby what he thought, and Bobby said, "Let's do it!" Phil put two fingers in his mouth and whistled over all that noise and champagne and everything.

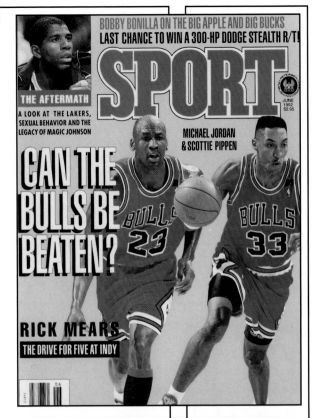

The last-second victory ignited a wild celebration in the Stadium.

He got everything quieted down. He said, "Grab that trophy. We're going back up to celebrate with our fans!" With that, Michael grabbed the trophy, and we went back upstairs. When we started emerging through the tunnel, we started to play the opening to our introduction music. It's very dramatic. It's 'Eye in the Sky' by the Alan Parsons Project. So the crowd knew when the music started playing something was happening. The team came up through the tunnel, and all of the sudden the crowd just exploded. It was a 10,000-goose bump experience. All of a sudden some of the players—Scottie and Horace and Hanson—those guys got up on the table so that everybody could see them in the crowd. Then Michael came up and joined them with the trophy, and they started dancing. It was just an electrifying experience, and I think for anybody that was there, it was a moment that they will never forget as long as they live.

Phil Jackson: I went upstairs with the players into this scene of bedlam. But I got tripped up by some television people, from the cables on their equipment. It occurred to me that this was a little bit wilder than I wanted it to be. I got hit and got tripped. I thought, "I guess this really isn't something I have to be a part of. This is a time for the fans and the players." I stood and watched them for a while celebrating on the tables. Then I went back downstairs and collected myself and my thoughts. My family stayed up there and was a part of the celebration. But I went back downstairs and enjoyed some private thoughts. How the first championship had been more of a glory ride, and the second one was more of a journey.

Michael and Bill tote the fruits of their labor.

CHICAGO BULLS

1991-92 CHICAGO BULLS
BACK TO BACK NBA WORLD CHAMPIONS

FRONT ROW (left to right):   Michael Jordan, Horace Grant, Bill
Cartwright, Scottie Pippen, John Paxson

BACK ROW (left to right):   B.J. Armstrong, Bobby Hansen, Stacey
King, Will Perdue, Scott Williams,
Cliff Levingston, Craig Hodges

It had been a special time of nine months together. Things had been up and down, but we had had this one goal together, and despite our differences, we had focused on that one goal.

I told the guys, "A back-to-back championship is the mark of a great team." We had passed the demarcation point. Winning that second title set us apart.

Again, the team opted for a rally in Grant Park. Again, hundreds of thousands gathered to scream and celebrate. "We will be back," Bill Cartwright promised.

"Let's go for a three-peat," Pippen suggested, and the crowd's roar in response made it clear no one in Chicago doubted that it was possible.

It was back to Grant Park for celebration number two.

225

Threesweet, 1992-93

JERRY KRAUSE HAD HOPED THAT SCOTTIE Pippen and Michael Jordan would decline their invitations to play for the United States on the Dream Team in the Olympic games in Barcelona over the summer of 1992. Krause wasn't being unpatriotic. He just wanted the Bulls' superstars to rest. They both agreed to the honor, however, and despite the United States' easy breeze to the gold medal that August, both players came home thoroughly exhausted by the experience.

Horace Grant, who had said many times that no one understood his importance to the Bulls, seemed jilted by the attention showered on Jordan and Pippen. And when Jackson allowed the two stars to take a casual approach to training camp in early October, Grant complained to the media about "double standards" and "preferential treatment."

Later in the season, he would accuse Pippen of arrogance. Ultimately, this sniping would prove to be a minor rift between the two friends, but both agreed that they weren't as close as they had been.

Besides the "divisiveness" that Jackson loathed, the Bulls encountered a rash of physical ailments. Cartwright, 35, and Paxson, 32, had offseason surgery on their creaky knees, and Pippen would be troubled by a bad ankle for most of the season. For Jordan, the pains were first his arch and then his wrist.

B. J. Armstrong, who had long struggled with the Bulls' triple-post offense, finally found enough of a comfort level to replace Paxson in the starting lineup. Finding his playing rythmn coming off the bench clearly stumped Paxson, and the media kept steady track of the difficulties brought on by the shift. But no rift developed between the two guards. The 25-year-old Armstrong was simply better equipped to play in the Bulls' pressure defense, and that would make the difference in the playoffs. Plus, he would lead the league in three-point shooting, hitting better than 45 percent.

For the regular season, however, Jackson backed off from the pressure defense, thinking that he needed to conserve their energies and health. But the other problem for this veteran club was boredom, and the slowed pace worked against them until at one point during the season Jordan called an on-court conference and told his teammates to resume the pressure. Later, Jordan debated Jackson's strategy with reporters. "Maybe we gamble and we lose our legs," Jordan said. "I still don't think we get conservative now. When we try to slow down, things get too deliberate."

All of these wrinkles ultimately proved no hindrance. Their only real downside was the sameness. Jordan called it "monotony." For most teams, they might have meant 38 wins. For the Bulls, it meant another divisional championship, 57 wins (their fourth straight 50-win season) and a seventh straight scoring crown for Jordan, tying him with Wilt Chamberlain.

On January 8th, Michael scored his 20,000 career point, having reached that total in just 620 games. The only man to do it faster was Chamberlain, who reached the milestone in

Chicago Tribune

Monday, June 21, 1993

NBA Championship Final

50¢ Newsstand 40¢ Home Delivery

147th Year — No. 172 © Chicago Tribune   6 Sections   N S NW L D SW   ★

Three-mendous!

- Paxson hits winning three-point shot
- Grant blocks KJ's last-second attempt
- Suns lose 4-point lead in last minute

GAME 6

BULLS **99**   SUNS **98**

- Jordan MVP, breaks scoring record
- Bulls 1st three-time champs in 27 years
- Rally at 10 a.m. Tuesday in Grant Park

The Bulls' bench jumps for joy as Game 6 of the NBA Finals comes to an end while Charles Barkley of the Suns stares ahead glumly.

Tribune photo by Michael Meinhardt

More than a victory, it's history

By Sam Smith
Pro basketball writer

The Bulls this time came stalking history, which is a most elusive goal. For history makes one both a target and an enduring memory.

It will be hard to forget this third consecutive NBA title, which the Bulls won by outlasting Phoenix in Game 6 Sunday 99-98 on a three-point shot by guard John Paxson with 3.9 seconds remaining. Horace Grant sealed the historic night by blocking the Suns' Kevin Johnson last-second shot attempt.

The night will forever be engraved in the conscience of sport. For few have gone this way, and only the aristocracy of sport

■ 2 killed, 2 cops shot in Bulls post-victory violence. Page 6.

reside here, names offered in solemn reverence, like Boston Celtics, Montreal Canadiens, New York Yankees, Notre Dame football, UCLA basketball.

And Chicago Bulls.

Right up there by virtue of winning a third straight NBA title in a time when such things are not done, when players are too spoiled, too wealthy and not determined enough. Or so the belief goes. They're not like those old-timers, it was said, who would just show up to play for free.

Well, the Bulls are those guys.

Many have tried the unique "three-peat," but few have succeeded. Sure, those famed Celtics won eight straight and the Canadiens and Yankees five straight and UCLA seven straight.

But that was before the big-money explosion, which was supposed to have taken the kid out of the man and replaced it with avarice and self-aggrandizement.

But it didn't for Michael Jordan or Scottie Pippen or Horace Grant or Bill Cartwright or B.J. Armstrong or John Paxson or Will Perdue or Scott Williams or Stacey King or the rest.

History repeats itself, it was once said, because nobody listens.

But they do when history repeats itself twice, when, despite all odds, a group takes on history and wins.

"When you win twice in a row, that's really all you're playing for," said former Lakers star Magic Johnson, whose 1989 team had won 11 straight playoff games before injuries to him and Byron Scott took them down against the Detroit Pis-

See **Bulls**, pg. 6

Bulls seal legacy with dramatic finish

By Melissa Isaacson
Chicago Tribune

PHOENIX—Michael Jordan had just three words for his Bulls teammates when he stepped onto the team bus before Sunday's game.

"Hello, world champs."

Maybe that's all you need to know about the Bulls' frame of mind, all you need to know about the Bulls, really.

Check that. All you need to know about the three-time world champion Bulls.

Make room in the Stadium rafters for one more banner and clear another page in the NBA record books. The Bulls' 99-98 victory over the Phoenix Suns in Game 6 of the NBA Finals on Sunday night gave them a 4-2 series win and placed them alongside the Boston Celtics of the '60s and the Min-

neapolis Lakers of the '50s as teams to win at least three consecutive NBA titles.

Jordan's scoring 9 of the Bulls' 12 fourth-quarter points, John Paxson's three-point shot with 3.9 seconds remaining and, finally, Horace Grant's block of Kevin Johnson's 10-footer with time running out spelled the difference on this improbable and amazing night.

"I can't think of a more dramatic finish for us," Bulls coach Phil Jackson said. "Three games on the road to win certainly typifies the emotional swings that went on in these playoffs."

With every intention of hanging on to their old moniker and re-establishing control in the NBA Finals, the Bulls defended their two world titles by surviving this night like they have survived this season—by fending off their opponent again and again and again.

The Bulls led by as many as 11 points in the second quarter, but the Suns closed the gap to five at halftime and wiped out an eight-point lead at the end of three quarters to lead by four with less than a minute remaining. "I honestly believe they had to win tonight to win the series," said Charles Barkley, who along with Dan Majerle, led the Suns in scoring with 21 points.

Jordan, unanimously named the series' Most Valuable Player for the

See **Champions**, pg. 6

Tribune photo by Jim Prisching

Michael Jordan drapes his arm around teammate Trent Tucker and the NBA championship trophy Sunday night.

Kids spell out their love for dads with winning words

"The man that I call dad is really my stepdad. My real dad died when I was very young. My stepdad is very large. When he stands in the door he blocks the sunlight. One day he said: 'Once I climbed a mountain when I was in the army in Europe and I saw God.' I do not think that he really saw God. I think he felt God there and found peace in the mountains, because he told me that he found out what was really important in life and what was not. . . .

"When I say my prayers, sometimes I see my real father smile at me. I do not really see him, but I can feel him smile. He is smiling because my stepdad is making me become the gentleman that my dad would want me to be."

—Christopher Shelton, 10, on why his father has the best view of life.

By Andrew Gottesman

Earl Young, Christopher Shelton's stepfather, cried the first time he read that Father's Day essay.

Young cried again Sunday, when his stepson accepted one of six first-place awards in the 8th annual John Hancock Observatory's

Father's Day Essay Contest.

"My own father had just passed away and I had gone out to write the obituary," said Young, a local businessman who married Shelton's mother on Mother's Day. "[Christopher and his twin sister] left their essays for me on the bed

See **Dads**, pg. 10

Somali warlord like Elvis: Everywhere and nowhere

By Liz Sly
Chicago Tribune

MOGADISHU, Somalia—For a while last week, as American bombs rained down on Gen. Mohamed Farrah Aidid's enclave, the defiant warlord looked set to become Somalia's version of Saddam Hussein, thumbing his nose at the international forces ranged against him and making regular appearances on CNN.

But now that he has gone into hiding from UN forces seeking to arrest him, he is turning into Mogadishu's Elvis.

It is believed that Aidid has taken refuge somewhere in the city's rabbit warren of sandy streets and little stone houses after he was bombed out of his enclave last week.

Rumors are al[so] Aidid sightings. H[e] mosque attending he was spotted market surround[ed] armed henchmen, this neighborhood he has been seen e[ver] nowhere to be foun[d]

"I recognize tha[t] here an Elvis ki[nd] some time," said

See

7 49485 0000

JOHN **PAXSON**

BULLS • G

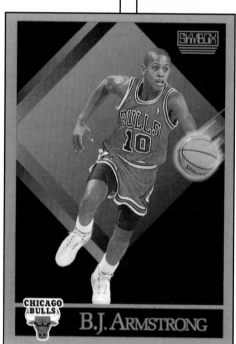

CHICAGO
BULLS

B.J. ARMSTRONG

Pax found himself sharing time with B.J. at the point.

499 games. "It looks like I fell short of Wilt again, which is a privilege," Jordan said. "I won't evaluate this until I'm away from the game. I'm happy about it, but we still have a long season to go. I'm sure as I get older, I'll cherish it more."

In another game, an overtime loss to Orlando, Jordan scored 64 points, although Pippen complained afterward that Jordan had taken too many shots.

Jordan would be named All-NBA first team again, and both he and Pippen would make the All-Defense first team. In the Finals, Jordan would collect an unprecedented third straight MVP award

For Jackson, December would bring his 200th win, reaching the mark faster than any coach in league history. Even with the accomplishments, it was not a regular season to treasure.

Chip Schaefer: They were tired. No question. Michael and Scottie were tired in the fall of '92. That was just a tough long year and really a tough year for Michael. It seemed like one thing after another. The press was picking on him, things just happening all year long. As soon as one thing would let up, it seemed like another came into play. It was really evident that he was getting tired. Tired physically, tired mentally of the whole thing.

Michael Jordan: Phil Jackson played a lot of mind games. He waged psychological warfare to make you realize the things you have to do to be a winner.

For two years, the New York Knicks had seen their championship hopes end in seven-game playoff battles with the Bulls. With good reason, they figured they needed the homecourt advantage to dethrone Jordan and his teammates. So coach Pat Riley turned the full force of his considerable intensity to driving New York to 60 wins and the homecourt advantage in the Eastern Conference.

The Bulls, meanwhile, slipped quietly into second place with 57 wins and seemed almost distracted heading into the playoffs. But they quickly picked up the pace, sweeping three from Atlanta in the first round, then devastating the Cleveland Cavaliers again by winning four straight. Jordan capped the series with a last-second game winner in Cleveland that closed the chapter on his domination of the Cavs.

Chip Schaefer: And then we faced New York again. We didn't have home-court so there really wasn't much reason to be optimistic about it.

Jordan loathed the Knicks' brutish style. "They play like the Pistons," he said testily. Perhaps New York's frustration made them worse. Plus, Jackson and Riley made no great effort to hide their dislike for one another. In Game 1 in Madison Square Garden, the Knicks banged Jordan into a 10-for-27 shooting performance and won, 98-90. "I told the team I let them down," Jordan said afterward.

The acknowledgment did little good because the same thing happened in Game 2. Jordan missed 20 of 32 shots, and the Knicks won again, 96-91. Afterward, the smugness in New York was tangible. "Now the Bulls are down two games and have to beat the Knicks four games out of five games if they are going to have a chance at three titles in a row," crowed New York Daily News columnist Mike Lupica.

A media firestorm then erupted after a New York Times report that Jordan had been seen at an Atlantic City casino in the wee hours before Game 2, suggesting that perhaps he wasn't properly rested for competition. The headlines brought Jackson and Krause quickly to his defense. "There is no problem with Michael Jordan," Krause told reporters. "He cares about winning and is one of the great winners of all time."

"We don't need a curfew," Jackson added. "These are adults…. You have to have other things in your life or the pressure becomes too great."

With this issue hovering over the events, the series moved to Chicago.

Cheryl Raye: The Bulls came back for practice at the Berto Center. I've never seen as much media gathered for an event. Michael stepped out of the training room, and I said, "Michael, would you just go over the chain of events for us? Would you tell us what happened and where this story is coming from?" He did, and then a television newsperson from a local Chicago station started grilling him as though he were an alderman being convicted of a crime. Chuck Gowdy from Channel 7 was saying things like, "Do you do this before every game? Do you have a gambling problem?" He kept hammering and hammering away, and eventually Michael just shut up and walked away. He didn't talk until the first game against Phoenix.

Jordan ceased speaking with the media, and his teammates followed suit. With Pippen taking charge, the Bulls won big in Game 3 in the Stadium, 103-83.

Jordan scored 54 points to drive Chicago to a win in Game 4, 105-95, and it was Jordan's triple-double (29 points, 10 rebounds, and 14 assists) that dominated the statistics column in Game 5, when Chicago took the series lead, 3-2. But it was Pippen's successive blocks of putback attempts by New York's Charles Smith late in Game 5 that closed off the Knicks' hopes. Then, when the Bulls completed their comeback in Game 6 in Chicago, it was Pippen again doing the final damage, a corner jumper and a trey, in a 96-88 victory.

The Bulls had persevered to return to their third straight NBA Finals. This time, Charles Barkley, now with the Phoenix Suns, was the opponent. They had won 62 games and had the homecourt advantage for their brand new America West Arena. The Bulls, though, had plenty of confidence. They had always done well against Barkley's Philadelphia teams.

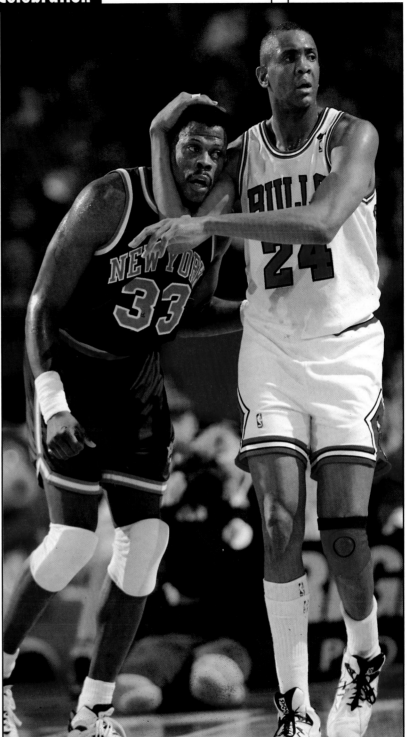

The Bulls wrapped up the Knicks in an amazing playoff reversal.

Pippen's and Grant's defense would shackle him again, and B. J. Armstrong had the quickness to stay with Phoenix point guard Kevin Johnson.

Those plans eventually worked out, but in the short term there was more turbulence ahead. No sooner had Jordan's Atlantic City casino

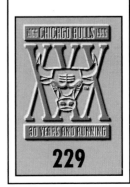

229

Aging Trent Tucker provided excellent spot duty off the bench.

230

jaunt slipped out of the news than Richard Esquinas, a San Diego businessman, stepped forward with a book claiming that Jordan owed him $1.2 million from high-stakes losses from betting on golf games.

In a taped interview on NBC at halftime of Game 1 of the Finals, Jordan answered, admitting that he had lost substantial sums to

Esquinas but nowhere near the figure claimed. However, questions about whether this distraction would hinder the Bulls were quickly put aside when Chicago claimed the first game, 100-92. The Suns then sank deeper into trouble in Game 2. Barkley and Jordan both scored 42 points, but the Bulls defense clamped down on Kevin Johnson and Phoenix guard Dan Majerle to take a 2-0 series lead.

Suddenly Phoenix faced three games in Chicago and the prospects of a sweep. The Suns answered by scratching out a 129-121, triple-overtime win in Game 3.

Sensing a vulnerability in his team, Jordan came on strong in Game 4, scoring 55 points and driving the Bulls to a 108-98 win and a 3-1 series lead. The victory had been aided by Armstrong's pressure and a key late steal. The Bulls, however, were strangely teetering at the brink of their accomplishment. Jordan swore to his teammates that he would not accompany them back to Phoenix if they failed to deliver Game 5 in the Stadium. Regardless, the Bulls stumbled, and the Suns got the win they needed to return the series back to their home court. There had been speculation that if the Bulls won Game 5 in Chicago, the city would be racked by the riotous celebration that had marred the team's previous championships. In fear of that, many merchants had boarded up their stores.

"We did the city a favor," Barkley said as he left town. "You can take all those boards down now. We're going to Phoenix."

So was Jordan, contrary to his vow, and the Bulls were fighting feelings that they had let their best opportunity slip away.

Tom Dore: Michael seems to sense what a team needs. They had just lost. But Michael walked on the plane going to Phoenix and said, "Hello, World Champs." He's got a foot-long cigar, and he's celebrating already because he knows the series is over.

Barkley had claimed that "destiny" belonged to the Suns, but over the first three quarters of Game 6 it seemed the Phoenix players were feeling pressure more than anything else. Meanwhile, the Bulls phalanx of guards—Jordan, Armstrong, Paxson and seldom-used reserve Trent Tucker—fired in nine three-

In the Finals, B.J. had the quickness to counter K.J.

pointers over the first three periods to stake Chicago to a 87-79 lead.

From there, however, it was the Bulls' turn to succumb to the pressure. They missed nine shots and had two turnovers the first 11 times they got the ball in the fourth quarter. The Suns closed within a point, then surged to take a 98-94 lead with 90 seconds left. Jordan pulled down a defensive rebound and wound his way through traffic to the other end for a short bank shot. It was 98-96 with 38 seconds to go. Majerle's shooting had helped the Suns back into the series, but on their next-to-last possession he shot an air ball.

The Bulls had another chance with 14.1 seconds to go. After a time-out, Jordan inbounded the ball to Armstrong, then got it back and passed ahead to Pippen. The ball was supposed to go back to Chicago's Superman, but Pippen saw that he was covered and motored into the lane, where he was greeted by Suns center Mark West.

Alone on the near baseline was Grant, who had scored a single point in the game, who had had a stick-back opportunity moments earlier and almost threw the ball over the backboard. Pippen whipped him the ball, and scrambling out of his personal terror, Grant passed up the shot to send the ball out to John Paxson, all alone in three-point land to the left of the key.

Michael Jordan: I knew it was in as soon as Pax shot it.

John Paxson: It was like a dream come true. You're a kid out in your driveway shooting shots to win championships. When you get down to it, it's still just a shot in a basketball game. But I think it allowed a lot of people to relate to that experience, because there are a lot of kids and adults who lived out their own fantasies in their backyards.

Jordan shook off the pressure.

232

The Bulls stiffled Sir Charles.

Pax hit the winning shot.

Scottie tightened up on Ainge.

234

And Horace Grant made the game-saving block in the final seconds.

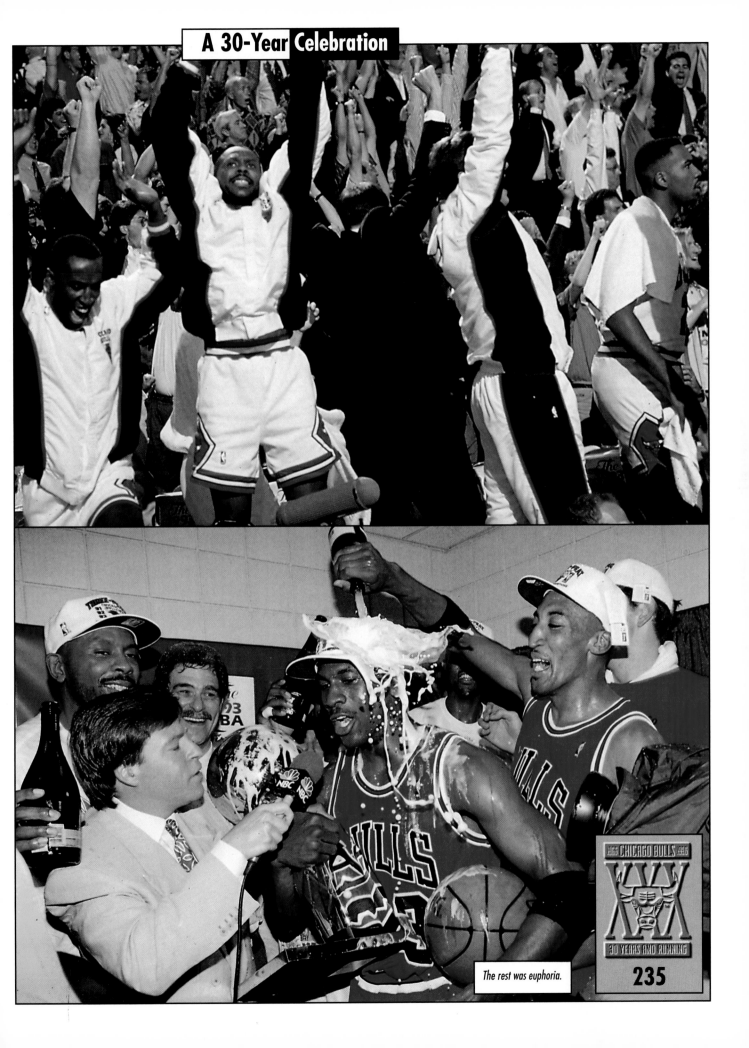

The rest was euphoria.

Jim Cleamons, Bach, Jackson and Winter with their hardware display.

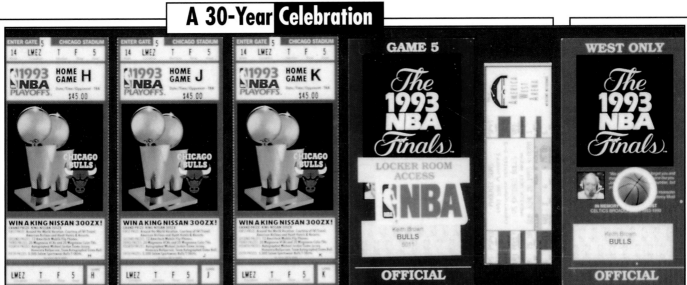

First and Second Game Tickets in Bulls History

SPECIAL PLAYOFFS & FINALS EDITION

hoop

THE OFFICIAL NBA PROGRAM MAGAZINE

1993 NBA PLAYOFFS

The 1993 NBA Finals

1966 CHICAGO BULLS 1996

XXX

30 YEARS AND RUNNING

James Jordan.

Michael tried his hand at baseball.

Jordan and mother Delores.

Move/Jordan's Retirement

AT THE CLOSE OF THE 1993 PLAYOFFS, Michael Jordan sat atop the NBA mountain. During the Finals, he had averaged 41 points per game, breaking the championship series record of 40.8 points per game set by Rick Barry in 1967.

Yet there was little question among Jordan's close associates that he had grown weary of the grind, of the lack of privacy. In his public comments, he made oblique references to his retirement. Yet in the locker room victory celebration, Jordan had said he would be back for another campaign come fall. "My love for this game is strong," he told reporters.

However, late that July, a dreadful turn of events hastened his departure from the game. Jordan's popular father, James Jordan, was found murdered in South Carolina, ostensibly the victim of a random roadside killing. Yet the news of Mr. Jordan's death was followed quickly by wild speculation that somehow Jordan's golf wagering might be a factor. That, as much as anything, seemed to be the final insult for Jordan. On October 6, 1993, he abruptly announced his retirement from the Bulls.

Phil Jackson: That's what killed us about Norm Van Lier, here in Chicago. He was broadcasting theories about Michael's father's death and gambling and the NBA and all this stuff. Michael had to go talk to

Chicago Tribune

Sports Final

Wednesday, October 13, 1993

147th Year – No. 286 © Chicago Tribune 8 Sections N ★★

Thanks for the memories

A tribute to the unforgettable Michael Jordan

Tribune photo by Ed Wa

'I knew when I walked away from the game that a lot of people,
especially kids, would be disappointed. But I'd like to let them know
that basketball is great as a hobby, but there's a lot to life
other than sports. My life goes on.'

1966 CHICAGO BULLS 1996

30 YEARS AND RUNNING

239

Jordan's number 23 was retired in a November 1994 ceremony at the United Center.

called the *Daily Nation*, Kenya's national newspaper. On the back page, there was a picture of Michael, and the headline said, " Michael Jordan Retires." I thought it was somebody's idea of a bad joke. But two days earlier, Michael had announced his retirement. Apparently, Michael's mom didn't know. I went up to her and thanked her for lending us her son for nine great years. She said, "What are you talking about?" I said, "Mrs. Jordan, your son retired two days ago." She said, "He did! I don't believe it." So I went and got the newspaper and showed her. That was how we found out about Michael retiring.

That night at dinner I bought some Dom Perignon for everybody, and we toasted Michael on his great career. But by the time I got back to Chicago, the festive mood was gone. People were definitely depressed. It happened with such suddeness, it was so out of the blue that it kind of took the wind out of people's sails.

Within months, Jordan announced that he would try his hand at minor league baseball in the Chicago White Sox farm system with the hopes that he might someday make it to the big leagues..

Phil Jackson: It was really his father's dream that he play baseball. His father wanted to play pro ball and did play semi-pro. When his father passed away, I think Michael was kind of living out his father's dream.

That's one of the things I thought when I heard it. "Geez, this guy wants to go play baseball in the major leagues!?!?" But then I realized basketball players are always fantasizing that they could play baseball.

Looking back on it, it was a beautiful thing Michael did. What a risk he took trying to play baseball. The whole idea that he's going to go out and give up everything to try that at his age. That's the wonderful thing about it. Michael is such a special person.

In November 1994, the Bulls retired Michael Jordan's number 23 and unveiled a statue of him outside their new arena, the United Center.

Van Lier and say, "Norm. Cool this stuff about gambling and the NBA and the grand scheme and all this other stuff about my father's death. There's no conspiracy going on here." That's the paranoia that builds in people's minds and sometimes drives you crazy.

Steve Schanwald: When we got the news, I was on safari in Nairobi with Michael's mom and a group of school kids. It had been so peaceful out there. We were on safari in a remote portion of Kenya, living in tents. No newspapers, no radio, no TV, no nothing. I told the people that the world could be coming to an end, and we wouldn't know. Two days later we flew back to Nairobi, where I got word that Michael had retired. The bus driver was reading a newspaper, a tabloid

Aftershock, 1993-95

MICHAEL JORDAN'S ABRUPT retirement came just as training camp was set to open in 1993. Suddenly, Jerry Krause found himself hustling to patch together a replacement combination for the backcourt. As he once explained, it had been nearly impossible to keep a young off guard as an understudy for Jordan because his immense competitiveness consumed them in practices. Now, Krause had to pull together a group of free agents. Ultimately, the coaches decided to go with an old standby, Pete Myers. He moved into the starting lineup on opening night and played solidly and consistently all season.

There were several other new faces on the roster. After years of trying, Krause had lured Toni Kukoc, the 6-11 Croation, from Europe. Krause had pursued Kukoc since the Bulls drafted him in the second round in 1990.

The general manager had also signed free agent Steve Kerr with the idea that he would eventually replace Paxson, who, like Cartwright, was struggling to return for one more season. For the frontcourt, Krause signed 7-foot journeyman Bill Wennington and later traded Stacey King to Minnesota for 7-foot-2 Luc Longley.

There was immediate speculation that these newly reconstituted Bulls would fail miserably without Jordan. But just the opposite happened. The coaching staff did perhaps its best job in Jackson's tenure with the team. And Scottie Pippen, Horace Grant and B. J. Armstrong showed that they had developed into outstanding players in their own right. All three were selected for the All-Star team, the first time that three Bulls had been selected.

Amazingly, these Jordanless Bulls won 55 games and made a strong-but-controversial run into the 1994 playoffs. Their first round opponents, the Cavaliers, fell easily, leaving the Bulls to face Pat Riley's Knicks in the Eastern semifinal.

Phil Jackson: We'd used more energy to get 55 wins than we'd ever had to use in the past. Maybe my better job was holding them back a little bit in years past so that when we went into the playoffs we had energy and expertise that could be

unleashed. This time, it was a matter of how much did we have left for the playoffs.

In Game 1 in New York, the Bulls had a 15-point lead but seemed to run out of energy. It was a bitter, frustrating loss, the kind that Jackson feared could do harm to his team. So, instead of practicing, he decided they needed a break, which turned out to be an impromptu ride on the Staten Island Ferry.

It did not, however, bring them a win in Game 2. The Knicks strong-armed a second win, and the series moved to Chicago with the Bulls down 2-0. There, in Game 3, they seemed set

After years of trying, the Bulls finally brought Croatian Toni Kukoc to Chicago in 1993 and immediately set him to work in legendary strength coach Al Vermeil's program.

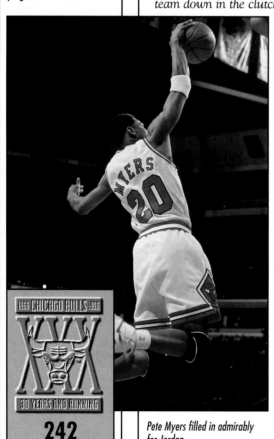

Pete Myers filled in admirably for Jordan.

to fall off the edge. The Knicks had a one-point lead with 1.8 seconds left. Chicago had the ball and called a time-out, during which Jackson set instructions for the ball to go to Kukoc for the final shot. Pippen was infuriated. He was the superstar of the team, burdened all season with the load of carrying the Bulls alone. He believed the shot should have been his to take. So he refused to go back in the game. Cartwright was at first stunned, then furious with Pippen.

Nonplussed, Jackson substituted, leaving Pippen on the bench, and Kukoc hit the game-winning shot. The aftermath, however, was soon awash in controversy. Pippen was roundly lambasted for letting his team down in the clutch.

"Those times are the moments in games that you live for," Pippen later explained. "And I thought it was an injustice the way Phil treated me, and I had to say something, right or wrong. So it wasn't what people wanted to hear."

Steve Schanwald: Phil handled it beautifully. With many coaches the situation would have escalated and gotten uglier.

Somehow, the team shook off the incident and claimed a 12-point win in Game 4 to even the series. The Bulls then could have

won crucial Game 5 in New York, but they let it slip away by a point. Back in Chicago for Game 6, they played well and evened the series at three-all.

It was in New York in Game 7 that the next great controversy landed. In the closing seconds, the Bulls had the lead and seemingly the win when referee Hue Hollins whistled Pippen for a late foul on New York's Hubert Davis beyond the top of the key. The Bulls incredulously protested, and supervisor of officials Darrell Garretson later said the call was terrible. But it still cost Chicago the game and series and a chance to win a fourth straight championship.

Jerry Reinsdorf: Hue Hollins obviously blew the call on Pippen, but a call has been blown before. These things happen. You can make yourself nuts if you worry about them. Referees will only beat you if you put yourself in a position to let it happen. We obviously had a chance to control that series in earlier games.

The loss brought a host of changes to the Bulls, one of the first being the release of longtime assistant coach John Bach.

Jerry Krause: In essence, Johnny fired himself. I told him many times that assistant coaches shouldn't be holding press conferences. Assistant coaches should have lower profiles. We cautioned him about that time and time again, yet he kept doing it.

Cheryl Raye: Johnny was too friendly to the media, but he helped us. He gave us information, not to hurt the team. He would explain why something was being done and how it was working.

In fact, he would say to me, "I can't talk to you, if management sees me, they'll get mad." But the more they told him not to, the more he wanted to do it.

Johnny Bach: That's the twist in life that fate does to you.

Phil Jackson: It was Jerry Krause's relationship with Johnny Bach that created a very uncomfortable situation. It made this have to happen eventually. It had gone all wrong. It was bad for the staff to have this kind of thing because we had to work together.

Jerry basically blamed Johnny Bach for a lot of the things in *The Jordan Rules*. And there's no doubt that Johnny did provide that information.

Jerry felt that Johnny talked too much. And Johnny, in retrospect, felt that animonsity that Jerry gave to back to him, the lack of respect, so Johnny refused to pay allegiance to Jerry just because he was the boss.

It had gone on for too long a period of time. I could have kept them apart, at bay from one another, I suppose, for a while longer. But I didn't like the fact that it wasn't good teamwork. That was my staff and my area. I agreed to do it. I felt it was a good opportunity because Johnny had an opportunity to get another job in the league quickly.

It worked out fine for Johnny, although I would just as soon have not put him through the disappointment, or have to go through the situation myself.

Horace suffered through a season of discontent.

The Bulls and Knicks battled through another Eastern Finals in '94.

CHICAGO BULLS MAGAZINE
BASKETB**ULL**

VOLUME 4 $5   NUMBER 8

DESTINY DENIED

Scottie Pippen's controversial foul of Hubert Davis in the closing seconds of Game 5 helped end the Bulls' historic run for a fourth title.

son contending with Grant's behavior, including incidents of games missed due to "blue flu."

John Paxson and Bill Cartwright retired, then Cartwright abruptly unretired when the Seattle Supersonics offered him a substantial two-year contract.

The bottom line to these changes meant a substantial struggle over the first months of the 1994-95 season. The on-court battles were made worse by a public dispute between Scottie Pippen and management over his efforts to have his multi-year contract renegotiated. The feelings between the forward and the organization had hardened after a summertime deal to trade him to Seattle for power forward Shawn Kemp fell through. In the aftermath, Pippen asked repeatedly to be traded.

The outcome came down to a controversial Game 7 foul call against Scottie Pippen.

1966 CHICAGO BULLS 1996

30 YEARS AND RUNNING

244

There were other major changes in the months leading up to the 1994-95 season. Scott Williams became a free agent and accepted a lucrative offer to play in Philadelphia. Then the re-signing of Horace Grant got mired in dispute, and he left the Bulls to sign with the Orlando Magic. The incident left Bulls' management angry and frustrated, particularly Jerry Reinsdorf, who said that Grant had reneged on a handshake agreement for a new $20-million contract. Making matters worse, Bulls' management had spent the '94-95 sea-

By early March 1995, the Bulls were struggling to stay above .500, and speculation abounded that once the season was over Pippen would be shipped to another team. Observers figured that, short of some miracle, the roster would have to be rebuilt, and the Bulls would have to start over.

Quite suddenly, the entire picture changed in mid March, and the good people of Chicago learned that the Jordan era wasn't over after all.

Epilogue/Back at Last

FOR 10 DAYS, IT WAS THE GREATEST tease in the history of sport. Was Michael Jordan returning to basketball or not? From Warsaw to Waukegan, the planet clamored to know.

Then on Saturday, March 18, 1995, he broke his silence with a two-word press release, issued through agent David Falk.

"I'm back."

Sure enough, the next day, shortly after noon, he emerged with his teammates from the visitors' locker room at Market Square Arena in Indianapolis, where the Bulls were scheduled to meet the Indiana Pacers.

Standing before the crowd gathered in the hallway outside the locker room was Superman himself, chomping his gum fiercely. The greatest basketball player in the history of the game was ready to resume the career that had been interrupted by an 18-month "retirement."

Instamatics flashed, and people wiggled with excitement. "This is just like the President appearing," commented one Chicago TV reporter.

"Are you kidding?" somebody else said. "Michael's more important than that."

Wearing number 45, Jordan made his comeback against the Pacers in March.

Chicago Tribune

Monday, March 20, 1995

Chicago
Sports Final

Relaunched

Tribune photo by Nancy Stone

Only now, just as he was raring to take the floor and restart his career, something was wrong. Jordan's face tightened. Somebody was missing.

The Bulls did a quick head count. Only eleven. "Who's not here?" Jordan asked as he searched the faces around him.

They all turned to see Scottie Pippen sheepishly slipping out of the locker room.

With his jaws working the gum and his glare policing the roster, Jordan gathered his teammates in a huddle, where they joined hands.

"What time is it?" forward Corie Blount yelled.

"It's game time!" they answered in unison.

With that, the Bulls broke and made their way out into the arena, opening the latest chapter in the strange, wonderful saga of Air Jordan.

Michael was back, and the news flashed around the world. Everywhere, it seemed, fans were reassuring themselves that basketball's heart was once again beating, that the sport they loved no longer needed life support.

"He is like a gift from God to the basketball game," Huang Gang, a 21-year-old professional player in Beijing, remarked upon hearing the news. "We try to imitate his ground moves. But you can't copy him in the air. He is unique."

Waiting for the competition to begin that Sunday in Indianapolis, Pacers coach Larry Brown quipped that the atmosphere was so zany, it seemed like "Elvis and the Beatles are back."

The proceedings did have a dreamlike feel about them. But that's how we define superstars, isn't it? By their ability to suspend reality? Jordan had always done that for Bulls fans. Yet the circumstances were never more ethereal than in early March, when the first rumors leaked out that he was contemplating another career move.

Chicago was agog over Jordan's return.

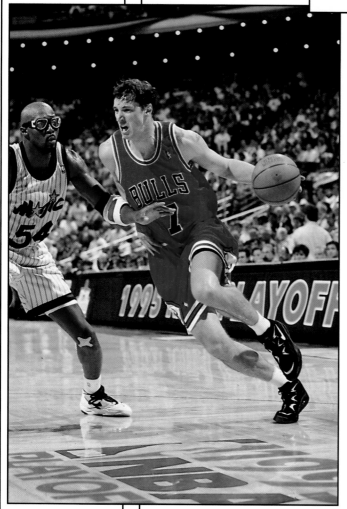

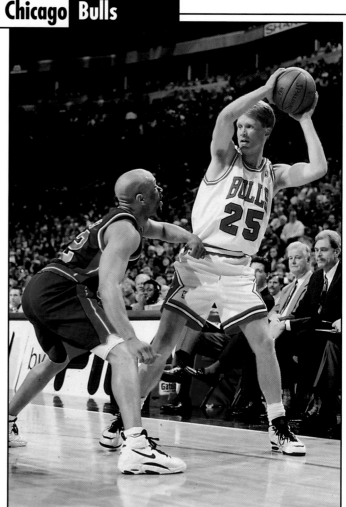

Upon Michael's return, he found a host of new teammates, including Kukoc, Steve Kerr, Luc Longley and Bill Wennington.

Without question, the Bulls were caught off guard by Jordan's decision to abandon the professional baseball career he had launched upon leaving basketball. Many people in baseball had questioned his skill level after he immersed himself in the White Sox minor league farm system, but no one doubted his work ethic. In his determination to learn to hit big league pitching, Jordan came early and stayed late each day at practice.

But the futility was obvious almost from the start. He was too tall, some said, and presented too big a strike zone. "He is attempting to compete with hitters who have seen 350,000 fastballs in their baseball lives and 204,000 breaking balls," Rangers pitching instructor Tom House appraised shortly after Jordan joined the AA Birmingham Barons for the 1994 season. "Baseball is a function of repetition. If Michael had pursued baseball out of high school, I don't doubt he would have wound up making as much money in baseball as in basketball. But he's not exactly tearing up Double A, and that's light years from the big leagues."

If he was light years away, Jordan, a 32-year-old .200 hitter, certainly didn't have time to waste with the protracted baseball strike that had loomed over the game for eight months. Hoping it would soon be resolved, he reported to spring training in Florida only to realize that the fight between owners and players over money wasn't going to end anytime soon. Then, he had a misunderstanding with White Sox management over dressing room and parking arrangements. So he packed up and went home.

Within days of his departure from Florida, a Chicago radio station reported that Jordan was secretly working out with the Bulls and contemplating a return to basketball.

On March 10, he announced his retirement from baseball, saying his minor league experience had been powerful because it allowed him to rediscover the work ethic that had made him a great basketball player. "I met thousands of new fans," he said, "and I learned that minor league players are really the foundation of baseball. They often play in obscurity and with little

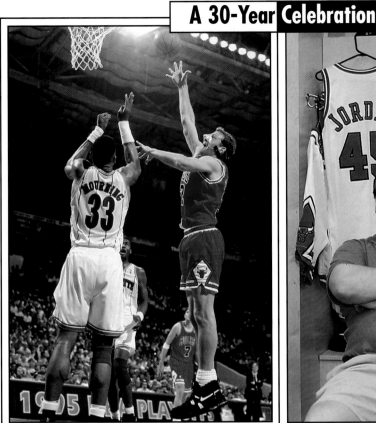

The Bulls dismissed Charlotte in the first round of the '95 playoffs.

recognition, but they deserve the respect of the fans and everyone associated with the game."

Michael Jordan hadn't failed baseball, Phil Jackson noted. "Baseball failed him."

Soon the Bulls confirmed that Jordan was working out with the team, and Jackson revealed that Jordan had actually been contemplating a return since October.

Like that, the situation exploded. Scores of media representatives from the major networks and national publications converged on the Berto Center, the Bulls' practice facility in suburban Deerfield, in anticipation of Michael holding a press conference announcing his return.

Yet each day at practice, large screens covered the picture windows through which reporters observed Bulls practices. The media could hear the shouts, the squeaking of sneakers on the gym floor. They were told that Michael was practicing with the team but that he hadn't yet made up his mind about returning, that the details were being worked out.

On the Berto Center floor, Michael displayed the intense competitiveness that for years had charged Bulls practice sessions. Wearing the yellow vest of the second team, he ran point

guard against the regulars and reminded them just what true greatness meant. "Just to be able to play with him is fun," said center Will Perdue. "Just to be able to watch him."

Still, Jordan wavered that week, pausing, as he would later explain, to contemplate whether he was returning to basketball out of disappointment over the baseball strike, or if he was in fact returning because he loved the game. This self-evaluation came at the urging of Jerry Reinsdorf, who didn't want Jordan to leave the game only to regret it later. While the media speculated and fans kept the lines buzzing on sports radio talk shows, Jordan remained silent. The closest he came to making a statement was the revving of his burgandy Corvette, warning the media to get out of the roadway as he left practice each day.

His silence drove reporters and fans alike to distraction, with some callers on Chicago's sports radio talk shows claiming that Jordan was toying with the public.

Meanwhile, USA Today reported that the stock value of companies who employed Jordan as a spokesman had zoomed up $2 billion on the various stock exchanges in recent days, leading to further speculation that Jordan was engaged in some kind of financial manipulation.

Finally, on Thursday March 16, Jackson told

In the second round, Jordan struggled in Game 1 against Orlando, prompting Magic guard Nick Anderson to say that no. 45 just wasn't as good as no. 23 used to be. Jordan replied by switching jerseys for Game 2. The move, which was engineered by longtime equipment manager John Ligmanowski, was met with substantial fines by the NBA. But Bulls owner Jerry Reinsdorf said that if Michael needed his old number back, the team would pick up the tab.

249

Jordan not to attend practice that day because the media crowd at the Berto Center had gotten too large. After practice, Jackson revealed to a swarm of reporters that Jordan and Reinsdorf were engaged in discussions and that a decision was three or four days away.

That Friday night, the Bulls capped a three-game winning streak and raised their record three notches above .500 by defeating the Milwaukee Bucks in the United Center. Speculation had been high that Jordan might make a sudden appearance in uniform for that game, but only his security advisers showed up to evaluate the arena.

Early the next morning, the Chicago radio waves were abuzz that Jordan would make his announcement that day, and that he would play Sunday on the nationally televised game against Indiana. Down on LaSalle Street, the managers at Michael Jordan's Restaurant heard the news and decided that they better restock the gift shop yet again. The restaurant's business had been slow in February, but the hint of Jordan's return had turned March into a boom, with crowds packing the place virtually every night.

As a result, the gift shop was doing a whopping

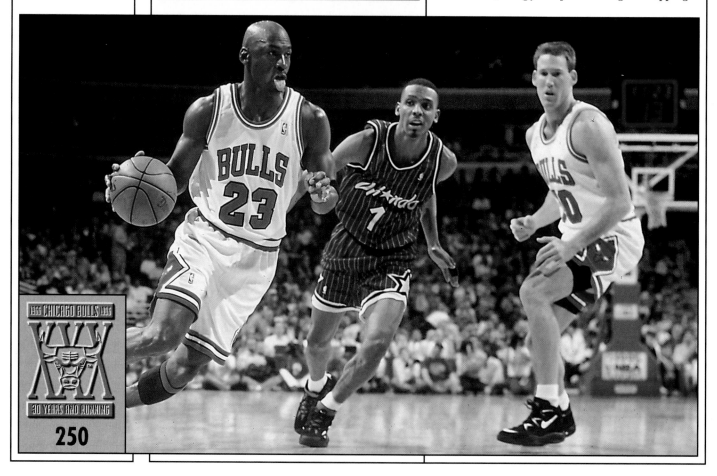

Part of Jordan's greatness is his focus in practice. "I have always liked practice, and I hate to miss it," he explained. "It's like taking a math class. When you miss that one day, you feel like you missed a lot. You take extra work to make up for that one day. I've always been a practice player. I believe in it."

business, selling miniature bats, trading cards, jerseys, posters, coffee mugs and other trinkets. Other fans gathered at the Jordan statue outside the United Center. Revealed in a nationally televised retirement ceremony in November, the statue had quickly become a hot spot for fans and tourists in Chicago. On this Saturday, as the anticipation grew, small groups were drawn to the statue.

"This is like the Colts returning to Baltimore," said one fan, "with Johnny Unitas as quarterback!"

Over at the Berto Center in Deerfield, crowds of fans and reporters milled about, with many fans hanging from the balconies and walls of the Residence Inn next door. Nine different TV satellite trucks hovered near the building, waiting to blast the news around the world.

Suddenly, practice was over, and like that,

Jordan's burgandy 'Vette appeared on the roadway, with him gunning his engine and the fans cheering wildly as he sped off. Next came Pippen in a Range Rover, pausing long enough to flash a giant smile through the vehicle's darkly tinted windows.

Moments later, NBC's Peter Vescey did a stand up report outside with the fans rooting in the background. He told the broadcast audience that Jordan was returning, that Jordan would play against Indiana on Sunday and probably wear his old number 23, which had been retired in November. The excitement coursed through the city. Chicago, quipped one radio sportscaster, was in a state of "Jorgasym."

Jordan did not fly to Indianapolis with the team that Saturday night. A crowd of fans and media gathered at the Canterbury Hotel, awaiting the Bulls' arrival. When a lim-

251

ousine with a police escort pulled up, the crowd surged forward. But out stepped a bride and groom. "Who are these people?" the stunned bride asked her new husband.

The team showed up moments later and was roundly cheered, but there was no Jordan. He flew down the next day on a private jet and arrived at the arena with an armada of limousines carrying his security force of 20 to help hold back the crowds.

That Sunday, Michael wore jersey number 45, his minor league and junior high number, instead of the number 23 that he had made so famous. Number 23 was the last number his father James saw him compete in, Jordan later explained, and he wanted to keep it that way.

Champion, the sportswear manufacturer that holds the NBA license for jerseys, immediately added an extra shift and began producing more than 200,000 No. 45's for sale around the world.

Jordan played against Indiana like someone who had taken two years off. He made just 7 of 28 shots, but his defensive intensity helped the Bulls take the division-leading Pacers to overtime before losing. Afterward, Jordan broke his silence to address the hoopla of the preceding 10 days. "I'm human," he said. "I wasn't expecting this. It's a little embarrassing."

He said he had taken his time evaluating his love of the game and had come to the conclusion that it was real. That, he said, was the reason he returned, not financial considerations. He pointed out that the league had a moratorium on renegotiating contracts while it worked out a new labor agreement with the NBA Players Association, so he was required to play for the $3.9 million salary he left behind in 1993. (Although not required to, the Bulls had paid his full salary for 1993-94, and they would cover the full amount for 1994-95, although Jordan only played a portion of the season.) He also added that he had received no assurances about Pippen or Armstrong, although he asked.

His return, he said, was based solely on his love for basketball.

"I wanted to instill some positives back into this game," he said of his return, indicating his displeasure at some of the NBA's highly paid young players. "There's been a lot of negatives lately, young guys not taking care of their part of the responsibility, as far as the love of the game. I think you should love this game, not take advantage of it... be positive people and act like gentlemen, act like professionals."

Three nights later, he scored 27 points by shooting nine of 17 from the floor in a win over the Celtics at Boston Garden. Next would come a last-second shot for a win against Atlanta, and a 56-point performance against the awestruck Knicks in Madison Square Garden. Between these displays of greatness, he struggled through bouts of very ordinary play. Regardless, in a few short games he had served notice that he was indeed back. Which, in turn, led to a revival of the NBA's fortunes. Sagging television ratings abruptly jumped, and suddenly the whole country was watching Michael Jordan's return.

"Everybody was complaining about the season," Phil Jackson said. "It was a lackluster year. It wasn't any fun. All of a sudden Michael comes back, and suddenly people start paying attention to the NBA. They see there's a lot of dynamic things going on here. A couple of television people told me, 'It brought back our audience.' And the NBA really enjoyed a very good postseason tournament because people got their minds set on pro basketball again because this great attraction."

The circumstances engendered an overwhelming belief among Chicagoans that Jordan was about to perform his grandest miracle of all: He would return after a two-year absence, play just 17 games of the regular season, then lead an undermanned Bulls team into the playoffs to capture a fourth title.

It had all the appeal of a storybook ending, which is what it proved to be. Instead of magic, Jordan's return created mostly unrealistic expectations. The Bulls finished in fifth place in the Eastern Conference and had no home-court advantage in the playoffs. Still, they managed to oust the Charlotte Hornets in six games. But it became increasingly obvious that Jordan still lacked the stamina and timing to deliver a miracle.

In the second round, against the Orlando Magic with Shaquille O'Neal, Anfernee

Hardaway and Horace Grant, the Bulls and Jordan found themselves out of sync, particularly in Game 1 in Orlando when Jordan committed two late turnovers that cost the Bulls the game. From there, Jordan missed shots, made miscues and watched Grant's play shift the balance in the series. At one point, Jordan donned his old jersey number 23 to get a second win, but the Magic took over from there to claim a 4-2 series victory.

"We agonized a little bit for him this year when he went through the postseason drama," Jackson said. "But knowing Michael so well, I put my arm around him after that first game against Orlando when he lost the ball and said, 'As many times as we won behind you, I never expected to see this happen. Let's use it for our tool. Let's use it to build a positive. You're our guy, and don't ever forget that.' You never think you'll have to go to Michael and talk about something like that."

Bulls fans were understandably stunned by the turn of events. In the days following the loss, the sports radio talk show airwaves were filled with comments that the team needed to rework its approach, that the triple-post offense had outlived its usefulness.

Even Tex Winter, the architect of the system, had his doubts. Michael Jordan had never expressed an opinion to Winter about the triple-post. But now Winter wanted to know, so he implored Jackson to ask Jordan's opinion when the two met for the postseason interview that Jackson annually holds with each of his players.

"With his impulsiveness," Jackson recalled, "Tex said, 'Phil, I'd like you to ask him, does he think we need to change the offense? Can we play this triple-post offense? Is it something we should plan on using next year? I want you to ask him just for me.' So I did, and Michael said, 'The triple-post offense is the backbone of this team. It's our system, something that everybody can hang their hat on, so that they know where to go and how to operate.'"

Winter, of course, was elated to hear that renewed commitment to the system he had spent his life perfecting. What the team really needed was a strong rebounding power forward, and late in the offseason, the Bulls got just that by trading Will Perdue to the San

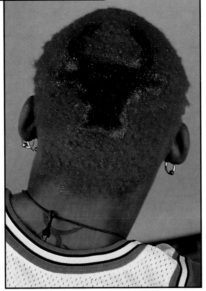

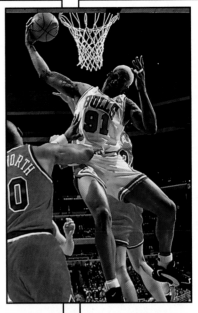

Antonio Spurs for Dennis Rodman, the onetime Piston Bad Boy who had claimed four straight league rebounding titles. In addition to inspired defense and board work, Rodman had become known for his dyed hair, numerous flamboyant tatoos and body piercings in recent seasons. There were charges that his eccentric behavior had been a distraction to the Spurs, but after numerous consultations and discussions—Pippen and Jordan were asked their opinion of the deal—Reinsdorf, Krause, and Jackson made the trade. Rodman arrived in Chicago with his hair dyed red and a black Bulls logo emblazoned in his crown, all matched by his nails which had been carefully manicured with a Bulls motif. Most important, though, Rodman brought his game.

Jackson soon began looking forward again to what he liked to call the mystery of each season, the unwritten stories. With Jordan back and Rodman now on the team, the mystery seemed to hold a very special potential.

Jackson had wanted a fourth title as badly as anyone. That hadn't happened, but neither had the opportunity passed. Instead, the circumstances were full of hope. Michael was back. Rodman was in town.

And the Bulls?

They're 30 and running.

Rodman brought his 'do and his game to Chicago for the 1995-96 season.

Jackson sporting a beard, and Krause were eager to greet him.